ARCHITECTURE AND WOMEN

GARLAND REFERENCE LIBRARY
OF THE HUMANITIES
(Vol. 886)

ARCHITECTURE AND WOMEN

*A Bibliography Documenting Women Architects,
Landscape Architects, Designers, Architectural
Critics and Writers and Women in Related Fields
Working in the United States*

Lamia Doumato

GARLAND PUBLISHING, INC. • NEW YORK & LONDON
1988

Library of Congress Cataloging-in-Publication Data

Doumato, Lamia.
    Architecture and women: a bibliogaphy documenting women
  architects, landscape architects, designers, architectural critics
  and writers, and women in related fields working in the United
  States / Lamia Doumato.
        p. cm. — (Garland reference library of the humanities; vol.
  886)
    Includes index.
    ISBN 0–8240–4105–4 (alk. paper)
    1. Architecture and women—United States—Bibliography.
  I. Title. II. Series.
  Z5944.U5D6886   1988
  [NA2543.W65]
  016.72'088042—dc19   88–17698
                                                            CIP

Printed on acid-free, 250-year-life paper
Manufactured in the United States of America

FOR

MIRIAM BARSOUM DOUMATO

CONTENTS

Contents

ACKNOWLEDGMENTS

Compiling any bibliography is both a time-consuming and detailed endeavor one that is rarely accomplished by a single person without assistance. Such is true in this case and I wish to thank all of the generous professionals in the field who unselfishly gave of their time and expertise. First and foremost the thanks go to Tony Wrenn, archivist of the AIA Information Center, who has compiled a unique resource of vertical files on women architects. This resource is matched only by Mr. Wrenn's knowledge of the field and his willingness to share all with the researcher. I must also thank Bob Kimberlin, again of the AIA information center and Therese Idlefonso, of the AIA, for their assistance with my many requests. Karen Morgan, Reference Librarian at the Schlesinger Library of Harvard University graciously answered many of my questions. Lila H. Katz, Archivist of the International Archive of Women in Architecture at Virginia Polytechnic Institute provided me with information. My colleagues at the National Gallery of Art, Thomas McGill and Ted Dalziel located materials for me through interlibrary loan. Several of the women documented in the volume generously supplied me with photographs of their work and in some instances also provided personal information. Finally, I must express my gratitude to my brother, Ephraim P. Doumato, without whom I would be unable to tell the time of day.

INTRODUCTION

Women architects, like many women artists, were
frequently initiated into their careers through the
intervention of male relatives; Cornelia Randolph,
granddaughter of Thomas Jefferson, served as draughtsman
for several of her grandfather's projects. Peter Hodson's
masters thesis at the University of Virginia, 1967,
entitled, <u>The Design and Building of Bremo: 1815-1820</u>
describes how these designs were..."drawn ca. 1825 under
Jefferson's guidance by his granddaughter as exercises in
architectural draughtsmanship. Jefferson was instructing
Cornelia at this time so that she could assist him with
drawings...Cornelia's inked and rendered elevations and
plans of the University's pavillions and rotunda, Poplar
Forest and Bremo display a neat and almost professional
skill." The same is often true in the early history of
landscape design where Elizabeth Bullard of Bridgeport,
Connecticut, learned her art while assisting her father.
Financial circumstances forced her to carry on her father's
work after his death. But unlike women painters or writers
who could quietly conduct their work in the secluded space
of a studio, the intrinsic nature of architecture and
landscape architecture demands public exposure both in the
working process and in the final product. Thus the work of
women in these fields (as well as the women themselves) was
exposed to a greater scrutiny. (Future generations would
continue to work alongside men and often, as in the case of
Marion Mahony Griffin and Victorine Homsey, marry their
associates or partners).
        Many of the women herein documented are pioneers in
one way or another, e.g., Harriet Morrison Irwin, advocate
of the octagonal house, was the first woman to patent a
house plan. Schenck and Mead composed the first American
female architectural firm (Howe, Manning and Almy was the
first female firm in Boston and the second such firm in the
United States). Margaret Hicks, while the only female
architecture student at Cornell University in 1878, became
the first to have a drawing published in an architectural
journal. Louisa C.H. Tuthill in 1848 published the first
history of architecture in the United States thus
establishing a tradition of women architectural writers and
critics, such as Mariana Griswold van Rensselaer, Esther
McCoy and Suzanne Stephens. Ruth Reynolds Freeman,
president of AIA's Vermont chapter was the first woman to

attain such an office. Eleanor Raymond, collaborating with
Maria Telkes in 1948, designed the first successful passive
solar house in the Northeast: this Dover, Massachusetts
house is still in use. The list of achievements goes on and
on.

The primary motivation for compiling this volume was
to encourage research on the history of women in
architecture. The intention was not to solve any polemic
discussions concerning the roles of women nor to assert in
any way their superiority to their male colleagues nor to
bemoan the difficulties encountered by women in the field.
Rather this selective bibliography was conceived from the
positive standpoint that women have made a vital contribution to the field and that their efforts are worthy of
recognition.   In a May 16, 1957, article in the Washington
Daily News entitled "Home Designing Is Last Job Choice"
Carol LeVarn posed the direct question to six female
architects, "Do women architects design better houses than
men?" These women agreed that, "An architect, man or woman,
uses skill and knowledge whether designing a house or a
hospital."

Why then are women not equally represented in the
literature of the field? Natalie Kampen and Elizabeth
Grossman in their study Feminism and Methodology: Dynamics
and Change in the History of Art and Architecture
(Wellesley, MA: Wellesley College Center for Research on
Women, Working Paper no. 122, 1983) relate that [Julia]
"Morgan's oeuvre of six to eight hundred commissions
[range] in style from bungalow to Roman villa, and from
Spanish to Gothic... yet the writing about Morgan is so
slight that she is more important in the histories as a
phenomenon than as an architect" (p. 12). This bibliography will, one hopes, serve as a motivation to scholars
and students, enabling them to study further the role of
women in American architecture. It becomes the work of
scholars to both pose and answer the questions inherent in
this topic.

The scope of this bibliography is by no means
comprehensive: monographs; dissertations and M.A. theses;
essays; articles and interviews in journals and other
serial publications; exhibition catalogs and reviews;
selective newspaper coverage; conference proceedings;
chapters in anthologies; manuscripts; and archival sources
are listed. Women playing an architectural role in numerous
capacities are included: architects; landscape architects;
architectural critics; writers on gardens and landscapes;

housing reformers; planners and women in related arts who
have made a significant contribution in their field. Book
reviews have intentionally been excluded unless they
establish an important thesis or discuss a new point.
General articles on women in architecture are limited to
the United States; the reader will find very few citations
that do not deal exclusively with American women. Those few
articles under the heading "general periodical articles"
are cited because they present universal arguments or
statements. Audio visual materials (films, slides,
videotapes, filmstrips, etc.) have been eliminated.

There are no educational criteria for inclusion; one
does not necessarily have had to attain a degree in any
discipline. Many of the early women had no formal training,
developing their skills through their working experience;
this is rarely the case with contemporary women. The book
has been limited to Americans defined as females who have
worked in the United States but not necessarily those born
or trained here. The obvious examples are Greta Grossman
and Diana Agrest, who emigrated to the United States.

A typical entry includes the woman's name as most
often cited; her birth and death dates (these were
eliminated when it was impossible to verify a date;
publishing a dubious date and thus perpetuating an error
seemed less desirable to providing no date at all);
locations for archival materials and manuscripts; primary
works, that is, publications by the woman (these have been
limited to include only writings relevant or directly
pertaining to architecture) followed by secondary works,
publications about her and her work, and finally citations
to exhibition catalogs and reviews.

Although no one history or handbook documenting women
architects is comprehensive, the extent volumes are
important sources, particularly: Doris Cole. From Tipi to
Skyscraper; Women in American Architecture. edited by
Susana Torre; and Dorothy M. Anderson Women, Design and the
Cambridge School. All three have been invaluable in the
compilation of this work. Architecture: A Place for Women.
edited by Ellen Perry Berkeley and Mathilda McQuaid is
still in the preparatory stages but will, no doubt, one day
stand with the above-mentioned titles as a classic in the
field.

The several bibliographic citations listed in this
volume are actually pamphlets, that consist of approxi-
mately ten pages. Compiling an initial bibliography in a
subject area that has no comprehensive antecedents and

relatively little documentation is a difficult task
allowing for a greater margin of error than might, for
example, be tolerated in a well-documented field. For any
errors or lacunae which the reader may encounter, I ask
their indulgence.

Lamia Doumato
January 1988
Washington, D.C.

Architecture and Women

MANUSCRIPT MATERIAL AND SPECIAL COLLECTIONS:

The Sophia Smith Collection at Smith College has the papers
of the Cambridge School of Architecture and Landscape
Architecture; this collection also houses scrapbooks,
clippings and biographical data on women's participation in
the World's Columbian Exposition.

The Schlesinger Library at Harvard University has in its
manuscript collection a five page typescript of the
"Isabella Idea" by Adelaide Nichols Baker, 1953. This is
the story of the Isabella Society founded in 1892 to
perpetuate the name of Isabella at the World's Columbian
Exposition through a statue and a pavilion at the Fair.

Women's National Farm and Garden Association's Records are
at Harvard's Schlesinger Library.

The Department of Registration and Education of the
Illinois State Archives has records on Illinois women
architects for the years, 1897-1951.

Architectural League of New York Records for 1888-1973 are
at the Archives of American Art.

The International Archive of Women in Architecture is at
the Virginia Polytechnic Institute and State University in
Blacksburg, Virginia; the archive consists of architectural
drawings, photographs, publications, correspondence and art
works by women architects.

Keystone, newsletter of the Association of Women in
Architecture, of Clayton, Missouri and their Yearbooks for
1957-1960 are at the American Institute of Architects
Archives, Women in Architecture Collection, Washington,
D.C.

The American Institute of Architects Archives in
Washington, D.C., has a collection of published and
unpublished papers and photographs documenting the role of
women in the profession; an asterisk indicates those
individuals represented in the "women in architecture"
collection.

1

BIBLIOGRAPHIES:

Coatsworth, Patricia. Women and Urban Planning: A
     Bibliography. Chicago, Ill.: Council of Planning
     Librarians, 1981.

Doumato, Lamia. Publications by Women on American Domestic
     Architecture. Monticello, Ill.: Vance Bibliographies,
     1984.

_____. Women: Architects of the Environment.
     Monticello, Ill.: Vance Bibliographies, 1981.

_____. Women and Landscape Architecture.
     Monticello, Ill.: Vance Bibliographies, 1986.

_____. Women as Architects: A Historical View.
     Monticello, Ill.: Vance Bibliographies, 1978.

_____. Women Architectural Critics. Monticello,
     Ill.: Vance Bibliographies, 1982.

Harmon, Robert B. The Feminine Influence in Architecture: A
     Selected Bibliography. Monticello, Ill.: Vance
     Bibliographies, 1980.

Huls, Mary Ellen. Women in Architecture, 1977 to the
     Present. Monticello, Ill.: Vance Bibliographies, 1986.

Johnson, Carolyn R. Women in Architecture. Monticello,
     Ill.: Council of Planning Librarians, 1974.

MONOGRAPHS:

American Institute of Architects. Task Force on Women in
     Architecture. Women in Architecture. Washington, D.C.:
     the Institute, 1974.

Anderson, Dorothy M. Women, Design and the Cambridge
     School. West Lafayette, Indiana: PDA Publishers Corp,
     1980.

Anscombe, Isabelle. A Woman's Touch: Women in Design from

1860 to the Present Day. New York: Viking, 1984.

Birch, Eugenie L., and Deborah Gardner. Unsheltered Woman:
    Women and Housing in the Eighties. New Brunswick:
    Center for Urban Policy Research, 1985.

Boston Architectural Center. Proceedings of the Conference
    for Women in Design and Planning, Boston Architectural
    Center. Boston: Boston Architectural Center, 1975.

Brainard, Jocelyn, and Linda Yowell. Built by Women: A
    Guide to Architecture in the New York Area. New York:
    Alliance of Women in Architecture, 1981.

Brown, Catherine R. Women and the Land. Baltimore, Md:
    Built Environment Studies, Morgan State Univ., 1979.

Class, Robert A. and Robert E. Koehler. Current Techniques
    in Architectural Practice. New York: Architectural
    Record Books, 1976.

Cole, Doris. From Tipi to Skyscraper. Boston: i Press,
    1973.

Dobyns, Winifred Starr. California Gardens. New York:
    Macmillan Co., 1932.

Epstein, Cynthia Fuchs. Woman's Place. Berkeley: University
    of California Press, 1970.

Fogarty, Michael P. Women in the Architectural Profession
    1978. London: Policy Studies Institute, 1979.

Frost, Henry Atherton. Women in Architecture and Landscape
    Architecture (Study for the Institute for
    Co-ordination of Women Interests Publication no. 7)
    Northampton, Mass: Smith College, 1931.

Gardner, E.C. The House that Jill Built After Jack's Had
    Proved a Failure. New York: Fords, Howard & Hulbert,
    1882.

Goldreich, Gloria, and Esther Goldreich. What Can She Be?
    An Architect. New York: Lothrop, Lee and Shepard,
    1974.

Gothein, Marie Luise. A History of Garden Art. New York:

E.P. Dutton, 1928.

Hadfield, Mills. Pioneers in Gardening. New York:
    Macmillan, 1957.

Hapgood, Karen C. Women in Planning: A Report on Their
    Status in Public Planning Agencies. Chicago: American
    Society of Planning Officials, 1971.

_____, and Judith Getzels. Planning, Women and
    Change. Chicago: American Society of Planning
    Officials, 1974.

Harrod, Nancy, and Susan Naimark editors. Proceedings of
    the Conference For Women in Design and Planning.
    Boston: Boston Architectural Center, 1975.

Hayden, Dolores. The Grand Domestic Revolution. Cambridge,
    Mass: MIT Press, 1981.

_____. Seven American Utopias. Cambridge, Mass:
    MIT Press, 1976.

Hollingsworth, Buckner. Her Garden Was Her Delight. New
    York: Macmillan, 1962

_____. Romance of the National Parks. New York:
    Macmillan Co., 1939.

Kampen, Natalie, and Elizabeth Grossman. Feminism and
    Methodology: Dynamics and Change in the History of Art
    and Architecture. Wellesley, MA: Wellesley College
    Center for Research on Women (Working Paper no. 122),
    1983.

Karras, Maria. The Woman's Building, Chicago, 1893; The
    Woman's Building, Los Angeles, 1973. Los Angeles: A
    Women's Community Press, 1975.

Keller, Suzanne. Building for Women. Lexington, MA: D.C.
    Heath and Co., 1981.

Kennedy, Roger G. Architecture, Men, Women and Money in
    America, 1600-1860. New York: Random House, 1985.

Klowdasky, Fran. Employment Opportunities for Women in

Architecture and Urban Planning. Ottawa: Labour
Canada, 1985.

Loeb, J. Feminist Collage: Educating Women in the Visual
Arts. New York: Teachers College Press, Columbia
University, 1979.

Lowthorpe School of Landscape Architecture, Gardening and
Horticulture for Women, Groton, Mass. Lowthorpe
School of Landscape Architecture, Gardening and
Horticulture for Women, Groton, Massachusetts.
Ayer, MA: H.S. Turner, 1914.

Marvin, Betty. The Residential Work in Berkeley of Five
Women Architects. Berkeley, CA: Berkeley Architectural
Heritage Association, 1984.

Meinhardt, Carl, Carolyn Meinhardt, and Alan E. Nourse. So
You Want to Be an Architect. New York: Harper and Row
Pub., 1969.

Monchow, Helen C. The Use of Deed Restrictions in
Subdivision Development. Chicago: Institute for
Research in Land Economics and Public Utilities, 1928.

Nassauer, Joan I. The National Survey of Career Patterns
Among Women in Landscape Architecture. Washington,
D.C.: American Society of Landscape Architects, 1983.

Newton, Norman T. Design on the Land. Cambridge, MA:
Belknap Press, 1971.

Prather-Moses, Alice Irma. The International Dictionary of
Women Workers in the Decorative Arts. Metuchen, New
Jersey: Scarecrow Press, 1981.

Rondanini, Nunzia. Making Room: Women and Architecture. New
York: Heresies Collective, 1981.
Special issue of Heresies (v. 3 no. 3, 1981) devoted
to this theme.

Saint, Andrew. The Image of the Architect. New Haven: Yale
University Press, 1983.

Torre, Susanna. ed. Women in American Architecture. New
York: Whitney Library of Design, 1977.

U.S. Women's Bureau. <u>The Outlook for Women in Architecture</u>
    <u>and Engineering</u>. Washington, D.C.: Government Printing
    Office, 1948.

Waters, Clara Clement. <u>Painters, Sculptors, and Architects</u>.
    Boston: J.R. Osgood and Co., 1882.

Weimann, Jeanne Madeline. <u>The Fair Women</u>. Chicago: Academy
    Chicago, 1981.

Wekerle, Gerda ed. <u>New Space for Women</u>. Boulder: Westview
    Press, 1980.

West Coast Women's Design Conference, University of Oregon,
    1974. <u>Proceedings of the West Coast Women's Design</u>
    <u>Conference</u>. Eugene: Univ. of Oregon Press, 1975.

Wright, Gwendolyn. <u>Moralism and the Model Home</u>. Chicago:
    University of Chicago Press, 1980.

Yondrof, Lisa B. <u>Women and Blacks in Planning, 1972</u>.
    Chicago: American Society of Planning Officials, 1972.

DISSERTATIONS AND THESES:

Beavers, Faye. <u>American Women Designers</u>. B.S. Thesis, Texas
    State College for Women, 1938.

Earnest, Katrena A. <u>Women and Walls: Eleven Architectural</u>
    <u>Figures</u>. M.F.A. Thesis, California State University,
    Long Beach, 1981.

Hargis, Jerlene W. <u>Attitudes Toward Women: A Study of the</u>
    <u>Urban Planning Profession</u>. M.A. Thesis, Ohio State
    University, 1971.

Leavitt, Jacqueline. <u>Planning and Women, Women in Planning</u>.
    Ph.D. Dissertation, Columbia University, 1980.

Martin, Rochelle. <u>The Difficult Path: Women in the</u>
    <u>Architectural Profession</u>. Ph.D Dissertation,
    University of Michigan, 1986.

Milwid, Mary Elizabeth. <u>Women in Male-Dominated</u>

Professions: A Study of Architects, and Lawyers. Ph.D
Dissertation, The Wright Institute, 1982.

Paine, Judith. Pioneer Women Architects. M.A. Thesis,
Columbia University, 1975.

Palmer, Donna. An Overview of the Trends, Eras, and Values
of Landscape Architecture in America from 1910 to the
Present with an Emphasis on the Contributions of Women
to the Profession. M.L.A. Thesis, North Carolina State
University, 1976.

Stevenson, Roseann C. Women Architects: Engineering New
Roles for Professionals. B.A. Thesis, Rutgers
University, 1976.

Vigil, Terry Ann. A Manpower Study of the Professional
Woman in Planning. M.A. Thesis in Regional Planning,
Syracuse University, 1972.

Wheeler-Meehan, Linda. Analysis of Factors Related to the
Increase in Women Graduates from Professional Schools
in the United States from 1960 through 1980. Ed.D.
Dissertation, Pepperdine University, 1983.

EXHIBITION CATALOGS AND REVIEWS:

A.I.R. Gallery, New York. Detail, the Special Task. New
York: the Gallery, 1984.

Art Insitute of Chicago. Chicago Architects Design: A
Century of Architectural Drawings from the Art
Institute of Chicago. New York: Rizzoli Inc. and the
Art Institute of Chicago, 1982.

Chicago Historical Society. Chicago Women in Architecture:
Progress and Evolution, 1974-1984. Chicago: The
Society, 1984.
Published as an insert in Inland Architect. 28
(November-December 1984).

"Chicago Women in Architecture." Progressive Architecture.
66 (January 1985), 30.

"Chicago Women in Architecture: Exhibition Review."
    Progressive Architecture. 66 (January 1985), 30.

Conroy, Sarah Booth. "Washington Women in Architecture: Out
    of the Broom Closet." Washington Post. (August 1,
    1976), F1, F3.

"Designing Women." Newsweek. 89 (March 7, 1977) 79-81.

Huxtable, Ada Louise. "The Last Profession To Be Liberated
    by Women." New York Times (March 13, 1977), D25, D33.

Kay, Jane H. "Architecture; Women in American Architecture,
    A History and Contemporary Perspective, Exhibition."
    Nation. 224 (April 16, 1977), 474-476.

_____. "Built by Women." Los Angeles Times. (November
    12, 1982), 62-63.

_____. "Women at Work...Woman, the Master Builder: An
    Exhibition of Women Architects' Work in the U.S.A."
    Building Design. 352 (June 24, 1977), 21.

"Kitchen Specialists: Report on the Exhibition Showing the
    Work of Women Architects in the U.S." Art Journal. 37
    (Fall 1977), 53.

Knight, C. "D.C. Women's Exhibit: Brief but Memorable."
    Progressive Architecture. 57 (October 1976), 31-32.

Lague, Louise. "Lady Architects Have Designs on Equality."
    Washington Star. (August 2, 1976), C1, C3.

"Major Exhibition on Women in Architecture Opens at
    Brooklyn." Architectural Record. 161 (March 1977), 38.

Paine, Jocelyn. "Hidden History of a Profession: Exhibit
    Recognizes Women's Largely Obscured Architectural
    Contributions." Los Angeles Times. (April 30, 1978),
    20, 22 +.

Treib, Marc. "Women Architects Shown in Finland: An
    Exhibition Produced by Architects, The Finnish
    Association of Women Architects." Progressive
    Architecture. 64 (January 1983), 33.

Washington Women in Architecture. Washington Women
     Architects. Washington, D.C.: Washington Women in
     Architecture, 1976.

"Women Design Space: Preview of a Major Exhibit." Ms. 5
     (March 1977), 62-67.

"Women in American Architecture: A Historic and
     Contemporary Perspective." Ms. 5 (March 1977), 62-67.

"Women in American Architecture: A Historic and
     Contemporary Perspective, Exhibition." Controspazio. 9
     (July-August 1977), 60-62.

"Women in Architecture and Design: An Historic and
     Contemporary Perspective: Brooklyn Museum." Interiors.
     136 (March 1977), 4.

"Women's Exhibit: A Timely Tribute." Progressive
     Architecture. 58 (April 1977), 32 +.

"Women's Role in Architecture Influence Lifestyles:
     Exhibition Sponsored by the Architectural League of
     New York." Theatre Design and Technology. 13 (Summer
     1977), 34.

PERIODICAL ARTICLES AND ESSAYS:

"AIA. Affirmative Action Plan Attacks Sex Dicrimina-
     tion." Architectural Record. 159 (March 1976), 35.

"AIA. Annual Convention: Proposed Study of Women's Status
     in Field." Architectural Forum. 139 (July 1973), 22.

"AIA. Convention: Women on the Move Towards Tomorrrow."
     Progressive Architecture. 58 (July 1977), 29.

"The Admission of a Woman to Associateship in the Royal
     Institute of British Architects." American Architect
     and Building News. 63 (January 21, 1899), 20-21.

"Advent of the Draughtswoman." Architectural Review. 41
     (April 1917), 86.

Agena, K. "Red Letter Count Down." Design and Environment.
    5 (Spring 1974), 31-33.

Ahrentzen, Sherry. "Women and Environments' Course in an
    Architecture School." Women and Environments. 7
    (Winter 1985), 13.

"American Women." Time. (March 20, 1972), 77.

Anderson, Dorothy M. "Women's Breakthrough via the
    Cambridge School." Landscape Architecture. 68 (March
    1978), 145-148.

"Architectural Criticism: Four Women." Progressive
    Architecture. 58 (March 1977), 56-57.

"Architecture: Feminist Ferment." New York Times (August
    9, 1975), 7.

"Architecture for Women." Southern Architect and Building
    News. 32 (January 1914), 7-8.

Banham, Reyner. "Death and Life of the Prairie School."
    Architectural Review. 154 (August 1973), 99-101.

Beaumont, Anne. "Women Planners: the Challenge of the Top."
    Women and Environments. 6 (Fall 1984), 20-21.

Beem, Lulu S. "Women in Architecture: A Plea Dating from
    1884." Inland Architect. 15 (December 1971), 6.

Benson, Mary Ellen. "Women in Architecture Revisited."
    Architecture News. (February 1985), 1-2, 4-5.

Berkeley, Ellen Perry. "Women in Architecture."
    Architectural Forum. 137 (September 1972), 45-53.

Berlo, J. C. "The Cambridge School: Women in Architecture."
    Feminist Art Journal. 5 (Spring 1976), 27-32.

Bethune, Louise. "Women and Architecture." Inland Architect
    and News Record. 17 (March 1891), 20-21.

Birch, Eugenie L. "Women Made America: The Case of Early
    Public Housing Policy." Journal of the American

Institute of Planners. 44 (April 1978), pp. 130-144.

Birkby, Phyllis. "Herspace." Heresies. 3 (March 1981),
    28-29.

_____ and Leslie Kanes Weisman. "A Woman Built
    Environment: Constructive Fantasies." Quest. 2
    (Summer 1975), 7-18.

Blitzer, D.C. "Unisex Architecture." Progressive
    Architecture. 55 (August 1974), 7.

Bliznakov, Milka. "A Brief Survey of the Women Architects
    in the First Half of the Twentieth Century."
    Structurist. 25-26 (1985-1986), 121-127.

"Black Women Architects: A Blueprint for Success." Ebony.
    39 (June 1984), 52-56.

Bowlby, Sophie, and others. "Women and the Environment."
    Built Environment. 10 no. 1 (1984), 4-68, 81-87.

Boys, Jo. "Shape of Work to Come: The Matrix Group's
    Feminist Approach to Architecture." Building Design.
    500 (June 13, 1980), 27.

Briggs, M.S. "Women as Architects." Architectural Review.
    26 (September 9, 1909), 121-122.

"Bringing Them Back Alive: Resourceful Women Restorers
    Authentically Re-create the Homes of our Colonial
    Ancestors." House and Garden. 153 (May 1981), 122-123,
    188, 192.

Brown, Catherine R. and Celia Maddox. "Women and the Land:
    A Suitable Profession." Landscape Architecture. 72
    (May 1982), 65-69.

Bruegel, Irene and Adah Kay. "Women and Planning." AD. 45
    (August 1975), 499-500.

"The Case for Flexible Work Schedules." Architectural
    Forum. 137 (September 1972), 53 + .

Charles, E. "Building Blocks." Spare Rib. 18 (December 1973), 37-40.

Charles, Ethel M. "A Plea for Women Practising Architecture." American Architect and Building News. 76 (April 19, 1902), 20-22.

Chatfield Taylor, Adele. "Hitting Home." Architectural Forum. 138 (March 1973), 58-61.

Clay, Grady. "Shapely Women and Cities." Landscape Architecture. 49 (Autumn 1958), 7.

Cliff, Ursula. "Three Exceptional Women." Design and Environment. 5 (Spring 1974), 34-37.

Cohen, J.H. and S.F. Berkon. "Letters." Feminist Art Journal. 4 (Spring 1975), 46-47.

Cole, Doris. "The Education of Women Architects: A History of the Cambridge School." Architecture Plus. 1 (December 1973), 30-35, 78-79.

Colybes, Annick. "Women Invade the Profession." Architecture Revue de l'Ordre des Architects. 7 (August-September 1979), 18-19, 21.

Davies, Paul. "Women in Architecture: Report of a Conference Held at North East London Polytechnic." The Architect. 4 (February 1974), 53-54.

Dean, Andrea O. "Board Acts on the Role of Women in Architecture." AIA Journal. 63 (March 1975), 33-34.

_____. "Women in Architecture: Individual Profiles and a Discussion of Issues." AIA Journal. 71 (January 1982), 42-51.

DeBretteville, S.L. "Some Aspects of Design from the Perspective of a Woman Designer." Iconographic. 6 (1973), 4-8.

Deitz, Paula. "Designing Women." Metropolis. (December 1982), 14-19.

_____. "Women in Landscape Architecture." New York

Times. (August 28, 1980), C10.

DeSaules, M. "Return of Married Women to Professional
    Life." _Royal Institute of British Architects Journal_.
    71 (April 1964), 136.

"Design Plus: The How and Why." _Interiors_. 140 (October
    1980), 20.

Dietsch, S. "Women at Columbia: A Century of Change."
    Progressive Architecture. 63 (June 1982), 22-23.

Dinerman, Beatrice. "Women in Architecture." _Architectural
    Forum_. 131 (December 1969), 50-51.

Dixon, John M. "Editorial: Women's Place." _Progressive
    Architecture_. 58 (March 1977), 7.

Dobson, Carla. "As Good As the Next Man: The Problems
    Confronting Women in the Construction Industry."
    Building. 235 (October 27, 1978), 52-53.

"The Domestic Domain." _Progressive Architecture_. 58 (March
    1977), 39-40.

Domett, H.W. "Women in Art and Architecture." _Building: an
    Architectural Monthly_. 1 (June 1883), 118.

Dona, Claudia. "Butterflies of Planning." _Modo_. 78 (April
    1985), 54-57.

Dott, Annabel. "The Woman Architect and Her Work."
    Architectural Review. 44 (1918), 31-32.

Dreyfus, Patricia Ann. "Women's Lib and Women Designers."
    Print. 24 (May 1970), 29-35.

Dunlop, Beth. "How One Firm Goes About 'Cutting In'
    Minorities and Women: Dalton, Dalton, Newport." _AIA
    Journal_. 63 (February 1975), 41-42.

Dwyer, Gary C. "A Critical Role for Women." _Landscape
    Architecture_. 74 (September-October 1984), 172.

Easton-Ruiz, Miriam. "The Missing Sex in Landscape
    Architecture Classrooms." _Landscape Architecture_. 68

(March 1978), 102-103.

Fein, Albert. A Study of the Profession of Landscape
    Architecture. McLean, Virginia: American Society of
    Landscape Architects Foundation, 1972.

"Female Architects." Builder. 19 (April 13, 1861), 254.

"Les Femmes Architectes." La Construction Moderne. 11
    (1896), 245-256.

"The First Woman Architect?" Country Life. 113 (April 9,
    1953), 1077.

"Four Fine Fellows." AIA Journal. 52 (September 1969),
    86-87.

"A Forty Thousand Dollar Dream House Designed by Sixty
    Women." Better Homes and Gardens. 52 (May 1974), 24.

Fowler, Pauline. "The Public and the Private in
    Architecture: A Feminist Critique." Women's Studies
    International Forum. 7 no. 6 (1984), 449-454.

_____. "Reclaiming Architecture: Women's Cultural
    Building." Women and Environments. 7 (Fall 1985),
    14-17.

Francis, Susan. "Women's Design Collective." Heresies. 3
    no. 3 (1981), 17.

Frost, Henry Atherton. "Letter to the Editor." Landscape
    Architecture. 32 (April 1942), 119.

_____ and William R. Sears. "Women in
    Horticulture." House and Garden. 47 (March 1925), 64.

"Gardening in New England Section." Horticulture. 18
    (December 15, 1940), 1-2.

Garrett, Susanne. "Women in Architecture." Buiding Design.
    195 (April 5, 1974), 12-13.

Goldberger, Paul. "Women Architects Building Influence in a
    Profession That Is 98.8 per cent Male." New York
    Times. (May 18, 1974), 33 + .

Greene, Zina. "The Changing Role of Women: Implications for
    Planners." HUD Challenge. (May 1974), 2-4.

Greer, Nora Richter. "The Plight of Minority Architects."
    Architecture. 74 (May 1985), 58-61.

_____. "Women in Architecture: A Progress
    Report and a Statistical Profile." AIA Journal. 71
    (January 1982), 40-41.

Gregg, J.W. "Universities Broaden Scope of Training in
    Landscape Design." Architect and Engineer. 131
    (November 1937), 43-46.

Greig, Doreen. "Women in Architecture." Planning and
    Building Developments. 20 (May-June 1976), 25-28.

Handlin, David. "Efficiency and the American Home."
    Architectural Association Quarterly. 5 (Winter 1973),
    50-54.

Hannaford, Iris. "Women in Building." Building. 239 (July
    18, 1980), 26-27.

Hartt, Mary B. "Women and the Art of Landscape Gardening."
    Outlook (March 28, 1908), 694-704.

Harvey, Ashley. "Women Principals." Interiors. 140 (June
    1981), 46, 48.

Hayden, Dolores. "Challenging the American Domestic Ideal."
    In: Women in American Architecture. New York: Whitney
    Library of Design, 1977, pp. 32-39.

Hayden, Dolores. "The Feminist Paradise Palace." Heresies.
    3 no. 3 (1981), 56-58.

Hayden, Dolores and Gwendolyn Wright. "Architecture and
    Urban Planning." Signs. 1 no. 4 (1976), 923-933.

Hodgdon, Rosaria F. "Influences: Positive and Negative on
    Women Entering the Profession." AIA Journal. 66
    (August 1977), 43-45.

Hollis, L.E. "Women and Planning: Why, What, When, Where
    and How." American Planners Association Journal. 46

(October 1980), 457-486.

Hudnut, Joseph. "The Architectress." AIA Journal. 15 (March 1951), 111-116; (April 1951), 181-184, 187-188.

Ibarguen, Jennie. "Designing Women." Raleigh Times (January 21, 1987), B1 + .

Jansson, Linda. "She's Built." Empire State Architect. 33 (December 1973), 26-27.

Johnson, Alice E. "Architecture as a Woman Sees It." Interstate Architect and Builder. 3 (April 13, 1901), 8.

Joynes, Jennifer R. "Women in the Architectural Profession." Habitat. 2 (July-August 1959), 2-6. Also: Royal Architectural Institute of Canada Journal. 36 (September 1959), 320-321.

Kanner, Allen D. "Femininity and Masculinity: Their Relationships to Creativity in Male Architects and Their Independence from Each Other." Journal of Consulting and Clinical Psychology. 44 (October 1976), 802-806.

Kaplan, Jane R. "Sexism in Planning: A Woman Examines a Man's Perception of Planning." Practicing Planner. 8 (September 1978), 35-36, 47.

Karten, Barbara. "Face to Face with an Architect of the Future." Seventeen. 24 (August 1965), 339.

Kaufman, Jerome L. "An Approach to Planning for Women." In Planning, Women and Change, edited by Karen C. Hapgood and Judith Getzels. Washington, D.C.: Department of Housing and Urban Development, 1974, pp. 73-76.

Kaunitz, Rita D. "Planner Suggests Strategy To Give Broader Role to Women." Institute of Planners Newsletter. 2 (November 1967), 9.

Kennedy, Margrit. "Seven Hypotheses on Male and Female Principles in Architecture." Heresies. 3, no. 3 (1981), 12-13.

Kohlberg, Edith Rose. "Battleground of the Spirit: The Pros
     and Cons of Architecture as a Career for Women."
     Mademoiselle. 63 (May 1966), 162.

Konrad, Walecia. "The Ten Worst Careers for Women." Working
     Women (July 1986), 72-73.

Lau, Barbara. "Designing Women: Black Women Architects."
     Savvy. 5 (February 1984), 88-89.

Leavitt, Jacqueline. "Women in Planning: There's More to
     Affirmative Action than Gaining Access." In: New Space
     for Women. Boulder: Westview Press, 1980, pp. 219-234.

_____. "Women in Planning Design." In Women's
     Studies and the Arts, edited by Elsa Honig Fine and
     others. New York: Women's Caucus for Art, 1978.

Lewis, Brian J. "How to Find Minority and Women-Owned
     Firms." Consulting Engineer. 57 (July 1981), 72-78.

Lewis, Ralph. "Ralph Lewis Adds a Little More About Women
     and Architecture." The Architect. 2 no. 11 (1972),
     65.

Lewis, Shawn D. "Their Fields Have Widened: Professional
     Women." Ebony. 32 (August 1977), 114-118.

"Life at the Top." Vogue. 173 (August 1983), 282-285,
     375-377.

Lindquist-Cock, Elizabeth and Estelle Jussim. "Machismo in
     American Architecture." Feminist Art Journal. 3
     (Spring 1974), 9-10.

Lippard, Lucy. "Centers and Fragments: Women's Spaces." In:
     Women in American Architecture. New York: Whitney
     Library of Design, 1977, pp. 186-197.

Lloyd, Bonnie. "Woman's Place, Man's Place." Landscape. 21
     (October 1975), 10-13.

Lobell, John. "American Women Architects." Artforum. 15
     (Summer 1977), 28-33.

Lofland, Lyn. "Women and Urban Public Space." Women and

Environments. 6 (April 1984), 12-14.

Lubbock, Jules. "Yin Quest." New Statesman. 108 (August 24, 1984), 27-28.

Mackintosh, Kate. "Women Architects: Victims by Design." Architects' Journal. 184 (September 17, 1986), 36.

Marcus, Elizabeth R. "WSPA Theme Is Social Change." Progressive Architecture. 59 (October 1978), 22 + .

Martin, Rochelle, Wendy Chamberlin, and Sarah Haselschwardt. "Women as Architects: Have We Come a Long Way?" Women and Environments. 7 (Spring 1985), 18-20.

Matthews, C.T. "Influence of Women on Architecture." American Architect and Building News. 59 (January 1, 1898), 3-4.

Nassauer, Joan Iverson. "Forked Paths: A New Survey Confirms the Gender Gap Among Professionals." Landscape Architecture. 73 (November-December 1983), 76-78.

_____. "Managing Career and Family: The Experience of Women Landscape Architects." Landscape Journal. 4 (Spring 1985), 31-38.

Nevins, Deborah. "The Triumph of Flora: Women and the American Landscape, 1890-1935." Antiques. 127 no. 4 (1985), 904-922.

"The New Professional: Coming of Age." Progressive Architecture. 58 (March 1977), 41-46.

"The New Professional: Historic Buildings." Progressive Architecture. 58 (March 1977), 47-50.

Norris, Doreen. "What It's Like To Be a Young Lady Architect." Architect and Building News. 2 (February 13, 1969), 36-37.

"One Hundred Years Ago: Lady Architects." Building. 229 (December 12, 1975), 49.

Osgood, James R. "Editorial." American Architect and
    Building News. 1 (October 1876), 1.

Paine, Judith. "The Woman's Pavilion of 1876." Feminist Art
    Journal. (Winter 1975/76), 5-13.

Patterson, Anne. "Woman Architects, Why So Few of Them?"
    Inland Architect. 15 (December 1971), 14-19.

Petersen, Anne. "Women Take Lead in Landscape Art: Field Is
    Dominated by a Group of Brilliant Designers of
    Horticultural Vistas." New York Times (March 13,
    1938), 5.

Pettit, Beatrice. "Women in W.A.L.A.P.: Women in
    Architecture, Landscape Architecture and Planning."
    ASLA Bulletin (July 1973), 14-15.

Pidgeon, W. "Women Architects Identify Identity: Extracts
    from the Resolution Drawn up at the International
    Conference of Women Architects, Ramsar, Iran, October
    1976." RIBA Journal. 83 (December 1976), 496-497.

"Portfolio of Women Architects." Architecture California. 7
    (January-February 1985), 24-29.

"Program Will Promote Women in Architecture." AIA Journal.
    65 (April 1976), 10.

"Quiet Waves in the Sexual Storm." Building Design and
    Construction. 15 (September 1974), 52-55.

Reed, J.D. "Their Plates Are Smashing: A Group of Top
    Architects Produce a Classy Line of Tableware." Time.
    124 (December 17, 1984), 90-91.

Rehman, Elsa. "An Ecological Approach." Landscape
    Architect. 23 (July 1933), 239-245.

Reif, Rita. "Fighting the System in the Male Dominated
    Field of Architecture." New York Times (April 11,
    1971), 60.

_____. "Women Architects, Slow to Unite, Find They're
    Catching Up with Male Peers." New York Times (February
    26, 1973), 37.

"Royal Institute of British Architects on Equality for
    Women." RIBA Journal. 82 (April 1975), 6-7.

Richardson, M. "Women Theorists." AD. 45 (August 1975),
    466.

Rochlin, Harriet. "All in a Day's Work: From High Rises to
    Restaurants Seven Architects Break Ground." Ms. 5
    (December 1976), 10.

_____. "Distinguished Generation of Women
    Architects in California." AIA Journal. 66 (August
    1977), 38-42.

Rock, Cynthia. "Building the Women's Club in Nineteenth
    Century America." Heresies. 3 no. 3 (1981), 87-90.

_____, Susana Torre, and Gwendolyn Wright. "The
    Appropriation of the House: Changes in House Design
    and Concepts of Domesticity." In: New Space for Women.
    edited by Gerda Wekerle and others. Boulder: Westview
    Press, 1980, pp. 83-100.

Roth, Darlene. "Feminine Marks on the Landscape: an Atlanta
    Inventory." Journal of American Culture. 3 (Winter
    1980), 673-685.

Sachs, Helen. "Aunty Tom Architects." Architectural Design.
    49 no. 2 (1974), 119-120.

_____. "Women's Self Help." Architectural Design. 45
    (1975), 493-496.

Schauman, Sally. "Women in Education." ASLA Bulletin. (July
    1973), 16.

Schultz, Robert Weir. "Architecture for Women."
    Architectural Review. 24 (September 1908), 153-154.
    Also: Architecture. 19 (1909), 13-15.

"Sexism in Design: The Evidence Builds Up." Design. 375
    (March 1980), 5.

"The Situation Today." Progressive Architecture. 58 (March
    1977), 50-55.

Speyer, Marian. "Women Who Build." Michigan Society of
    Architects Monthly Bulletin. 18 (September 12, 1944),
    144.

Standley, Kay, Bradley Soule and Jo Standley. "Women and
    Architecture." Journal of Architectural Education. 27
    no. 4 (1974), 78-82.

"Status of Women in the Profession." ASLA Bulletin (July
    1973), [7-14].

Stephens, Suzanne. "The Women Behind the T-Square."
    Progressive Architecture. 58 (March 1977), 37-38.

Stephens, Suzanne. "Women in Architecture: Breaking New
    Ground." House and Garden. 153 (March 1981), 146-149,
    196-197.

Stern, Madeleine B. "America's First Woman Architect?"
    Society of Architectural Historians Journal. 18 (May
    1959), 66.

Stevens, M. "Struggle for Place: Women in Architecture,
    1920-1960." In: Women in American Architecture. New
    York: Whitney Library of Design, 1977, pp. 88-102.

Strong, Sarah. "A Man's World, A Woman's Place."
    Architectural Design. 45 (1975), 463-465.

"Survey Finds Numerous Black Female Architects." Jet. 61
    (January 28, 1981), 29-30.

"Survey of Women in Architecture." Memo. 659 (January 12,
    1984), 1.

"Surveying the Role of Women in the Profession." AIA
    Journal. 61 (June 1974), 9.

Taylor, Ann Richards. "Landscape Architecture: A Summary
    Description." Landscape Architecture. 3 (October
    1945), 7-9.

Taylor, Maureen. "The Official View of the Female User."
    Architectural Design. 45 (1975), 471-472.

Thompson, J.M. "World at the Double Win: Male and Female

Principles in Design." Feminist Art Journal. 5 (Fall 1976), 16-20.

"A Thousand Women in Architecture I & II." Architectural Record. 103 (March 1948), 105-113; (June 1948), 108-115.

Torre, Susana. "A Current Portfolio of Projects and Ideas." In: Women in American Architecture. New York: Whitney Library of Design, 1977, pp. 162-182.

_____. "The Pyramid and the Labyrinth." In: Women in American Architecture. New York: Whitney Library of Design, 1977, pp. 198-202.

_____. "Space as Matrix." Heresies. 3 (March 1981), 51-52.

_____. "Women in Architecture and the New Feminism." In: Women in American Architecture. New York: Whitney Library of Design, 1977, pp. 148-161.

Tripp, A.F. "Lowthorpe School of Landscape Architecture, Gardening and Horticulture for Women." Landscape Architecture. 3 (1912-1913), 15.

Turpin, Dick. "More Women Architects To Be Sought." Los Angeles Times (May 11, 1973), 2.

Tyng, Emma M. "Women's Chances as Bread Winners, Part VIII: Women as Interior Decorators." Ladies Home Journal. 8 (October 1891), 4.

vanPeborgh, Sonia. "Le Premier Congres International des Femmes Architectes." UIA: Revue de l'Union Internationale des Architectes. 23 (October 1963), 14-15.

Vrchota, J. "Women in Design." Design and Environment. 5 (Spring 1974), 18-25.

WALAP: Women Architects, Landscape Architects and Planners, Boston. "The Case for Flexible Work Schedules." Architectural Forum. 137 (September 1972), 53, 66.

Walker, Lynne. "The Entry of Women into the Architectural

Profession in Britain." <u>Woman's Art Journal</u>. 7
(Spring-Summer 1986), 13-18.

Waxman, Barbara. "The Woman Architect--Myth or Mrs.?"
<u>Architecture New Jersey</u>. 2 (September-October 1965),
14-15.

Weatherford, E. "Women's Traditional Architecture."
<u>Heresies</u>. 2 (May 1977), 35-39.

White, Deborah. "Women and Architecture: A Personal
Observation." <u>Meanjin Quarterly</u>. 34 (December 1975),
399-403.

White, Naomi R. "Equal Career Opportunities: Does
Architecture Offer Equal Career Opportunities to Men
and to Women?" <u>Architecture Australia</u>. 74 (March
1985), 67-69.

_____. "On Being one of the Boys: An Exploratory
Study of Women's Professional and Domestic Role
Definitions." <u>Women's Studies International Forum</u>. 7
no. 6 (1984), 433-440.

Willis, Stan. "Woman Architects." <u>The Architect</u>. (July 18,
1919), 44-46.

Withers, Margaret. "Margaret Withers Thinks Out Loud About
Women and Architecture." <u>Architect</u>. 2 (September
1972), 36-39.

_____. "Women in Architecture." <u>Architect and
Building News</u>. 233 (March 27, 1968), 492-496.

"Women and the American City." <u>Signs: Journal of Women in
Culture and Society</u>. 5 (1980), S1-S276.

"Women and the City." <u>International Journal of Urban and
Regional Research</u>. 2 (1978), 389-576.

"Women Architects." <u>Revolution</u>. 5 (April 7, 1870), 220 + .

"Women Architects." <u>UIA: Revue de l'Union Internationale
des Architectes</u>. 35 (September 1965), 28-29.

"Women Architects Demand a Better Deal." <u>Architects'</u>

Journal. 167 (June 21, 1978), 1193-1194.

"Women Architects Say Home Designing Is Last Job Choice."
    Washington Daily News (May 16, 1957), 38.

"Women Architects Seek Wider Role in Profession, End to
    Discrimination." Architectural Record. 153 (April
    1973), 36.

"Women Architecture Students Meet in St. Louis."
    Architectural Record. 155 (May 1974), 35.

"Women as Architects." Revolution. 5 (February 3, 1870),
    74.

"Women as Landscape Architects." Southern Architect and
    Building News. 22 (February 23, 1909), 15-16.

"Women Delete 'Women' from A.I.A. Resolutions." Progressive
    Architecture. 57 (June 1976), 23-24.

"Women in Architecture." Architectural and Engineering
    News. 1 (April 1959), 13.

"Women in Architecture." Architectural Design. 45 (August
    1975), entire issue devoted to this theme.

"Women in Architecture." Bauwelt. 70 (August 24, 1979),
    1297-1323.

"Women in Architecture." Progressive Architecture. 58
    (March 1977), 37-57.

"Women in Architecture: A Symposium at Washington
    University." Interiors. 133 (March 1974), 221.

"Women in Design." Design and Environment. 5 (Spring
    1974), entire issue is devoted to this theme.

"Women in the Profession: A Report on NYSAA/AIA
    Professional Survey." Empire State Architect. 33
    (December 1973), 23-25.

"Women's Architectural School Is Scheduled." AIA Journal.
    67 (April 1978), 90 +.

"Women's Design Awards." AIA Journal. 69 (December 1980),
66.

"Women's Firms Sought by EPA to Build Wastewater Plants."
AIA Journal. 69 (June 1980), 21.

Wright, Gwendolyn. The Model Domestic Environment: Icon or
Option." In: Women in American Architecture. New York:
Whitney Library of Design, 1977, pp. 18-31.

_____. "On the Fringe of the Profession: Women
in American Architecture." In: The Architect, edited
by Spiro Kostof. New York: Oxford University Press,
1977, pp. 280-308.

_____. "The Woman's Commonwealth: A Nineteenth
Century Experiment." Heresies. 3, pt. 3 (1981), 24-27.

Wright, Richardson. "Women in Landscaping." House and
Garden. 49 (January 1926), 150.

Yarwood, George. "History of Women in Landscape Architecture." ASLA Bulletin (July 1973), [3-7].

Zanca, Jacqueline. "New Choices for Women: Career
Opportunities in Ten Major Fields." Nutshell
(1977-1978), 62-67.

AGREST, DIANA (1944-)   ARCHITECT

PRIMARY WORKS:

"Architecture of Mirrors/Mirror of Architecture."
Oppositions. 26 (Spring 1984), 118-133.

"Architectural Anagrams: The Symbolic Performance of
Skyscrapers." Oppositions. 11 (Winter 1977), 26-51.

"La arquitectura de espejo: espejo de la arquitectura."
Summa. 202 (July 1984), 42-47.

Chanin, Irwin S. A Romance with the City. New York: Cooper
Union Press, 1982, edited by Diana Agrest.

"Le Ciel est La Limite." Architecture d'Aujourd'hui. 178
(March-April 1975), 62-64.

"City as the Place of Representation." Design Quarterly.
113-114 (May 1980), 8-13.

"Design versus Non-design." Oppositions. 6 (Fall 1976),
45-68.

"Imaginary Typological Wars: Park Square, Boston, 1978.
Lotus International. 39 (1983), 59-60.

"Portrait d'un artiste." Architecture d'Aujourd'hui. 184
(March 1976), 54-57.

"Toward a Theory of Production of Sense in the Built
Environment." In: On Streets, edited by S. Anderson.
Cambridge, MA: MIT Press, 1978, pp. 213-222.

"La Villette, Paris, 1976." Design Quarterly. 113/114
(January-February 1980), 24-26.

and Mario Gandelsonas. "Architecture, Architecture."
Architecture d'Aujourd'hui. 186 (August-September
1976), 73-74.

and Mario Gandelsonas. "Architecture Between Memory and
Amnesia: A Project in the Minneapolis Grid, 1976."
Lotus International. 39 (1983), 55-58.

and Mario Gendelsonas. "Architecture Between Memory and
Amnesia: la Vilette." Design Quarterly. 113/114 (May
1980), 22-25.

and Mario Gandelsonas. "Diana Agrest and Mario Gandelsonas:
On Practice, Architecture as a Cultural Practice."
Architecture and Urbanism. 114 (March 1980), 31-110.

and Mario Gandelsonas. "Manhattan Additions - The Case for
and Against Diana Agrest and Mario Gandelsonas' Scheme
for a Tower in Manhattan's Upper East Side Historic
District." Architectural Design. 52 no. 5/6 (1982),
44-48.

and Mario Gandelsonas. "Projects, 1970-1978." Architecture
and Urbanism. 3 (March 1980), 31-110.

and Mario Gandelsonas. "Semiotica e architettura."
    Casabella. 41 (October 1977), 25.

and Mario Gandelsonas and Rodolfo Silvetti. "Concours pour
    l'amenagement des anciennes halles de la Villette."
    Architecture d'Aujourd'hui. 187 (October-November
    1976), 86-87.

and Barbara Jakobson. "Deep Ellum, Dallas, Texas." Lotus
    International. 50 (1986), 46-61.

and Allesandra Latour. "Roosevelt Island Housing
    Competition." Architecture d'Aujourd'hui. 186
    (August-September 1976), 22-35.

and others. North American Semiotics Colloquium, 1975.
    University of South Florida. A Perfusion of Signs.
    Bloomington: University of Indiana Press, 1977.

and others. "Projet Agrest/Gandelsonas/Machado/Silvetti,
    Roosevelt Island, New York City." Architecture
    D'Aujourd'hui. 186 (August-September 1976), 34-35.

and others. "Selection of Urban and Architectural Designs
    from 'City Segments' Exhibition Held at the Walker Art
    Center." Design Quarterly. 113-114, (1980) 1-80.

SECONDARY WORKS:

Colquhoun, A. "On Writing Architecture: Urban Fragments,
    Building I, Buenos Aires." Progressive Architecture.
    64 (June 1983), 80-85.

"Diana Agrest and Mario Gandelsonas: Projects."
    Controspazio. 13 (April-June 1981), 72-79.

"Diana Agrest and Mario Gandelsonas: Visionary Archi-
    tecture: Four Follies: the Forms of a Legend."
    Architecture and Urbanism. 1 (January 1985), 59-62.

Diaz, Tony, and Miguel Angel Roca. "After Modernism: Diana
    Agrest and Mario Gandelsonas." Summa. 178/179
    (September 1982), 21-66.

Dittman, Gunther, and others. "City Segments: Exhibition on

Urban Design and Architectural Depiction." Design
    Quarterly. 113/114 (1980), 4-79.

"Les Echelles: Home for a Musician on Majorca, Spain."
    Lotus International. 31 (1981), 45.

"Les Echelles: la maison d'un musicien a Majorque."
    Architecture d'Aujourd'hui. 186 (August-September
    1976), 73-74.

Filler, Martin. "Harbingers: Ten Architects." Art in
    America. 69 (Summer 1981), 114-123.

Forster, Kurt. "Sense of Construction, Buenos Aires: Urban
    Fragment I." Lotus International. 40 (1983), 90-100.

_____. "Agrest and Gandelsonas." Architecture and
    Urbanism. 8 (August 1984), 25-64.

"The Gramercy Condominium, New York City." Architectural
    Record. 173 (April 1985), 124-129.

"Les Grandes Demeures: Residence d'ete, Punta del Este,
    Uruguay; Diana Agrest and Mario Gandelsonas,
    architects." Architecture d'Aujourd'hui. 200 (December
    1978), 23-26.

Kimball, Roger. "Bill Robinson Showroom, New York City."
    Architectural Record. 174 (Mid-September 1986),
    134-141.

Lucain, Pierre. "The New American Skyscrapers: The Fifth
    Generation." Architecture d'Aujourd'hui. 220 (April
    1982), 71-106.

Mack, Mark. "Autonomous Architecture." Harvard Architecture
    Review. 3 (Winter 1984), 6-153.

"Manhattan Additions: Apartment House Project: Diana Agrest
    and Mario Gandelsonas with others." Domus. 627 (April
    1982), 4-5.

"Manhattan Additions: Proposed Apartment Building in Upper
    East Side Historic District." AD. 52 (May 1982),
    44-48.

"New York, Historical District: Design and Preservation."
    Lotus International. 33 (1981), 79-83.

"New Trends in Contemporary Architecture: Formalism,
    Realism, Contextualism." Space Design. 157 (October
    1977), 5-80.

"Park of La Villette: Architecture as Mise-en-sequence."
    Lotus International. 31 (1981), 82-84.

"Per la serie, in Austria: edificio-campione per edilizia
    universitaria." Domus. 552 (November 1975), 13-16.

"Projet de quartier a Minneapolis, 1979: Architects, Diana
    Agrest and Mario Gandelsonas." Architecture
    d'Aujourd'hui. 202 (April 1979), 19-21.

Rayon, Jean-Paul. "La Macchina per riciclare/ The Machine
    for Recycling." Lotus International. 13 (December
    1976), 102-126.

"Residence d'ete, Punta del Este, Uruguay." Architecture
    d'Aujourd'hui. 200 (December 1978), 22-25.

"Shingle Schinkel: Design for a Holiday House." Lotus
    International. 44 (1984), 55-57.

Stephens, Suzanne. "What Becomes a Monument Most?"
    Progressive Architecture. 60 (May 1979), 88-89.

_____. "Women in Architecture." House and
    Garden. 153 (March 1981), 149, 196.

Stern, Robert A. "40 Under 40." Architecture and Urbanism.
    73 (January 1977), 70-71.

"Two Pavilion House: Parents and Children." Lotus
    International. 44 (1984), 51-53.

"La Vilette: Amenagement des Anciens abattoirs et des
    abords du bassin." Paris Projet. 15/16 (1976), 96-97.

"Visionary Architecture: Diana Agrest and Mario

Gandelsonas, Four Follies - The Forms of a Legend."
Architecture and Urbanism. 1 (January 1985), 59-62.

"Un'attualita dell'architettura U.S.A." Controspazio. 7
(September 1975), 2-75.

EXHIBITIONS:

Agrest, Diana, and others. "Selection of Urban and
Architectural Designs from 'City Segments' Exhibition
Held at the Walker Art Center." Design Quarterly.
113-114 (1980), 1-80.

Desideri, P. "Le contraddittorie verita di Agrest &
Gandelsonas: Galleria AAM, Roma." Casabella. 47
(October 1983), 29.

Doubilet, S. "Agrest/Gandelsonas: Yale School of
Architecture, New Haven, Exhibit." Progressive
Architecture. 62 (March 1981), 33 + .

Galerie Nina Dausset, Paris. Dessins d'architectes: D.
Agrest, M. Gandelsonas, Michael Graves, Antoine
Grumbach, OMA, Massimo Scolari. Paris: L'Equerre,
1980.   Preface by Frederic Edelman.

Institute of Contemporary Arts, London. Drawings by
Architects/Diana Agrest. London: Institute of
Contemporary Arts, 1983.

Yale School of Architecture, New Haven. Diana Agrest/Mario
Gandelsonas: Exhibition. New Haven: Yale School of
Architecture, 1981.

ALMY, MARY (1883-1967) ∺   ARCHITECT

The M.I.T. Archives has the papers of the firm Howe,
Manning and Almy Architects; the first firm of women
architects in Boston and the second such firm in the U.S.

SECONDARY WORKS:

Cole, Doris. "New England Women Architects." In: Pilgrims
    and Pioneers: New England Women in the Arts, edited by
    Alicia Faxon and Sylvia Moore. New York: Midmarch Arts
    Press, 1987, p. 58.

"Mary Almy." American Women, 1935-1940. Detroit: Gale
    Publishers, 1981, p. 17.

"Mary Almy's Membership to be Voted Upon, Boston Chapter."
    AIA Journal. 14 (August 1926), 371.

Morse, Gail. The Firm: A Study of the First Women's
    Architectural Firm in Boston: Howe, Manning and Almy.
    Boston University, B.A. Thesis, 1979.

Parks, Warren W. Mariemont Story. Cincinnati: Creative
    Writers and Publishers, 1967, p. 75

EXHIBITION:

AIA and Architectural League, New York. Architectural and
    Allied Arts Exposition. New York: AIA and Architec-
    tural League, 1925, p. 34.

ANDERSON, DOROTHY MAY (1908-)   ARCHITECT

Smith College Archives has some of Dorothy May Anderson's
papers.

PRIMARY WORKS:

The Era of the Summer Estates. Canaan, New Hampshire:
    Phoenix Pub., 1985.

"Modern Gardens for Modern Houses." Landscape Architecture.
    32 (July 1942), 159-162.

"What Is a Landscape Architect?" Pencil Points. 23
    (February 1942), 111-112.

Women, Design and the Cambridge School. West Lafayette,
    Indiana: PDA Publishers, 1980.

"Women's Breakthrough via the Cambridge School." <u>Landscape
    Architecture</u>. 68 (March 1978), 145-148.

SECONDARY WORKS:

Anderson, Dorothy May. <u>Women Design and the Cambridge
    School</u>. West Lafayette, Indiana: PDA Pub., 1980.
    References to Anderson and photographs of her
    throughout the book.

ANDREWS, LAVONE DICKENSHEET (1912-) ⁑   ARCHITECT

SECONDARY WORKS:

"International Style of Living." <u>Architektur & Women of
    Winterhalbjahr</u>. (1972/73), 196-199.

"Third Annual International House Tour." <u>House Beautiful</u>.
    (January 1974), 44-51.

"A Thousand Women in Architecture I." <u>Architectural Record</u>.
    103 (March 1948), 105-113.

ARMSTRONG, LESLIE (1940-) ⁑   ARCHITECT

PRIMARY WORKS:

<u>The Little House</u>. New York: Macmillan Pub. Co., 1979.

and Roger Morgan. <u>Space for Dance: An Architectural Design
    Guide</u>. Washington, D.C.: Public Center for Cultural
    Resources, 1984.

SECONDARY WORKS:

"Designing Woman." <u>Woman's Day</u> (June 15, 1982), 36-37.

Lelen, Kenneth "Being Constructive: Planning a 'Little
    House' You Can Build on Your Own." <u>House Beautiful</u>.
    121 (March 1979), 27, 30.

"Record Interiors: Krasnow Apartment." Architectural
    Record. 169 (Mid-February 1981), 76-77.

Richards, Donna. "Building by the Book: A Low Cost 'Little
    House' from an Architect's Published Plans." Fine
    Homebuilding. 1 (February-March 1981), 56-58.

Slavin, Maeve. "Having It All." Interiors. 144 (November
    1984), 104-109.

"Temporary Alteration of the Broadway Theatre."
    Architectural Record. 152 (December 1972), 114-115.

"Uneasy Bedfellows: Multiple Frames." Metropolis. 5 (April
    1986), 32.

EXHIBITION:

Built By Women: A Guide to Architecture in the New York
    Area. New York: Alliance of Women in Architecture,
    1981, p. 29.

BAKER, ANNE (1890-1949)   LANDSCAPE ARCHITECT

SECONDARY WORKS:

"Anne Baker." New York Times (February 17, 1949), 23.

"Anne Baker: Biographical Minute." Landscape Architecture.
    40 (October 1949), 34-35.

Brown, Catherine R. Women and the Land. Baltimore: Morgan
    State University, 1979, p. [2].

Palmer, Donna. An Overview of the Trends, Eras and Values
    of Landscape Architecture in America. M.L.A. North
    Carolina State Univ., 1976, pp. 36-37.

BASHFORD, KATHERINE (1885-1953) LANDSCAPE ARCHITECT

SECONDARY WORKS:

Brown, Catherine R. Women and the Land. Baltimore: Morgan
    State University, 1979, p. [3].

"Honors in Landscape Architecture." Landscape Architecture.
    27 (July 1937), 208.

"Industrial Section." California Arts and Architecture. 59
    (November 1942), 51-68.

"Katherine Bashford: Biographical Minute." Landscape
    Architecture. 44 (October 1953), 29.

"Merienda, A Modern House at Palm Springs in California."
    California Arts and Architecture. 52 (October 1937),
    26-27.

Palmer, Donna. An Overview of the Trends, Eras and Values
    of Landscape Architecture in America. M.L.A. North
    Carolina State Univ., 1976, p. 36.

"Public Housing, Harbor Hills Housing Project, Housing
    Authority, County of Los Angeles." California Arts and
    Architecture. 58 (July 1941), 32.

"Residence Old and New: K. Bashford, Landscape Architect."
    Landscape Architecture. 29 (January 1939), 66-67.

Weston, Eugene Jr. "Ramona Gardens Housing Project."
    California Arts and Architecture. 57 (December 1940),
    34-35.

BASSETT, FLORENCE KNOLL (1917-)   DESIGNER

SECONDARY WORKS:

Ball, Victoria K. The Art of Interior Design. New York:
    Macmillan, 1960, p. 300.

Boles, D.D. "The Cranbrook Connection." Progressive
    Architecture. 65 (January 1984), 49-50.

"CBS: a New York au siege de la Columbia Broadcasting
      System, le Grand Style des Annees Soixante." Oeil. 142
      (October 1956), 18-23.

"CBS Offices." Architectural Forum. 102 (January 1955),
      134-139.

"Distinguished Interior Architecture for CBS." Architec-
      tural Record. 139 (June 1966), 129-134.

"Florence Knoll." In: Studio Dictionary of Design and
      Decoration. New York: Viking Press, 1973, p. 337.

"Florence Knoll Bassett." In: Macmillan Encyclopedia of
      Architects. New York: Free Press, 1982, v. 1, p. 151.

"Florence Knoll Bassett Receives 1977 ASID Total Design
      Award." Interior Design. 48 (August 1977), 39.

"Florence Knoll Receives ASID Award." Residential
      Interiors. 2 (September 1977), 22.

"Florence Knoll Resigns." Industrial Design. 12 (March
      1965), 14.

"Florence Shust Knoll Bassett." In: Britannica Encyclopedia
      of American Art. New York: Simon and Schuster, 1973,
      59-60.

"Furniture Preview: Knoll's Spare Parallel Bar System."
      Interiors. 116 (January 1957), 106-107.

"Gold Medal Award." Interior Design. 32 (June 1961), 120.

Gueft, O. "Florence Knoll and the Avant Garde." Interiors.
      116 (July 1957), 58-66.

Hayward, Helena, editor. World Furniture. New York: McGraw-
      Hill, 1965, pp. 303 and plates 1143-1144.

"Human Campus for the Study of Man." Architectural Forum.
      102 (January 1955), 130-133.

"Interior Design of C.B.S. Building, 51 West 53rd Street,
      New York." Architect and Builder. 16 (July 1966),
      12-15.

Kelvin, Alice. "Designing the Workplace." Working Woman. 7
    (March 1982), 76-78.

"Knoll Without Knolls?" Interiors. 126 (August 1966), 151.

Larrabee, Eric. Knoll Design. New York: Abrams, 1981.
    References to Knoll throughout the book.

"Life at the Top." Vogue. 173 (August 1983), 375.

"L'Oeil aux Aguets sur la SAD et le SICOB." Oeil. 155
    (November 1967), 58.

"Only in the U.S.A." House and Garden. 96 (July 1949),
    30.

"Personalities." Progressive Architecture. 42 (June 1961),
    75.

Shea, John G. Contemporary Furniture. New York: Van
    Nostrand Reinhold, 1980, pp. 4, 7.

Slavin, Maeve. "Aesthetic Revolutionary." Working Woman. 9
    (January 1984), 74-79.

Smith, C. Ray, and Allen Tate. Interior Design in the 20th
    Century. New York: Harper & Row, 1986, pp. 431,
    435-436, 478.

"Total Design Award to Florence Knoll." Contract Interiors.
    137 (August 1977), 8.

"Vingt-cinq ans de dessin a l'avant-garde." Oeil. 206/207
    (February-March 1972), 64-67.

EXHIBITIONS:

"All that Glitters: Knoll's Recent Exhibition." Industrial
    Design. 19 (April 1972), 62-67.

Boles, D.D. "The Cranbrook Convention." Progressive
    Architecture. 65 (January 1984), 49-50.

Detroit Institute of Arts. An Exhibition for Modern
    Living. Detroit: the Museum, 1949.

Musee des Arts Decoratifs, Paris. <u>Knoll au Louvre</u>. New
    York: Chanticleer Press, 1971.

National Collection of Fine Arts, Washington, D.C. <u>A Modern</u>
    <u>Consciousness: D.J. De Pree, Florence Knoll</u>.
    Washington, D.C.: Smithsonian Institution, 1975.
    Exhibition organized by L.E. Herman also traveled to
    Cranbrook Academy of Art, Bloomfield Hills, Michigan.

Neue Sammlung, Munchen. <u>Die Gute Industrieform</u>. Munchen:
    Neue Sammlung, 1955.

Plump, Barbara. "Pioneers: Designers." <u>Vogue</u>. 174 (April
    1984), 235-236.

BAUER (WURSTER), CATHERINE (1905-1964) ∺ PLANNER
                                        ARCHITECTURAL CRITIC

Her papers for 1940-1964 are at the Bancroft Library, University of California at Berkeley.

PRIMARY WORKS:

<u>Architecture in Government Housing</u>. New York: The Museum of
    Modern Art, 1936.

"Cities in Flux: A Challenge to the Postwar Planners."
    <u>American Scholar</u>. 13 (1943-1944) 70-84.

<u>A Citizens Guide to Public Housing</u>. Poughkeepsie, New York:
    Vassar College, 1940.

"Do Americans Hate Cities?" <u>Journal of the American</u>
    <u>Institute of Planners</u>. 23 (1957), 2-8.

"The Dreary Deadlock of Public Housing." <u>Architectural</u>
    <u>Forum</u>. 106 (May 1957), 140-143.

"Exhibition of Modern Architecture: Museum of Modern Art,
    New York. "<u>Creative Arts</u>. 10 (March 1932), 201-206.

<u>Facts for a Housing Program</u>. Washington, D.C.: U.S.
    Housing Authority, 1938.

Framework for an Urban Society. President's Commission on
     National Goals. New York: Prentice-Hall, 1960.

The Future of Cities and Urban Redevelopment. Chicago:
     University of Chicago Press, 1953.

"Garden Cities and the Metropolis: A Reply." Journal of
     Land and Public Utility Economics. 22 (February 1946),
     65-66.

"Good Neighbors." Annals of the American Academy of
     Political Science. 284 (1945), 104-115.

"Historia de la vivienda en los Estados Unidos." Nuestra
     Arquitectura. 7 (July 1947), 238-247.

"Homes: Front Line Defense for American Life." Survey
     Graphic. 29 (February 1940), entire issue devoted to
     this topic.

"Houser Wins Guggenheim Award." Architectural Record. 79
     (May 1936), 341.

"Housing, Planning, and the New Emergency." Community
     Planning Review. 1 (August 1951), 78-82.

"Housing Progress and the Architect." Michigan Society of
     Architects Bulletin. 28 (April 1952), 9, 11.

"HUD Building Seen as Turning Point for Department and
     Public Architecture." Journal of Housing. 25
     (September 1968), 405-408.

"Increasing the Social Responsibility of the City
     Planners." Proceedings of the American Institute of
     Planners and Institute of Professional Town Planners
     Joint Meeting. Boston: American Institute of Planners,
     1950.

"Indian Vernacular Architecture: Wai and Cochlin."
     Perspecta. 5 (1959), 37-48.

International Labour Office: Housing in the United States,
     Problems and Policy. Montreal: n.p., 1915.

Labor and the Housing Program. Washington, D.C.: U.S.

Housing Authority, 1938.

"Leadership Responsibilities in Planning for Human Needs."
   Proceedings American Municipal Association. Chicago:
   American Municipal Association, 1957.

"Lessons from War Housing: A Summary." AIA Journal. 1
   (March 1944), 143-144.

Low Rent Housing and Home Economics. Baltimore, MD: U.S.
   Housing Authority, 1939.

"Machine-Made." American Magazine of Art. 27 (May 1934),
   267-270.

Modern Housing. Boston: Houghton Mifflin, 1934.

"Nathan Straus: Administrator of USHA, 1937-1942." NAHU
   News. 6 (March 14, 1942), 18-20.

"The Pattern of Urban and Economic Development: Social
   Implications." Annals of the American Academy of
   Political Science. 305 (1956), 60-69.

"Planned Large Scale Housing." Architectural Record. 39
   (May 1941), 89-105.

"Planning Is Politics - But Are Planners Politicians?"
   Pencil Points. 25 (March 1944), 66-70.

"Prize Essay: Art in Industry." Fortune (May 1931),
   94-110.

"Reconstruction: France." Task. 7/8 (1948), 34.

"Redevelopment: A Misfit in the Fifties." In: The Future of
   Cities and Urban Redevelopment. edited by Coleman
   Woodbury. Chicago: University of Chicago Press, 1953.

"Row House Construction." Pencil Points. 28 (July 1947),
   73-77.

"The Social Effects of Decentralization." Proceedings of
   the University of California Conference on City and
   Regional Planning. Berkeley:University of California,
   1954.

"The Social Front of Modern Architecture in the 1930's."
    Society of Architectural Historians Journal. 24 (March
    1965), 48-52.

"Social Questions in Housing and Community Planning."
    Journal of Social Issues. 5 (1949) 1-34.

Social Questions in Housing and Town Planning. London:
    University of London Press, 1952.

"Social Responsibility of the Planners." Town and Country.
    20 (April 1952), 169-173.

"Sources of Information on Housing." Architect and
    Engineer. 150 (August 1942), 13.

"Toward a Green and Pleasant England? Critical Review of
    English Publications on Postwar Planning." Pencil
    Points. 25 (April 1944), 78 + .

"Typenware in Amerika." Die Form. 7 (September 15, 1932),
    275-280.

"Urban and Regional Structure: The Belated Challenge and
    the Changing Role of the Physical Planners."
    Proceedings of the Annual Conference of the American
    Institute of Planners. Washington, D.C.: American
    Institute of Planners, 1961.

"Wartime Housing in Defense Areas." Architect and Engineer.
    151 (October 1942), 33-35.

"We Present Catherine Bauer in Her Own Words." Journal of
    Housing. 1 (November 1944), 27, 31.

"A Year of the Low-Rent Housing Program." Shelter. 3
    (November 1938), 4-8.

and Henry Russell Hitchcock. Modern Architecture in
    England. New York: Museum of Modern Art, 1937.

and Clarence S. Stein. "Store Buildings and Neighborhood
    Shopping Centers." Architectural Record. 75 (1934),
    175-187.

SECONDARY WORKS:

"Architectural Criticism: Four Women." Progressive
    Architecture. 58 (March 1982), 72-73.

Birch, Eugenie L. "Woman-Made America: The Case of the
    Early Public Housing Policy." AIA Housing Journal. 44
    (April 1978), 130-144.

"Catherine K. Bauer." Macmillan Encyclopedia of Architects.
    New York: Free Press, 1982, v. 1, p. 154.

"Catherine Bauer." National Cyclopedia of American
    Biography. New York: James T. White, 1904, pp. 268-69.

"Catherine Krouse Bauer." Notable American Women: The
    Modern Period. Cambridge: Belknap Press, 1980, pp.
    66-68.

Cole, Susan. Catherine Bauer and the Public Housing
    Movement, 1926-1937. Ph.D. Dissertation, George
    Washington University, 1975.

Elsen, Sylvia. "Early Heroics: Catherine Bauer." Working
    Woman. 7 (March 1982), 72-73.

"Housing: A Memorandum." California Arts and Architecture.
    60 (February 1943), 18-19, 41-42.

"Housing's White Knight." Architectural Forum. 84 (March
    1946), 116-119,146, 148, 150.

Mumford, Lewis. My Works and Days: A Personal Chronicle.
    New York: Harcourt Brace Jovanovich, 1979.
    References to her throughout the book.

_____. Roots of Contemporary American
    Architecture. New York: Reinhold, 1952, p. 421.

"Portrait." Architectural Forum. 75 (July 1941), 10.

"Portrait." Architectural Forum. 77 (September 1942), 2.

Stevens, Mary Otis. "Struggle for Place: Women in
    Architecture, 1920-1960. "In: Women in American
    Architecture. New York: Whitney Library of Design,

1977, pp. 88-102.

Stephens, Suzanne. "Voices of Consequence: Four
    Architectural Critics." In: Women in American
    Architecture. New York: Whitney Library of Design,
    1977, pp. 136-143.

"Woman Hiker Dead: Aided Three Presidents on City
    Planning." New York Times (November 24, 1964), 40.

BERKELEY, ELLEN PERRY (1931-   ) ☆   EDUCATOR
                                ARCHITECTURAL CRITIC

PRIMARY WORKS:

"Architecture: Towards a Feminist Critique." In: New Space
    for Women. Boulder: Westview Press, 1980, pp. 205-218.

"Evaluation: Seeing a House Through the Reactions of
    Others." AIA Journal. 67 (February 1978), 42-43.

"Evaluation: Three Small Dormitories in Vermont." AIA
    Journal. 68 (April 1979), 58-63.

"New York Style: Architect's Guide to Apartment Houses."
    Skyline (April 1982), 12-13.

"Seeking an Agenda for Urban Design: Conference Held by the
    AIA's National Urban Planning and Design Committee."
    AIA Journal. 69 (February 1980), 54-55, 66, 76.

"Where Architects and Behavioralists Meet: The Tenth Annual
    Conference of the Environmental Design Research
    Association at the State University of New York at
    Buffalo." AIA Journal. 68 (August 1979), 56-57, 72,
    74.

"Where People are 'Users': Reflections on the 1985 FDRA
    Conference." Architecture. 74 (November 1985), 76-79.

"Women and the Man-Made Environment." In: Modern Social
    Reforms, edited by Arthur B. Shostak. New York:
    Macmillan, 1974.

and Paul F. Friedberg. Play and Interplay: A Manifesto for
    New Design in Urban Recreational Environment. New
    York: Macmillan, 1970.

and others. "Computers for Design and a Design for the
    Computer." Architectural Forum. 128 (March 1968), 60.

SECONDARY WORKS:

"Ellen Perry Berkeley." In: Contemporary Authors. Detroit:
    Gale, 1984, v. 110, p. 52.

BETHUNE, LOUISE (1856-1913) ::   ARCHITECT

PRIMARY WORKS:

Bethune, Louise. "Women and Architecture." Inland Architect
    and News Record. 17 (March 1891), 20-21.
    Reprinted In: Inland Architect. 27 (July-August 1983),
    46-47.

SECONDARY WORKS:

Becker, John E. A History of the Village of Waterloo, New
    York. Waterloo, New York: n.p., 1949, p. 200.

Buffalo/Western New York Chapter AIA. Louise Bethune, FAIA
    1856-1913. researched by Adriana Barbasch. Buffalo:
    AIA, 1986.

Greenstein, Louis. "History of Buffalo-Western New York
    Chapter of the AIA." Empire State Architect. 4
    (September-October 1944), 19-21.

Hitchcock, Henry Russell. "Buffalo Architecture in Review."
    Art News. 38 (January 20 1940), 8 + .

Logan, Mrs. John A. The Part Taken by Women in American
    History. Wilmington, Delaware: Perry Nalle Publishing
    Co, 1912, pp. 787-788.

"Louise Bethune." Architectural Era (August 1888), 149;

(November 1888), 214; (August 1889), xiv, 286;
(February 1890), 47; (March 1890), 64; (June 1890),
138.

"Louise Bethune."Buffalo Courier (July 20, 1915), 7.

"Louise Bethune." National Cyclopedia of American
Biography. New York: White and Co., 1904, p. 9.

"Louise Bethune." Who's Who in America, 1914-1915. Chicago:
Marquis Pubs., 1942, v. 1, p. 184.

"Louise Bethune." Who Was Who in America, 1897-1942.
Chicago: Marquis Pubs., 1942, v. 1, p. 90.

"Louise Blanchard Bethune." International Dictionary of
Women's Biography. New York: Macmillan Co., 1982, p.
57-58.

Paine, Judith. "Pioneer Women Architects." In: Women in
American Architecture. New York: Whitney Library of
Design, 1977, pp. 54-69.

Pettengill, G.E. "How A.I.A. Acquired Its First Woman
Member, Mrs. Louise Bethune." A.I.A. Journal. 63
(March 1975), 35.

Stern, Madeline B. We the Women: Career Firsts of
Nineteenth Century America. New York: Schulte
Publishing Co., 1963, pp. 61-67.

_____. "America's First Woman Architect?"
Society of Architectural Historians Journal. 18 (May
1959), 66.

Waters, Clara E.C. Women in the Fine Arts from the 7th
Century B.C. to the 20th Century A.D. New York:
Houghton Mifflin, 1904, p. 43.

Williard, Frances E., and Mary A. Livermore. A Woman of the
Century. New York: Moulton, 1893, pp. 80 ff.

Withey, Henry F., and Elsie R. Withey. Biographical
Dictionary of American Architects. Los Angeles:
Hennessey and Ingalls Inc., 1970, p. 55.

"Women in Architecture: The New Professional: Historic
    Beginnings." Progressive Architecture. 58 (March
    1977), 41-42.

BROOKS, KATHERINE   LANDSCAPE ARCHITECT

SECONDARY WORKS:

Anderson, Dorothy May. "Women's Breakthrough Via the
    Cambridge School." Landscape Architecture. 68 (March
    1978), 145-148.

Brown, Catherine and Celia Maddox. "Women and the Land: A
    Suitable Profession." Landscape Architecture. 72 (May
    1982), 65-69.

BROWN, CATHERINE R. (1950-   )   LANDSCAPE ARCHITECT

PRIMARY WORKS:

Women and the Land. Baltimore, MD: Built Environment
    Studies, Morgan State University, 1979.

and Celia Maddox. "Women and the Land: A Suitable
    Profession." Landscape Architecture. 72 (May 1982),
    65-69.

and others. Building for the Arts.   Santa Fe: Western
    States Art Foundation, 1984.

BROWN, DENISE SCOTT (1931-   )   ARCHITECT
                                        PLANNER

PRIMARY WORKS:

"Architectural History." Arts and Architecture. 84 (May
    1967), 30.

"Architectural Taste in a Pluralistic Society. "Harvard
    Architectural Review. 1 (Spring 1980), 40-51.

"Changing Family Forms." American Planning Association
     Journal. 49 (Spring 1983), 133-137.

"The Crosstown Is Dead: Long Live the Crosstown,
     Philadelphia's Controversial Crosstown Expressway."
     Architectural Forum. 135 (October 1971), 42-44.

"Design for the Deco District: Architects for Renovation
     Venturi, Rauch, and Scott Brown." Lotus International.
     39 (1983), 119-120.

"Development Proposal for Dodge House Park." Arts and
     Architecture. 83 (April 1966), 16.

"Drawing for the Deco District." Archithese. 12
     (March-April 1982), 3-4.

"Elitismo e/o establishment." Architettura. 22 (February
     1977), 548.

"Invention and Tradition in the Making of American Place."
     Harvard Architecture Review. 5 (1986), 163-171.

"Las Vegas." Casabella. 44 (November-December 1980), 112.

"Learning from Pop." Casabella. 357 (May-June 1971), 14-40.

"Little Magazines in Architecture and Urbanism." American
     Institute of Planners Journal. 34 (July 1968),
     223-233.

"Looking at the Future Into the Immediate Past."
     Architecture. 76 (May 1987), 116.

"Mapping the City: Symbols and Systems." Landscape. 17
     (Spring 1968), 22-25.

"Mass Communication on the People Freeway, or Piranesi Is
     Too Easy." Perspecta. 12 (1969), 49-56.

"On Architectural Formalism and Social Concern: A Discourse
     for Social Planners and Radical Chic Architects."
     Oppositions. 5 (Summer 1976), 99-112.

"On Formal Analysis as Design Research." Journal of
     Architectural Education. 32 (May 1979), 8-11.

"On Pop Art, Permissiveness, and Planning." Architects'
     Yearbook. 13 (1971), 63-64.

"Il 'Pop' Indegna: Learning from Pop." Casabella. 35
     (December 23, 1971), 14-23.

"Planning the Expo." American Institute of Planners
     Journal. 47 (April 1967), 81-83.

"Planning the Powder Room." AIA Journal. 47 (April
     1967), 81-83.

"Realissmus in der Architektur." Archithese. 19 (1976),
     entire issue devoted to this theme.

"Revitalising Miami: A Plan for Miami Beach's Washington
     Avenue." Urban Design International. 1 (January-
     February 1980), 20-25.

"Risposta per Frampton." Casabella. 35 (December 1971),
     39-46.

"Suburban Space, Scale and Symbols." VIA 3 (1977), 40-47.

"Venturi, Rauch and Scott Brown: Arts and Crafts Museum,
     Frankfurt am Main." Architectural Design. 51 no. 12
     (1981), 124-129.

"Visions of the Future Based on Lessons from the Past."
     Center: a Journal for Architecture in America. 1
     (1985), 44-63.

"Will Salvation Spoil the Dodge House?" Architectural
     Forum. 125 (October 1966), 68-71.

"With People in Mind." Journal of Architectural Education.
     35 (Fall 1981), 43-45.

"A Worm Eye's View of Recent Architectural History."
     Architectural Record. 172 (February 1984), 69, 71, 73,
     75, 77, 79, 81.

and Gordon Cullen. "Communications." Connection. 4 (Spring
     1967), entire issue is devoted to this theme.

and Robert Venturi. Aprendiendo de Todas Las Cosas.
    Barcelona, 1971.

and Robert Venturi. "L'architecture en tant qu'espace,
    l'architecture en tant que symbole." Architecture
    d'Aujourd'hui. 39 (September 1968), 36-37.

and Robert Venturi. "Co-op City: Learning to Like It."
    Progressive Architecture. 51 (February 1970), 64-73.

and Robert Venturi. L'Enseignement de Las Vegas, Ou, Le
    Symbolisme oubli'e de la Forme Architectural.
    Brussels: P. Mardaga, 1977.

and Robert Venturi. "Functionalism, Yes, but..."
    Arquitecturas Bis. 5 (January 1975), 1-2.

and Robert Venturi. "The Highway." Modulus. 9 (1973), 6-14.

and Robert Venturi. "Interview: Robert Venturi and Denise
    Scott Brown." Harvard Architecture Review. 1 (May
    1980), 228-239.

and Robert Venturi. "Robert Venturi and Denise Scott
    Brown." In: American Architecture Now II. New York:
    Rizzoli, 1983, pp. 231-239.

and Robert Venturi. "A Significance for A & P Parking Lots
    or Learning from Las Vegas." Architectural Forum. 128
    (March 1968), 36-41, 91.
    Also published in Lotus. 5 (1968), 70-91.

and Robert Venturi. "Some Houses of Ill-repute." Perspecta.
    13/14 (1971), 259-267.

and Robert Venturi. "Ugly and Ordinary Architecture or the
    Decorated Shed." Architectural Forum. 135 (November
    1971), 64-67.

and Robert Venturi. "Venturi, Rauch and Scott Brown."
    Architecture & Urbanism. 12 (December 1981), 4-223.

and Robert Venturi. "Venturi vs. Gowan." Architectural
    Design. 39 (January 1969), 31-36.

and Robert Venturi. <u>A View From the Campidoglio</u>. New York:
    Harper and Row, 1984.

and Robert Venturi, and Steve Izenour. <u>Learning From Las
    Vegas</u>. Cambridge, Mass.: MIT Press, 1972.

and Robert Venturi, and Steve Izenour. <u>Signs of Life:
    Symbols in the American City</u>. New York, 1976.

and others. "Crosstown Community, Philadelphia, 1968."
    <u>Architecture d'Aujourd'hui</u>. 159 (December 1971),
    94-97.

and others. Institute of Contemporary Art, University of
    Pennsylvania. <u>The Highway</u>. Philadelphia: the
    Institute, 1970.

SECONDARY WORKS:

Beck, Haig. "Letter from London." <u>Architectural Design</u>. 46
    (February 1976), 121.

Bruegmann, Robert. "Two Post Modernist Visions of Urban
    Design: Venturi, Scott Brown and Rob Krier."
    <u>Landscape</u>. 26 no. 2 (1982), 31-37.

Cliff, Ursula. "Are the Venturis Putting Us On?' <u>Design and
    Environment</u>. 2 (Summer 1971), 52-59, 65-66.

Cook, J.W. and H. Klotz. <u>Conversations with Architects</u>. New
    York: Praeger Publishers, 1973, pp. 247-266

"Co-op City, Bronx, New York: Learning To Like It."
    <u>Progressive Architecture</u>. 51 (February 1970), 64-72;
    51 (April 1970), 8.

Corrigan, Peter. "Reflections on a New North American
    Architecture: the Venturis." <u>Architecture in
    Australia</u>. 61 (February 1972), 55-66.

"Denise Scott Brown." In: <u>International Dictionary of
    Women's Biography</u>. New York: Macmillan Co., 1982,
    p. 421.

"Education in the 1970's: Teaching for an Altered Reality."
     Architectural Record. 148 (October 1970), 133.

"Erhaltung historischer Bauten und wirtschaftliche
     Neubelebung: Eine Studie uber den Old Mauch Chunk
     Historic District der Stadt Jim Thorpe, Pennsylvania,
     USA." Archithese. 10 (May-June 1980), 20-24.

Filler, Martin. "Personal Patterns: Pioneers in the Revival
     of Ornament and Decoration, Architects Robert Venturi
     and Denise Scott Brown Have Made Their Own Home into a
     Laboratory of Design." House and Garden. 156 (January
     1984), 90-99.

_____. "Venturi, Rauch, and Scott Brown:
     Drawings." House and Garden. 154 (October 1982), 8-10.

Frampton, Kenneth. "America 1960-1970: Notes on Urban
     Images and Theory." Casabella. 35 (December 1971),
     24-38.

Gandee, C.K. "At Home." Architectural Record. 171
     (September 1983), 108-113.

Gilbert, Lynn, and Gaylen Moore. Particular Passions. New
     York: Crown, 1981, pp. 310-323.

"Historic Preservation and Commercial Revitalization Plan
     for Jim Thorpe, Pennsylvania: Architects Venturi,
     Rauch, and Scott Brown, Partner in Charge, Denise
     Scott Brown." Progressive Architecture. 62 (January
     1981), 98-99.

"Humanities Building, State University of New York at
     Purchase." Architectural Record. 156 (October 1974),
     119-124.

Huxtable, Ada Louise. Will They Ever Finish Bruckner
     Boulevard? New York, 1970.

Jencks, Charles. "Points of View at the Architectural
     Association." AD. 39 (December 1969), 644.

Kurtz, A. Wasteland: Building An American Dream. New York,
     1973.

Larsen, Jonathan Z. "Venturi and Scott Brown." Life. 7
    (November 1984), 23 + .

"Learning the Wrong Lessons from the Beaux-arts." AD. 48
    (1978), 30-33.

"Life at the Top." Vogue. 173 (August 1983), 283.

Lytton, Bart. "Will Salvation Spoil the Dodge House?"
    Architectural Forum. 125 (October 1966), 68.

McGroarty, J. "New Professional Identities: Four Women in
    the Sixties." In: Women in American Architecture. New
    York: Whitney Library of Design, 1977, pp. 115-131.

Maddex, Diane, editor. Master Buildings. Washington, D.C.:
    Preservation Press, 1985, pp. 178-181.

Moos, S. von. "Las Vegas etcetera." Archithese. 13 (1975),
    5-52.

Polak, M.L. "Denise Scott Brown." Biography News. 2 (May
    1975), 495-496.

"Princeton Urban Design Study, Borough of Princeton, New
    Jersey: Architects: Venturi, Rauch and Scott Brown,
    principal in charge, Denise Scott Brown." Progressive
    Architecture. 63 (January 1982), 186-189.

"Progressive Architecture's Twenty-first Awards Program: A
    Year of Issues." Progressive Architecture. 55 (January
    1974), 52-89.

Rykwert, J. "Ornament Is No Crime." Studio. 190 (September
    1975), 95-97.

Schmertz, Mildred F. "Learning from Denise." Architectural
    Record. 170 (July 1982), 102-108.

_____. "Mosque as Monument." Architectural
    Record. 172 (June 1984), 142-149.

Stephens, Suzanne. "Women in Architecture." House and
    Garden. 153 (March 1981), 147, 196.

"Venturi, Rauch and Scott Brown." Macmillan Encyclopedia of

Architects. New York: Free Press, 1982, v. 4, p. 305.

"La Ville en tant que moyen de communication." Werk. 66
    (September 1979), 33-39 + .

"Women in Architecture, The New Professional: Coming of
    Age." Progressive Architecture. 58 (March 1977), 48.

"Zeichnen fur dem Deco District." Archithese. 12 (March-
    April 1982), 17-25.

BUDD, KATHERINE COTHEAL (1860-1951) * ARCHITECT

PRIMARY WORKS:

"The American Pantry." Architectural Record. 18 (September
    1905). 225-231.

"Japanese Houses." Architectural Record. 19 (January 1906),
    1-26.

"The Kitchen and Its Dependent Services." Architectural
    Record. 25 (June 1908), 463-476.

"Saragossa." Architectural Record. 19 (May 1906), 327-343.

SECONDARY WORKS:

Moulton, Robert. "Housing for Women War Workers."
    Architectural Record.37 (November 1918), 422-429.

EXHIBTION:

Built by Women: A Guide to Architecture in the New York
    Area. New York: Alliance of Women in Architecture,
    1981, p. 17.

BULLARD, ELIZABETH (fl. ca. 1899)   LANDSCAPE ARCHITECT

SECONDARY WORKS:

Brown, Catherine R. Women and the Land. Baltimore: Morgan
    State University, 1979, p. [5].

Palmer, Donna. An Overview of the Trends, Eras and Values
    of Landscape Architecture in America. M.L.A. North
    Carolina State University, 1976, p. 3.

Pond, Bremer. "Fifty Years in Retrospect." Landscape
    Architecture. 40 (January 1950), 59.

BUTTERFIELD, EMILY H. (?1885-1958)   ARCHITECT

SECONDARY WORKS:

"Emily H. Butterfield: Obituary." Michigan Society of
    Architects Monthly Bulletin. 32 (May 1958), [4].

"Emily Helen Butterfield." American Women, 1935-1940.
    Detroit: Gale Publishers, 1981, p. 136.

"A Thousand Women in Architecture: II." Architectural
    Record. 103 (June 1948), 108-115.

CAUTLEY, MARJORIE SEWEL (1891-)   LANDSCAPE ARCHITECT

PRIMARY WORKS:

Building a House In Sweden. New York: Macmillan Co., 1931.

Garden Design, The Principles of Abstract Design as Applied
    to Landscape Composition. New York: Dodd, Mead and
    Co., 1935.

"Landscaping the Housing Project." Architecture. 72
    (October 1935), 182-186.

"Planting at Radburn." Landscape Architecture. 21 (October
    1930), 23-29.

SECONDARY WORKS:

Brown, Catherine R. Women and the Land. Baltimore: Morgan
     State University, 1979, p. [6].

_____, and Celia Maddox. "Women and the Land:
     A Suitable Profession." Landscape Architecture. 72
     (May 1982), 65-69.

"Garden Design: The Principles of Abstract Design as
     Applied to Landscape Composition." Landscape
     Architecture. 26 (October 1935), 44-45.

"Marjorie Sewel Cautley." American Women, 1935-1940.
     Detroit: Gale Publishers, 1981, pp. 155-156.

"New Horizons from Aloft." Landscape Architecture. 3
     (December 1930), 17-19.

Newton, Norman J. Design on the Land. Cambridge, Mass.:
     Belknap Press, 1971, p. 489, 493.

CAVENDISH, VIRGINIA G. (1896-1951)   LANDSCAPE ARCHITECT

SECONDARY WORKS:

Palmer, Donna. An Overview of the Trends, Eras and Values
     of Landscape Architecture in America. M.L.A. North
     Carolina State Univ., 1976, p. 37.

"Virginia G. Cavendish: Biographical Minute." Landscape
     Architecture. 42 (October 1951), 28.

CLOSE, ELIZABETH SHEU (1912-)   ARCHITECT

SECONDARY WORKS:

"Cabin, St. Croix River, Minnesota." Progressive
     Architecture. 29 (December 1948), 78-79.

"Design by Chance." AIA Journal. 37 (May 1962), 43-44.

"Four Fine Fellows: Husband and Wife Teams Who Have Become
    Fellows of AIA." AIA Journal. 52 (September 1969),
    86-87.

"House at Minneapolis." Architectural Forum. 74 (April
    1941), 274.

"Interstate Clinic, Red Wing, Minnesota." Architectural
    Forum. 76 (February 1942), 129-133.

"Minneapolis House." Progressive Architecture. 28 (November
    1947), 87-89.

"Portrait." Progressive Architecture. 28 (November 1947),
    16.

"Portrait." Progressive Architecture. 29 (December 1948),
    79.

Richter, Bonnie. "Elizabeth Close, Minnesota's Premiere
    Woman Architect." Architecture Minnesota. 4
    (March-April 1978), 27-29.

"A Thousand Women in Architecture: I" Architectural Record.
    103 (March 1948), 112.

"Two Ideas Make This Two-Story House a Minnesota Pioneer."
    House and Home. 10 (October 1956), 186.

COFFIN, MARIAN CRUGER (1876-1957)   LANDSCAPE ARCHITECT

Marian Coffin's papers are at the Henry Francis duPont
Winterthur Museum in Winterthur, Delaware.

PRIMARY SOURCES:

"Roses in Landscaping." Journal of the New York Botanical
    Garden. 48 (September 1947), 197-204.

"A Suburban Garden Six Years Old." Country Life in America.
    21 (February 15, 1912), 19-22, 64-68.

Trees and Shrubs for Landscape Effects. New York: Charles
    Scribners' Sons, 1940.

SECONDARY SOURCES:

Boswell, H. "Exhibition, Studio Guild." *Art Digest.* 16
    (January 15, 1942), 23.

Brown, Catherine R. *Women and the Land.* Baltimore: Morgan
    State University, 1979, p. [7].

Deitz, Paula. "Designing Women." *Metropolis.* (December
    1982), 14-19.

Fowler, Clarence. "Three Women in Landscape Architecture."
    *Cambridge School of Architecture and Landscape
    Architecture. Alumnae Bulletin.* 4 (1932), 7.

Hartt, Mary B. "Women and the Art of Landscape Gardening."
    Outlook (March 28, 1908), 694-704.

"Marian Coffin." In: *Public Space.* Cambridge: Harvard
    University Graduate School of Design, 1975, p. 74.

"Marian Cruger Coffin: Biographical Minute." *Landscape
    Architecture.* 47 (April 1957), 431.

Newton, Norman. *Design on the Land.* Cambridge, MA:
    Harvard University Press, 1971, pp. 441-443.

Palmer, Donna. *An Overview of the Trends, Eras and Values
    of Landscape Architecture in America.* M.L.A. North
    Carolina State Univ., 1976, p. 33

Pond, B.W. "Trees and Shrubs for Landscape Effects."
    Landscape Architecture. 30 (April 1940), 153.

Prather-Moses, Alice I., compiler. *The International
    Dictionary of Women Workers in the Decorative Arts.*
    Metuchen, N.J.: Scarecrow Press, 1981, p. 33

Teutonico, Jeanne Marie. *Marian Cruger Coffin: The Long
    Island Estates.* M.A. Thesis, Columbia University,
    1983.

COIT, ELISABETH (1892-1987) ::   ARCHITECT

PRIMARY SOURCES:

Coit was editor of the Met-Nahro Reporter (The newsletter
of the National Association of Housing and Redevelopment
Officials) for 1968-1984.

"Georgina Pope Yeatman." Technology Review. 39 (1937), 255.

"Housing from the Tenant's Viewpoint." Architectural
    Record. 91 (1942), 71-84.

"Notes on the Design and Construction of the Dwelling Units
    for the Lower Income Family." Octagon. 13 (October
    1941), 10-30; (November 1941), 7-22.

Report on Family Living in High Apartment Buildings.
    Washington, D.C.: Public Housing Administration, 1965.

SECONDARY WORKS:

Cole, Doris. From Tipi to Skyscraper: A History of Women in
    Architecture. Boston: i Press, 1973, pp. 108-109.

"Elisabeth Coit." American Women, 1935-1940. Detroit: Gale
    Publishers, 1981, p. 177

"Elisabeth Coit." Macmillan Encyclopedia of Architects. New
    York: Free Press, 1982, v. 1, p. 436.

"Elisabeth Coit, 94, Architect and a Specialist on
    Housing." New York Times (April 8, 1987), D30.

"Elisabeth Coit: Portrait." AIA Journal. 24 (July 1955),
    25.

Ford, James. "1932 Better Homes in American Small Houses
    Architectural Competition." Architectural Record. 73
    (March 1933), 196-216.

"Houses of Miss M. Burnham, Yorktown Heights, New York and
    M.P. Hayes, Holderness, New Hampshire; E. Coit,
    Architect." Architecture. 73 (May 1936), 271, 290.

"Inspired by Cows and Milk Bottles, The New York Office of
   the Walker-Gordon Company." American Architect. 139
   (April 1931), 56, 86, 88.

"Portrait." Pencil Points. 19 (August 1938), 43.

"Shrub Oak, New York: Remodeled House of P. Maguire; E.
   Colt, Architect." American Architect. 147 (September
   1935), 15-20.

"The Smaller Airport." Pencil Points. 18 (November 1937),
   739-741.

Stevens, Mary Otis. "Struggle for Place." In: Women in
   American Architecture. New York: Whitney Library of
   Design, 1977, pp. 100-102.

"Symposium: In Building Low-Priced Homes Have We Carried
   the Doll House Idea Too Far? If So, How Can We Give
   People More Elbow Room ?" Tomorrow's Home. 1 (January
   1944), 2-3.

"Thirty Houses Costing Under $10,000." House and Garden. 78
   (August 1940), 7-38.

"A Thousand Women in Architecture: II" Architectural
   Record. 103 (June 1948), 114.

"Women in Architecture, The New Professional: Coming of
   Age." Progressive Architecture. 58 (March 1977), 47.

EXHIBITION:

Built by Women: A Guide to Architecture in the New York
   Area. New York: Alliance of Women in Architecture,
   1981, p. 29.

COLE, DORIS (1938-) *   ARCHITECT
                                            EDUCATOR

PRIMARY WORKS:

Eleanor Raymond/Architect. Boston, Mass: Institute of
   Contemporary Arts, 1981.

From Tipi to Skyscraper. Boston: i Press, 1973.

"New England Women Architects." IN: Pilgrims and Pioneers: New England Women in the Arts. edited by Alicia Faxon and Sylvia Moore. New York: Midmarch Press, 1987, pp. 56-61.

"Eleanor Raymond." In: Women in American Architecture. New York: Whitney Library of Design, 1977, 103-107.

SECONDARY WORKS:

"Doris Cole." Contemporary Authors. Detroit: Gale Pub., 1980, vols. 89-92, p. 104.

Coulacos, Cate. "A Space Solution." Boston Herald. (February 13, 1986), 45, 50.

"New England Women Architects." In: Pilgrims and Pioneers: New England Women in the Arts. edited by Alicia Faxon and Sylvia Moore. New York: Midmarch Press, 1987, p. 61.

"Rent Out Your Family Room." Better Homes and Gardens. (January 1983), 34-35.

COLTER, MARY (1869-1958) ⋇   ARCHITECT

PRIMARY WORKS:

Manual for Drivers and Guides Descriptive of the Indian Watchtower at Desert View and Its Relations, Architecturally, to the Prehistoric Ruins of the Southwest. Grand Canyon: Fred Harvey, 1933.

SECONDARY WORKS:

Ahlborn, Richard E. "The Hispanic Horseman: A Sampling of Horse Gear from the Fred Harvey Collection." Palacio. 89, no. 2 (1983), 12-21.

"The Alvarado of Albuquerque, New Mexico." Hotel Monthly. (October 1922), 50.

Bare, William K. "Mary E.J. Colter, Architect and
    Designer." Arizona Highways. 60 (May 1984), 16-17.

Black, W.J. Hotel El Tovar On the Rim of Grand Canyon.
    Grand Canyon: Fred Harvey, 1909.
    This publication was revised and reprinted in 1977.

"Centennial of the First Railway Postal Car." Montana. 12
    no. 4 (1962), 60-61.

Chappell, Gordon. "Railroad at the Rim: The Origin and
    Growth of Grand Canyon Village." Journal of Arizona
    History. 17 no. 1 (1976), 89-107.

Davies, Cynthia. "Frontier Merchants and Native Craftsmen:
    The Fred Harvey Company Collects Indian Art." Journal
    of the West. 21, no. 1 (1982), 120-125.

"El Navajo Hotel Reflects the Painted Desert." Hotel
    Monthly. (July 1923), 40.

"La Fonda, Santa Fe, New Mexico." Hotel Monthly (March
    1932), 24-29.

"La Fonda, Tripled in Size Becomes Spanish Fairyland." New
    Mexican. 18 (May 1929), 2.

"Food Service on the Santa Fe's New Streamlined Trains."
    Hotel Monthly (September 1938), 17-19.

Force, Kenneth. "Kansas City Likes Westport Room."
    Restaurant Management (February 1938), 82-85.

"Fred Harvey Caterer, Chicago Union Station." Hotel
    Monthly (August 1925), 38.

"Fred Harvey Catering at Grand Canyon." Hotel Monthly
    (October 1928), 31.

"Fred Harvey Welcomes You." Los Angeles Times (May 3 1939),
    6.

"Full Corps of Teachers, Mechanic Arts School Same as Last
    Year." Globe (August 18, 1898), 8.

Gebhard, David. "Architecture and the Fred Harvey Houses."
    New Mexican Architect (July-August 1962), 11-17.

_____. "Architecture and the Fred Harvey Houses."
New Mexican Architect (January-February 1964), 18-25.

Gleed, Charles S. "The Rehabilitation of the Santa Fe
Railway." Santa Fe Magazine (December 1912), 24.

Goodman, Vera. "The Stamp of a Woman Architect: Mary
Colter." New Directions for Women. 13 (January-
February 1984), 12 + .

Grattan, Virginia L. Mary Colter: Builder upon the Red
Earth. Flagstaff Arizona: Northland Press, 1980.

Harvey, Byron. "The Fred Harvey Collection: 1889-1963."
Plateau (Fall 1963), 35-53.

Henderson, James D. Meals by Fred Harvey. Fort Worth,
Texas: Christian University Press, 1969.
References to Colter's work throughout the book.

_____. "Meals by Fred Harvey." Arizona and the
West. 8, no. 4 (1966), 305-322.

"Impressions of El Ortiz." Santa Fe Magazine (October
1910), 55.

"John F. Huckel, Fred Harvey Official Passes Away." Santa
Fe Magazine (May 1936), 15.

Kelley, Carla. "Fred Harvey's Railroad Cuisine." American
West. 19 (September-October 1982), 14-15.

"La Posada and Harveycars, Winslow." Hotel Monthly
(February 1931), 44.

"La Posada for Sale." Wall Street Journal (February 13,
1957), 6.

"La Posada: The Resting Place." Hospitality. (March 1949),
1.

"Mary Colter." Macmillan Encyclopedia of Architects. New
York: Free Press, 1982, v. 1, pp. 441-442.

"Mary Colter Dies Here." New Mexican (January 8, 1958), 2.

"Mary Jane Colter Helps Canyon Library." Arizona Republic

(August 2, 1957), 12.

Mather, Christine. "Mexican Artifacts Collected by the Fred
     Harvey Company." Antiques. 124 (December 1983). 1206-
     1211.

Meadows, Amy. "Miss Colter Does It Again." Hospitality
     (September 1949), 3.

"Miss Colter's Indian Jewels on Public Exhibition at Lab."
     New Mexican (April 18, 1952), A6.

"Miss Mary Colter Dies in Santa Fe." Hospitality
     (January-February 1958), 3.

Mitchell, Harold D. "Architecture in America: Its History
     up to the Present Time." California Architect and
     Building News (February 1882), 29.

"Navajo Sand Paintings as Decorative Motif." El Palacio
     (June 15, 1923), 175-183.

"The New Bright Angel Lodge and Cabins." Hotel Monthly
     (December 1936), 13.

Pace, Michael. "Emory Kolb and the Fred Harvey Company."
     Journal of Arizona History. 24, no. 4 (1983), 339-364.

Saunders, Sallie. "Indian Watchtower at Grand Canyon Is
     Dedicated by Hopi Indians." Santa Fe Magazine (July
     1933), 27.

Strong, Douglas H. "Ralph H. Cameron and the Grand Canyon."
     Arizona and the West. 10. no. 1/2, (1978), 41-64,
     155-172.

"Taxi into Streetcar." Kansas City Star. 14 (March 1929),
     17.

"Union Station Still Magnet for Sight-Seeing Throngs." Los
     Angeles Times (May 5, 1939), part II, p. 1.

Watkins, T.H. "Pilgrim's Pride." American East. 6, no. 5
     (1969) 49-54.

"Woman's Railroad Hotel Threatened: Harvey House Hotel,

Barstow, California by Mary Colter." _Progressive_
Architecture. 58 (March 1977), 18.

CONNOR, ROSE (1892-1970) ⁙   ARCHITECT

The Schlesinger Library of Harvard University has in its
manuscript collection the Papers of Union Internationale
des Femmes Architectes given by Rose Connor; they include:
Announcement, Program, Reports of Second Congress 1969,
Statutes, 2 letters.

Rose Connor has some drawings at the University Art Museum,
University of California at Santa Barbara.

SECONDARY WORKS:

"A Thousand Women in Architecture: II." _Architectural_
        Record. 103 (June 1948), 111.

COVINGTON, GARNETT K. ⁙   ARCHITECT

SECONDARY WORKS:

"Black Women Architects: A Blueprint for Success." _Ebony_.
        39 (June 1984), 55.

EXHIBITION:

Built by Women: A Guide to Architecture in the New York
        Area. New York: Alliance of Women in Architecture,
        1981, p. 9.

CRAWFORD, MARY ANN (1901-) ⁙   ARCHITECT

The Architectural Archives of the Art Institute of Chicago
has some of Mary Ann Crawford's papers.

SECONDARY WORKS:

Markoutsas, Elaine. "Architect's Creative Genius Material-
    izes--Fifty Years Late." Chicago Tribune (October 26,
    1981), 1, 3.

"Portrait." Pencil Points. 13 (December 1932), 846.

EXHIBITIONS:

Art Institute of Chicago. Chicago Architects Design: A
    Century of Architectural Drawings. Chicago: Art
    Institute of Chicago, 1982.

Artemisia Gallery, Chicago. Chicago Women Architects.
    Chicago: the Gallery, 1978.

CUNNINGHAM, MARY P. (? -1934) *   LANDSCAPE ARCHITECT

Monthly column called "Month by Month in the Garden" in
House Beautiful.

SECONDARY WORKS:

"Barcelona Exposition." Landscape Architecture. 21 (January
    1931), 101-102.

Brown, Catherine R. Women and the Land. Baltimore: Morgan
    State University, 1979, p. [8].

Cole, Doris. From Tipi to Skyscraper: A History of Women in
    Architecture. Boston: i Press, 1973, p. 92

"Early American Details." Architectural Forum. 38 (January
    1923), plate 46.

"Mary P. Cunningham." Landscape Architecture. 25 (October
    1934), 38.

"Old and the New at the Exposition at Barcelona, Spain."
    American Landscape Architect. 3 (September 1930),
    22-23.

Palmer, Donna. An Overview of the Trends, Eras and Values of Landscape Architecture in America. M.L.A. North Carolina State University, 1976, p. 34.

DE BLOIS, NATALIE (1921 -) ⁑   ARCHITECT

SECONDARY WORKS:

Huxtable, Ada Louise. "The Last Profession To Be Liberated by Women." New York Times (March 13, 1977), D33.

Lobell, John. "American Women Architects." Artforum. 15 (Summer 1977), 31.

Oliver, Richard, ed. The Making of an Architect, 1881-1981. New York: Rizzoli, 1981, p. 144.

Owings, Nathaniel. The Spaces in Between. Boston: Houghton Mifflin Co, 1973, p. 264-265.

Paine, Judith. "Some Professional Roles: 1920-1960." In: Women in American Architecture. New York: Whitney Library of Design, 1977, pp. 112-114.

Patterson, Anne. "Women Architects--Why So Few of Them?" Inland Architect. 15 (December 1971), 13-19.

Smith, C. Ray, and Allen Tate. Interior Design in the 20th Century. New York: Harper & Row, 1986, p. 404.

"Women in Architecture, The New Professional: Coming of Age." Progressive Architecture. 58 (March 1977), 48.

EXHIBITION:

Built by Women: A Guide to Architecture in the New York Area. New York: Alliance for Women in Architecture, 1981, pp. 11, 13.

DE WOLFE, ELSIE (1865-1950) ⁑   DECORATOR

Theatre Collections of the New York Public Library at

Lincoln Center has scrapbooks of Robinson Locke that deal
with Elsie de Wolfe's career.

The Archives of American Art has somme Elsie de Wolfe
letters to Everett Shinn.

PRIMARY WORKS:

After All. London: Heinemann, 1935.

"Chateaux in Touraine." Cosmopolitan. 10 (February 1891),
    394-405.

"Freedom in Period Decoration as Expressed by Elsie de
    Wolfe in an Interview with Hildegarde Hawthorne."
    Touchstone. 8 (February 1921), 374-377.

The House in Good Taste. New York: Century Co., 1913.

Recipes for Successful Dining. New York: D. Appleton-
    Century, 1934.

"A Romance of Old Shoes." Cosmopolitan. 12 (April 1892),
    653-658.

"Stray Leaves from My Book of Life." Metropolitan Magazine.
    14 (December 1901), 809-820.

SECONDARY WORKS:

Armstrong, William. "Silhouettes: Miss Elsie de Wolfe."
    Leslie's Weekly (January 16, 1902), 64.

Baldwin, William. "Who's Afraid of Elsie de Wolfe?" Vogue.
    141 (June 1963), 116.

Bemelmans, Ludwig. To the One I Love Best. New York:
    Viking, 1955.
    Entire volume deals with de Wolfe.

Binney, Marcus. "Swan House, Georgia: The Property of the
    Atlanta Historical Society." Country Life. 173 (May 5,
    1983), 1168-1171.

Duquette, T. "Historic Interiors: Lady Mendl--Her Beloved Villa Trianon." Architectural Digest. 39 (June 1982), 66-73.

"Elsie de Wolfe." Biographical Cyclopaedia of American Women. New York: Halvord, 1924, v. 1, p. 70.

"Elsie de Wolfe." Dictionary of American Biography. New York: Charles Scribner's Sons, 1974, supp. 4, pp. 228-230.

"Elsie de Wolfe." National Cyclopedia of American Biography. New York: J.T. White, 1942, csv. 6, pp. 443-444.

"Elsie de Wolfe: The Birth of Professional Decorating." In: Interior Design in the 20th Century. New York: Harper & Row, 1986, pp. 235-242, 321.

Emery, S.R. "Elsie de Wolfe: the Legend Lives on." Interior Design. 53 (August 1982), 141.

Flanner, Janet. An American in Paris. New York: Simon & Schuster, 1940, pp. 103-118.

Geran, M. "Women in Design." Interior Design. 51 (February 1980), 261.

_____. "The Villa Trianon." Vogue (March 1, 1914), 45-49, 54-55.

Hadley, Rollin van. "Elsie de Wolfe and Isabella Stewart Gardner." Fenway Court (1981), 38-41.

"Lady Mendl Dies in France at 84." New York Times (July 13, 1950), 25.

Lynes, Russell. The Tastemakers. New York: Harper and Brothers, 1954, pp. 180-195.

Marbury, Elizabeth. My Crystal Ball: Reminiscences. New York: Boni and Liveright, 1923.
    Reference to de Wolfe throughout the book.

"Meenan, Monica. "Who's Afraid of Elsie de Wolfe?" Town and Country. 133 (July 1979), 78-79.

"Miss de Wolfe's Exquisite Gowns." Harper's Bazaar
     (February 3, 1900), 94.

"Miss de Wolfe Who Decorated." Architectural Forum. 124
     (March 1966), 88.

Moats, Alice-Leone. "The Elsie Legend." Harper's Bazaar
     (May 1949), 110-111, 168-172, 177, 180.

Platt, Frederick. "Elsie de Wolfe: The Chintz Lady." Art
     and Antiques. 3 (September-October 1980), 62-67.

"Porch Decorated by Elsie de Wolfe." Arts and Decoration.
     41 (September 1934), 39.

"Portrait." Architectural Forum. 65 (October 1936), 11.

"Portrait." Interiors. 110 (April 1951), 125.

"Re-do for the Plaza: Brings the Outdoors in." Architec-
     tural Forum. 84 (February 1946), 24.

Richardson, Nancy. "Elsie de Wolfe." House and Garden. 154
     (April 1982), 126-136.

Smith, Jane S. Elsie de Wolfe: A Life in the High Style.
     New York: Atheneum, 1982.

Sorensen, H. "American in Paris: the Villa Trianon, Lady
     Mendl's House in Versailles." Connoisseur. 208
     (November 1981), 202.

EXHIBITION:

Metropolitan Museum of Art, New York. Women of Style. New
     York: the Museum, 1975.

EAMES, RAY KAISER *   DESIGNER

PRIMARY WORKS:

A Computer Perspective. Cambridge: Harvard University
     Press, 1973.

Girard Foundation. The Magic of a People: Folk Art and Toys
     from the Collection of the Girard Foundation. New
     York: Viking Press, 1968.
     Photos by Ray and Charles Eames.

Le Monde de Franklin et de Jefferson. New York: Auspices of
     the American Revolution Bicentennial Administration
     and the Metropolitan Museum of Art, 1977.

SECONDARY WORKS:

"Charles and Ray Eames Receive First Kaufmann International
     Award." Industrial Design. 7 (December 1960), 14 + .

"Charles and Ray Eames Win First $20,000 Kaufmann Award."
     Architectural Record. 128 (October 1960), 25.

"Dallo Studio de Eames." Domus. 402 (May 1963), 26-42.

Donath, Jackie R. Design as Mass Communication: An
     Iconological Case Study of the Work of Charles and Ray
     Eames. Ph.D. Dissertation, Bowling Green State Univer-
     sity, 1986.

"Eames Awarded Royal Gold Medal for 1979." Progressive
     Architecture. 60 (June 1979), 25.

"Eames House Is Winner of AIA 25-year Award." AIA Journal.
     67 (April 1978), 11 + .

"Eames Images Still Fresh: The RIBA Gold Medal Award."
     Building Design. 450 (June 15, 1979), 2.

"Eames Television Show to Air in February." Architectural
     Record. 157 (January 1975), 34.

"Eameses and Nelson Receive Elsie de Wolfe Awards."
     Interiors. 134 (May 1975), 10.

"Elsie de Wolfe Award Presented." Interior Design. 46 (May
     1975), 28.

"First Kaufmann International Design Award Given to
     American Designers." Arts. 35 (October 1960), 10.

Hill, Mike. "Eames' Epitaph: Eames' Last Place, The Soft
    Pad Sofa, Just Launched in this Country." Building
    Design. 628 (February 11, 1983), 26.

Lacy, D.N. "Warehouse Full of Ideas." Horizon. 23
    (September 1980), 20-27.

McCoy, Esther. "An Affection for Objects, Interior Design:
    The Charles Eames Office." Progressive Architecture.
    54 (August 1973), 64-67.

_____. "Eames House, Santa Monica, California: On
    Attaining a Certain Age." Progressive Architecture. 58
    (October 1977), 80-83.

McQuade, Walter. "Charles Eames Isn't Resting on His
    Chair." Fortune. 91 (February 1975), 96-105.

"Office of Charles and Ray Eames Get Royal Gold Medal."
    RIBA Journal. 86 (April 1979), 143.

"Le Prix Kaufmann Annuel International est decerne pour
    1960 a Charles et Ray Eames." Architecture
    d'Aujourd'hui. 31 (December 1960), XLI.

"Ray Eames." California Arts and Architecture. 60
    (September 1943), 16-17.

"Royal Gold Medallists 1848-1984." RIBA Journal. 91 (May
    1984), 39-83.

Rubino, Luciano. Ray and Charles Eames: Il Collettivo della
    Fantasia. Rome: Kappa, 1981.

Saatchi, Doris. "All About Eames: Their 1949 House in Santa
    Monica, Put Together from Prefab Parts by Ray and
    Charles Eames Is Now Historic High Tech." House and
    Garden. 156 (February 1984), 122-129, 200.

Smith, C. Ray and Allen Tate. Interior Design in the 20th
    Century. New York: Harper & Row, 1986, pp. 404-405,
    416, 432, 436.

Walker, D. "Eames House, Pacific Palisades: Charles and Ray
    Eames." In: Los Angeles. London: Architectural Design
    Profile, 1981, pp. 76-77.

EXHIBITIONS:

Carnegie Arts Center. 10 Twentieth Century Houses. London:
     Arts Council of Great Britain, 1981.

"Connections: the Work of Charles and Ray Eames, Sainsbury
     Centre, East Anglia University, Mostra." Casabella. 43
     (February 1979), 4.

"Connections - the Work of Charles and Ray Rames: Sainsbury
     Centre for Visual Arts and University of East Anglia,
     Norwich, Exhibition." Burlington Magazine. 120
     (December 1978), 870.

"Connections: The Work of Charles and Ray Eames, Wight
     Gallery, University of California, Los Angeles;
     Exhibit." Art Journal. 36 (Winter 1976-1977), 147.

"Connections: The Work of Charles and Ray Eames, Wight
     Gallery, University of California, Los Angeles;
     Exhibit." Domus. 564 (November 1976), vi.

"Eames Celebration". Architectural Design. 36 (September
     1966), entire issue is devoted to this theme.

"Eames, Weeds and Colored Paper: Exhibition at Museum of
     Modern Art." Interiors. 110 (January 1951), 10.

Frederick S. Wight Art Gallery, University of California.
     Connections: The Works of Charles and Ray Eames. Los
     Angeles: the Gallery, 1976.

Lacy, B.N. "Warehouse Full of Ideas." Horizon. 23 (Septem-
     ber 1980), 20-27.

"Los Angeles Museum's Third Group Show." Arts and Architec-
     ture. 61 (October 1944), 20.

"Nelson, Eames, Girard, Propst: The Design Process at
     Herman Miller." Design Quarterly. 98/99 (1975), entire
     issue devoted to this exhibition at the Walker Art
     Center.

Tondreau, Bill. Images of Early America. [s.l.]: C. and R.
     Eames, 1976.

EDELMAN, JUDITH (1923 -) ∷   ARCHITECT

PRIMARY WORKS:

American Institute of Architects. Task Force on Women in
     Architecture, Judith Edelman, chair. Women in
     Architecture: Report to the AIA Board of Directors.
     Washington, D.C.: The Institute, 1974.

SECONDARY WORKS:

Oliver, Richard ed. The Making of an Architect, 1881-1981.
     New York: Rizzoli, 1981, p. 144.

Rochlin, Harriet. "All in the Day's Work." Ms. 5 (December
     1976), 15.

"Women in Architecture, Current Work: The Situation Today."
     Progressive Architecture. 58 (March 1977), 55.

EXHIBITION:

Built by Women: A Guide to Architecture in the New York
     Area. New York: Alliance for Women in Architecture,
     1981, p. 3, 5.

ELY, HELENA RUTHERFORD (1858-1920)   WRITER ON GARDENS

PRIMARY WORKS:

Another Hardy Garden Book. New York: Macmillan, 1905.

The Practical Flower Garden. New York: Macmillan, 1928.

A Woman's Hardy Garden. New York: Macmillan, 1903.

SECONDARY WORKS:

Brown, Catherine R. Women and the Land. Baltimore: Morgan
     State University, 1979, p. [9].

"Helena Rutherford Ely: Prophet of a New Era in Gardening."
    In: <u>Her Garden Was Her Delight</u>. by Buckner
    Hollingsworth. New York: Macmillan, 1962, pp. 139-142.

FARRAND, BEATRIX JONES (1872-1959) LANDSCAPE ARCHITECT

The College of Environmental Design at University of
California at Berkeley has the papers and drawings of
Beatrix Farrand.

Dumbarton Oaks has some letters and plans concerning
Farrand's work at their Gardens.

Houghton Library at Harvard has some letters of Farrand.
The Schlesinger Library at Harvard University has in its
manuscript collection a biographical file on Beatrix Jones
Farrand.

PRIMARY WORKS:

"The Debt of Landscape Art to a Museum of Trees."
    <u>Architectural Record</u>. 44 (November 1918), 407-413.

"Dumbarton Oaks." <u>Landscape Architecture</u>. 34 (July 1944),
    133.

"The Garden as a Picture." <u>Scribners</u>. 43 (1907), 2-8.

"The Garden in Relation to the House." <u>Garden and Forest</u>.
    (April 7, 1897), 132-133.

SECONDARY WORKS:

Auchincloss, Louis. <u>Edith Wharton: A Woman in Her Time</u>. New
    York: Viking Studio Books, 1971.
    Edith Wharton was Farrand's aunt and had a profound
    influence on her work.

Balmori, Diana. "Beatrix Farrand: Pioneer Landscape
    Architect." <u>Preservation League of New York State
    Newsletter</u>. 11 (November-December 1985), 4-5.

_____. "Beatrix Farrand at Dumbarton Oaks."
    Heresies. 3 (March 1981), 83-86.

_____ and others. Beatrix Farrand's American
    Landscapes: Her Gardens and Campuses. Sagapona, New
    York: Sagapress, 1985.

"Beatrix Cadalader Jones Farrand." Dictionary of American
    Biography. New York: Charles Scribner's Sons, 1980,
    pp. 196-197.

"Beatrix Farrand." American Women 1935-1940. Detroit: Gale
    Publishers, 1981, p. 280.

"Beatrix Jones Farrand." Notable American Women: The Modern
    Period. Cambridge, MA: Belknap Press, 1980, pp.
    221-223.

Bliss, Mildred B. "An Attempted Evocation of a
    Personality." Landscape Architecture. 49 (July 1959),
    216-224.

Brown, Catherine R. Women and the Land. Baltimore: Morgan
    State University, 1979, p. [10].

Byrd, W.T. "Comparative Anatomy: Donnell Garden and
    Dumbarton Oaks." Landscape Architecture. 73
    (March-April 1983), 53-59.

Deitz, Paula. "Designing Women." Metropolis (December
    1982), 14-19.

"Dumbarton Oaks." Landscape Architecture. 34 (July 1944),
    131-135.

Dumbarton Oaks Colloquium on the History of Landscape
    Architecture. Beatrix Jones Farrand: Fifty Years of
    American Landscape Architecture. Washington, D.C.:
    Dumbarton Oaks Trustees for Harvard University, 1982.

Hartt, Mary B. "Women and the Art of Landscape Gardening."
    Outlook (March 28, 1908), 694-704.

Iovine, Julie V. "University Pleasures of Landscape." Yale
    Alumni Magazine. 49 (November 1985), 24-27.

Joseph Regenstein Library, University of Chicago. The Uses

of Gothic: Planning and Building the Campus of the
University of Chicago, 1892-1932. Chicago: University
of Chicago, 1983.
By Jean F. Block, foreword by Neil Harris.

Littlefield, Susan S. "Dumbarton Oaks: From a Georgetown
Farm, Beatrix Farrand Created One of America's
Greatest Gardens." House and Garden. 158 (December
1986), 156-165, 221-222.

McGuire, Diane K. Ed. Beatrix Farrand's Plant Book for
Dumbarton Oaks. Washington, D.C.: Dumbarton Oaks,
1980.

_____. "The Gardens: Dumbarton Oaks, Washington,
D.C. " Apollo. 119 (April 1984), 268-273.

Masson, Georgina. Dumbarton Oaks: A Guide to the Gardens.
Washington, D.C., 1968.

Newton, Norman. Design on the Land. Cambridge, MA:
Harvard University Press, 1971, pp. 387-388.

Palmer, Donna. An Overview of the Trends, Eras and Values
of Landscape Architecture in America. M.L.A. North
Carolina State Univ., 1976, p.4.

Patterson, R.W., and M.B. Bliss "Beatrix Farrand--1872-
1959: An Appreciation of a Great Landscape Gardener."
Landscape Architecture. 49 (Summer 1959), 216-224.

Prather-Moses, Alice I. compiler. The International
Dictionary of Women Workers in the Decorative Arts.
Metuchen, N.J.: Scarecrow Press, 1981, p. 53.

"Reef Point Gardens: the Start and the Goal of a Study in
Landscape Gardening." Landscape Architecture. 37
(October 1946), 12-13.

Richardson, M. "Women Theorists." AD. 45 (August 1975),
466.

Roper, Lanning. "Perfection in Detail: The Gardens of
Dumbarton Oaks, Washington, D.C." Country Life. 155
(January 3-10, 1974), 6-8.

Salon, Marlene. Beatrix Farrand, Landscape Gardener: Her
    Life and Her Work. M.A. Thesis, University of Califor-
    nia at Berkeley, 1976.

_____. "Beatrix Jones Farrand: Pioneer in Gilt-
    Edged Gardens." Landscape Architecture. 67 (January
    1977), 32, 69-77.

Strong, Donna. "Beatrix Farrand: Landscape Gardener."
    Inland Architect. 30 (January-February 1986), 36-41.

Vaughan, H.L. "Library Gift to California Collection of
    Mrs. Farrand." Landscape Architect. 47 (October 1956),
    298 + .

Whitehill, Walter Muir. Dumbarton Oaks: The History of a
    Georgetown House and Garden, 1800-1966. Cambridge,
    MA: Harvard University Press, 1967.

Yarwood, George. "History of Women in Landscape
    Architecture." ASLA Bulletin (July 1973), [3-7].

EXHIBITIONS:

University of Chicago, Joseph Regenstein Library. The Uses
    of Gothic: Planning and Building the Campus of the
    University of Chicago, 1892-1932. Chicago: the
    University, 1983.

Powers, A. "Art of the Artless: Architectural Association,
    London." Architects Journal. 174 (November 25, 1981),
    1029.

FLANDERS, ANNETTTE HOYT (1887-1946) LANDSCAPE ARCHITECT

PRIMARY WORKS:

Consulting Garden editor for Good Housekeeping 1933-1934.

Landscape Architecture. New York: the author, 1932.

SECONDARY WORKS:

"Annette Hoyt Flanders." American Women, 1935-1940.
    Detroit: Gale Publishers, 1981, pp. 293-294.

"Annette Hoyt Flanders: Biographical Minute." Landscape
    Architecture. 37 (October 1946), 29-30.

Brown, Catherine R. Women and the Land. Baltimore: Morgan
    State University, 1979, p. [10].

_____, and Celia Maddox. "Women and the Land:
    A Suitable Profession." Landscape Architecture. 72
    (May 1982), 65-69.

Deitz, Paula. "Designing Women." Metropolis (December
    1982), 14-19.

"Exhibition of Photographs and Models of Landscape
    Architecture." Milwaukee Institute Bulletin. 5 (April
    1932), 10.

"House and Garden's Own Hall of Fame." House and Garden. 63
    (June 1933), 50.

Newton, Norman. Design on the Land. Cambridge, MA:
    Harvard University Press, 1971, p. 443.

Palmer, Donna. An Overview of the Trends, Eras and Values
    of Landscape Architecture in America. M.L.A. North
    Carolina State Univ., 1976, pp. 32-33.

"Sculpture Landscapes." Arts and Decoration. 43 (November
    1935), 36-37 + .

FLETCHER, JEAN BODMAN (1915-1965) ::   ARCHITECT

PRIMARY WORKS:

"Architecture, Family Style: Two Women Architects Look at
    Today's Houses, Tell How They Affect Family Life."
    House Beautiful. 92 (October 1947), 146-149.

and Gropius, Walter eds. The Architects Collaborative,
    1945-1965. New York: Architectural Book Publishing

Co., 1966.

and others. The Architects Collaborative Inc: TAC
    1945-1972. Barcelona, 1972.

SECONDARY WORKS:

Berlo, J.C. "Women in American Architecture: The Cambridge
    School." Feminist Art Journal. 5 (Spring 1976), 27-32.

Cole, Doris. "New England Women Architects." In: Pilgrims
    and Pioneers: New England Women in the Arts, edited by
    Alicia Faxon and Sylvia Moore. New York: Midmarch Arts
    Press, 1987, p. 60.

"A Competition to Select an Architect for a Proposed
    Dormitory Group for Smith College: First Prize winners
    Norman C. Fletcher, Jean Bodman Fletcher and Benjamin
    Thompson." Pencil Points. 27 (April, 1946), 52-61.

Gropius, Walter and others. "The Architects Collaborative:
    The Heritage of Walter Gropius." Process Architecture.
    19 (1980), 1-163.

"Johns Manville World Headquarters, near Denver Colorado,
    1976: Architects, the Architects Collaborative."
    Process Architecture. 19 (1980), 46-55.

"Motor Traveler's Hotel." Architectural Record. 98 (July
    1945), 75-77.

"Norwell High School, Norwell, Mass., 1973: Architects, the
    Architects Collaborative." Process Architecture. 19
    (1980), 122-125.

"Partitions and Lights Work as a Modular Pair to Create
    Luminous Space: CIGNA Office Building, Bloomfield,
    Conn.: The Architects Collaborative." Architectural
    Record. 171 (April 1983), 160-167.

"Pittsburgh Architectural Competition." Pencil Points. 26
    (May 1945), 51-92.

"Portrait." Pencil Points. 26 (May 1945), 52.

"Portrait." Pencil Points. 27 (April 1946), 18.

"Proposed Academic Center, Boston University, Boston,
    MA: Architects:the Architects Collaborative."
    Architectural Record. 165 (January 1979), 47.

"Regional Integration in Central Valley." Arts and
    Architecture. 62 (May 1945), 25-29.

Stevens, Mary Otis. "A Struggle for Place." In: Women in
    American Architecture. New York: Whitney Library of
    Design, 1977, pp. 93-95.

"TAC: The Architects Collaborative." Macmillan Encyclopedia
    of Architects. New York: Free Press, 1982, v. 4, pp.
    201-202.

"There Should Be Regional Integration in Central Valley."
    Arts and Architecture. 62 (May 1945), 25-29.

"Willimantic: Proposed Public Library." Arts and
    Architecture. 63 (August 1946), 28-29.

FREDERICK, CHRISTINE (1883-1970) DOMESTIC MANAGER

The Schlesinger Library at Harvard University has in its
manuscript collection a biographical file on Christine
Frederick.

PRIMARY WORKS:

Household Engineering: Scientific Management in the Home.
    Chicago: American School of Home Economics, 1923.

The New Housekeeping: Efficiency Studies in Home
    Management. New York: Doubleday, 1912.
    Appeared initially as a series in the Ladies Home
    Journal, 1911.

SECONDARY WORKS:

Handlin, David P. "Efficiency and the American Home."
    Architectural Association Quarterly. 5 (October-
    December 1974), 50-54.

Rybczynski, Witold. Home: A Short History of an Idea. New
    York: Viking, 1986, pp. 156-157, 163-167, 178.

Stein, S.A. "Composite Photographic Image and the
    Composition of Consumer Ideology." Art Journal. 41
    (Spring 1981), 42-44.

Women of Achievement. New York: House of Field, 1940, p.
    85.

FREEMAN, RUTH REYNOLDS (1913-1969) ::   ARCHITECT

SECONDARY WORKS:

"Architect and His Community." Progressive Architecture. 30
    (October 1949), 53-64.

"Burlington, Vermont: Saint Mark's Church." Architectural
    Forum. 81 (July 1944), 85-90.

"Burlington, Vermont: Thayer School." Liturgical Arts. 17
    (February 1949), 60.

Lavanoux, M. "Burlington, Vermont: Saint Mark's Church."
    Liturgical Arts. 11 (August 1943), 82-85.

"Portrait." Progressive Architecture. 27 (December 1946),
    14.

"Portrait." Progressive Architecture. 30 (October 1949),
    53.

"Residential Development, Burlington, Vermont."
    Architectural Forum. 80 (April 1944), 127-133.

"Rice Memorial High School, Burlington." Liturgical Arts.
    28 (February 1960), 47, 50.

"Synagogue, Burlington, Vermont." Progressive Architecture.
    35 (August 1954), 74-75.

"A Thousand Women in Architecture: I " Architectural
    Record. 103 (March 1948), 107.

FROMMER, MARIE (flourished ca. 1940's) * ARCHITECT

PRIMARY WORKS:

"Inexpensive Design for Specialty Shop, New Rochelle, New York." Pencil Points. 27 (August 1946), 73-76.

"New Light on Forensic Interiors." Interiors. 107 (May 1948), 96-98.

SECONDARY WORKS:

"Quaternian House." Architectural Record. 104 (July 1948), 164.

"Radio Frank's Knight Club, New York City." Pencil Points. 25 (July 1944), 60-61.

"Shops and Small Stores: Architectural Record's Building Type Study no. 154." Architectural Record. 106 (October 1949), 121-138.

"Showroom and Building for Creative Looms." Architectural Record. 106 (October 1949), 124-125.

"A Thousand Women in Architecture: I " Architectural Record. 103 (March 1948), 110.

GIDONI, ELSA (1901-1978) * ARCHITECT

The Library of Congress Prints and Photographs Section has an Elsa Gidoni Collection.

PRIMARY WORKS:

"Small Library of 5,000 Books for Council for Pan-American Democracy Doubles as Exhibition Room." Architectural Forum. 85 (October 1946), 126-127.

SECONDARY WORKS:

"Portrait." Architectural Forum. 85 (October 1946), 68.

"A Thousand Women in Architecture: I " Architectural
    Record. 103 (March 1948), 106.

GILBRETH, LILLIAN MOLLER (1878-1972) ✕ DOMESTIC MANAGER

The Schlesinger Library at Harvard University has in its
manuscript collection a biographical file on Lillian Moller
Gilbreth.

PRIMARY WORKS:

The Foreman in Manpower Management. New York: McGraw-Hill
    Co., 1947.

The Home-maker and Her Job. New York: Appleton, 1927.

Kitchen Practical. Brooklyn: Brooklyn Borough Gas Company,
    1931.

Living with Our Children. New York: Norton, 1928.

The Psychology of Management. New York: Macmillan, 1919.

The Quest of the One Best Way. Bridgeport, Conn: Society of
    Women Engineers, 1925.

and Orpha May Thomas and Eleanor Clymer. Management in the
    Home. New York: Dodd, Mead, 1954.

SECONDARY WORKS:

Boynick, David K. Pioneers in Petticoats. New York:
    Crowell, 1972, pp. 150-177.

Clymer, Eleanor. Modern American Career Women. New York:
    Dodd, Mead, 1959, pp. 1-11.

Fleischman, Doris E. Careers for Women. New York:
    Doubleday, 1928, p. 166.

Lerner, Gerda. The Woman in American History. Menlo Park, CA: Addison-Wesley Publishing Co., 1971, p. 183.

"Lillian Moller Gilbreth." Academy Management Journal. 15 (March 1972), 7-8.

"Lillian Moller Gilbreth." American Women, 1935-1940. Detroit: Gale Publishers, 1981, p. 332.

"Lillian Moller Gilbreth." Progressive Woman. 2 (May 2, 1972), 7.

Logie, Iona. Careers in the Making. New York: Harper, 1935, pp. 312-326.

Rybczynski, Witold. Home: A Short History of an Idea. New York: Viking, 1986, pp. 169-170, 171.

Stoddard, Anne. Topflight. New York: T. Nelson and Sons, 1946, pp. 88-99.

Yost, Edna. American Women of Science. Philadelphia: J.B. Lippincott, 1952, pp. 99-121.

GOODY, JOAN E. (1935-) ※   ARCHITECT

PRIMARY WORKS:

"Do You See New Directions?" Architecture. 74 (May 1985), 240-251, 312-320.

New Architecture in Boston. Cambridge, Mass: MIT Press, 1965.

"Our Images Today Are Less Restricted by Moral Dicta." Architecture. 74 (May 1985), 318 + .

"A Rare and Rich Response to Context: Keio University Library, Tokyo, Japan." Architectural Record. 171 (May 1983), 106-113.

"Ten Brief Essays." Progressive Architecture. 65 (July 1984), 82-87.

SECONDARY WORKS:

"Joan Goody." In: <u>American Architecture Now II</u>. New York:
    Rizzoli, 1983 pp. 111-119.

GRAY, GRETA (fl. ca. 1930's-40's) HOME ECONOMIST
                                              EDUCATOR

PRIMARY WORKS:

<u>House and Home</u>. Philadelphia: J.B. Lippincott, 1923.

SECONDARY WORKS:

"Greta Gray." <u>American Women, 1935-1940</u>. Detroit: Gale
    Publishers, 1981, p. 350.

Hayden, Dolores. "Challenging the American Domestic Ideal."
    In: <u>Women in American Architecture</u>. New York: Whitney
    Library of Design, 1977, pp, 22-24.

"New Houses in Southern California." <u>California Arts and
    Architecture</u>. 47 (March 1935), 22-23 + .

Wright, Gwendolyn. "On the Fringe of the Profession: Women
    in American Architecture." In: <u>The Architect,</u> edited
    by Spiro Kostof. New York: Oxford University Press,
    1977, pp. 297-298.

GREGORY, ANGELA (1903-)   ARCHITECTURAL SCULPTOR

PRIMARY WORKS:

<u>The Art of Woodworking and Furniture Making</u>. Leicester:
    Dryad Press, 1962.

SECONDARY WORKS:

"Angela Gregory." <u>American Women, 1935-1940</u>. Detroit: Gale
    Publishers, 1981, p. 355.

"Newcomb's Artist-in-Residence." Art Digest. 15 (October
    15, 1940), 29.

"Portrait." American Magazine of Art. 21 (April 1930), 218.

"Portrait." Art Digest. 16 (June 1942), 11.

GRIFFIN, MARION MAHONY (1871-1961) ✻   ARCHITECT

Some of her drawings are at the Northwestern University Art
Department, the New York Historical Society, Avery Library
at Columbia, and the Burnham Library at the Art Institute
of Chicago.

MIT Archives has her thesis drawings and papers.

PRIMARY WORKS:

Wright, Frank Lloyd. Ausgefuhrte Bauten und Entwurfe von
    Frank Lloyd Wright. Berlin: E. Wasmuth ,1910.
    Many of the drawings in this publication were by
    Griffin.

"Church of All Souls, Evanston, Illinois."   Western
    Architecture. 18 (September 1912), plate and plans.

The Magic in America. unpublished manuscript dated 1949. In
    the Collection of the New York Historical Society
    Library and the Burnham Library of the Art Institute
    of Chicago.

SECONDARY WORKS:

Art Institute of Chicago. Walter Burley Griffin, Marion
    Mahony Griffin: Architectural Drawings in the Burnham
    Library of Architecture. Chicago: the Institute, 1982.

Banham, R. "Death and Life of the Prairie School."
    Architectural Review. 154 (August 1975), 99-101.

Berkon, Susan F. "Some Professional Roles, 1860-1910." In:
     Women in American Architecture. New York: Whitney
     Library of Design, 1977, pp. 75-79.

_____, and Jane K. Holtz. "The First Lady: Marion
     Mahony." Building Design. 250 (May 16, 1975), 15.

_____, and J.H. Kay. "Marion Mahony Griffin,
     Architect." Feminist Art Journal. 4 (Spring 1975),
     10-14.

Birrell, James. Walter Burley Griffin. Brisbane: University
     of Queensland Press, 1964, p. 13.

Boyd, Robin. "Griffin in Melbourne." Architectural Review.
     137 (February 1965), 133-136.

Brooks, H. Allen. "Frank Lloyd Wright and the Wasmuth
     Drawings." Art Bulletin. 48 (1966), 193-202.

_____. The Prairie School: Frank Lloyd Wright
     and His Midwest Contemporaries. Toronto: Univ. of
     Toronto Press, 1972.
     Information on Griffin throughout the text.

_____, and J.H. Kay. "Marion Mahony Griffin,
     Architect." Feminist Art Journal. 4 (Spring, 1975)
     10-14.

1894 Class Book. Cambridge: Massachusetts Institute of
     Technology, 1898.

Johnson, Donald L. Architecture of Walter Burley Griffin.
     South Melbourne: Macmillan of Australia, 1977.

Kalec, Donald. "The Prairie School Furniture." Prairie
     School Review. 1, no. 4 (1964), 7.

Larson, Paul. "Marion Mahony and Walter Burley Griffin: The
     Marriage of Drawing and Architecture." Print
     Collector's Newsletter. 13 (May-June 1982), 38-41.

Lobell, John. "American Women Architects." Artforum. 15
     (Summer 1977), 31.

McCoy, R.E. "Rock Crest/Rock Glen: Prairie Planning in
    Iowa." Prairie School Review. 5, no. 3 (1968), 18 + .

Manson, Grant C. Frank Lloyd Wright to 1910: The First
    Golden Age. New York: Reinhold, 1958, p. 213.

"Marion Mahony Griffin." Macmillan Encyclopedia of
    Architects. New York: Free Press, 1982, v. 2, p. 248.

"Marion Mahony Griffin." Western Architect. 19 (April
    1913), p.38; (May 1913), 33; (October 1913), 88 ff.

Peisch, Mark L. The Chicago School of Architecture: Early
    Followers of Sullivan and Wright. New York: Random
    House, 1964, 33-35, 43-46, 48-51, 57-58.

Van Zanten, David. "The Early Work of Marion Mahony
    Griffin." Prairie School Review. 3, no. 2 (1966), 1-2,
    5-23, 27.

_____. Walter Burley Griffin, Selected Designs.
    Palos Park, Illinois: Prairie School Press, 1970.
    Illustrations of the designs are the presentation
    drawings by Marion Mahony Griffin.

von Holst, Hermann. "A Small Stone Church of Unusual
    Merit." Modern American Homes. Chicago: American
    School of Correspondence, 1912, plate 108.

White, Deborah. "Women and Architecture." Meanjin
    Quarterly. 34 (December 1975), 399-404.

"The Woman Architect." Southern Architecture Building News.
    27 (April 1912), 27-28.

"The Woman Architect and Low Cost Homes." Architect and
    Engineer of California. 28 (February 1912), 103.

"Women in Architecture, the New Professional: Coming of
    Age." Progressive Architecture. 58 (March 1977), 45 +.

EXHIBITIONS:

The Art Institute of Chicago. Chicago Architects Design: A
    Century of Architectural Drawings from the Art
    Institute of Chicago. New York: Rizzoli Inc. and the
    Art Institute of Chicago, 1982, p. 3

GROSSMAN, GRETA MAGNUSSON (fl. ca. 1940's-50's) DESIGNER

SECONDARY WORKS:

"Case in California." Domus. 335 (October 1957), 9-14.

"Design of Furniture." California Arts and Architecture. 58
     (March 1941), 20-21 + .

"Designer's House, Open Above the Hill." Interiors. 117
     (February 1958), 106-107.

"Deux Habitations a Beverly Hills." Architecture
     d'Aujourd'hui. 27 (October 1956), 16-17.

"For Sale, Custom Design." Interiors. 102 (September 1947),
     98-99.

"Four Foot Module--No Limitation on Design: House in
     Beverly Hills." Progressive Architecture. 38 (November
     1957), 136-139.

"Furniture and Lamps by G. Magnusson Grossman." Arts and
     Architecture. 67 (January 1950), 30-31.

"Greta Grossman's Own New House." Interiors. 117 (August
     1957), 96-97.

Henderson, R. "Swedish Furniture Designer in America:
     Interview." American Artist. 15 (December 1951),
     54-57.

"Hillside Apartment House, California." Interiors. 112
     (September 1952), 92-93.

"Hillside House." Arts and Architecture. 66 (July 1949),
     36-37.

"Hillside House." Arts and Architecture. 74 (June 1957),
     24-25.
"Hillside House." Arts and Architecture. 77 (October 1960),
     24-25.

"Hillside Houses." Arts and Architecture. 72 (July 1955),
     16-17.

"House." Arts and Architecture. 67 (September 1950), 32-33.

"House." Arts and Architecture. 74 (March 1957), 22-23.

"House in California." Domus. 319 (June 1956), 15-16.

"Interiors." Arts and Architecture. 63 (April 1946), 40-41.

"Living High, on a Steep Hill, with a Low Budget."
    Interiors. 112 (January 1953), 97.

"La Maison de Greta Magnusson Grossman a Beverly Hills."
    Architectured'Aujourd'hui. 29 (June 1958), 50-51.

"Rental Housing." Arts and Architecture. 69 (May 1952), 32.

"Rusticity Improved: Hillside Home, Furniture and Fabrics
    Designed by Greta Grossman." Interiors. 109 (February
    1950), 68-75.

"San Francisco House." Arts and Architecture. 67
    (September, 1950) 32-33; 68 (February, 1951) 32-33;
    (June 1951), 34-35.

"San Francisco Stilted House Ignores Its Site." Interiors.
    110 (January 1951), 90-91.

"Small House." Arts and Architecture. 70 (February 1953),
    32.

"Space Age Design: The Forecast Oven." Design for Industry.
    66 (June 1959), 19.

Stevens, Mary Otis. "Struggle for Place: Women in American
    Architecture: 1920-1960." In: Women in American
    Architecture. New York: Whitney Library of Design,
    1977, p. 98.

HALL, LOUISE (1905-   ) ⁂   ARCHITECT

PRIMARY WORKS:

Artificer to Architect in America. Ph.D. Dissertation,
     Radcliffe College, Cambridge, Mass., 1954.

"The Design of the Old Patent Office." Society of Architec-
     tual Historians Journal. 15 (March 1956), 27-30.

"First Architectural School. No, But..." AIA Journal. 14
     (August 1950), 79-82.

"Founding of the Company, Loxley's Provocative Note."
     Society of Architectural Historians Journal. 15
     (December 1956), 26-27.

"Mills, Strickland and Walter: Their Adventures in a World
     of Science." Magazine of Art. 40 (November 1947),
     266-271.

HALSBAND, FRANCES (1943 -   ) ⁂   ARCHITECT

PRIMARY WORKS:

Technical Requirements for Small Museums: An Annotated
     Bibliography. Hamilton: Gallery Asso., 1982.

SECONDARY WORKS:

Buttolph, Suzanne and others. "Digressions on the
     Architectural Model. "North Carolina State University.
     The Student Publication of the School of Design. 27
     (1978), 1-95.

Byron, Elizabeth and others. "The Strength of Tradition:
     Designer Mariette Himes Gomez and Architects R.M.
     Kliment and Frances Halsband Enhance the Instrinsic
     Charm of Seaside Cottages." House and Garden. 158
     (July 1986), 11-13.

"Computer Science Building at Columbia University."
    Building Stone Magazine. 3, no. 4 (1984), 20-21.

"Corporate Headquarters William M. Mercer Inc., New York,
    New York; Architects, R. M. Kliment and Frances
    Halsband." Architectural Record. 167 (June 1980),
    112-113.

Gaskie, M. "Classical Complexity." Architectural Record.
    172 (March 1984), 126-133.

Greene, E. "The Great Cover-Up." House and Garden. 155
    (July 1983), 124-129.

"Guiding Light: in Three Different Offices." Interiors. 145
    (May 1986), 300-311.

"An Interview with Commissioner Frances Halsband." Village
    Views. 2 (Spring 1985), 19-40.

"Reviving the Arts and Crafts: Projects by Kliment and
    Halsband." Architectural Record. 167 (June 1980),
    104-113.

Stephens, Suzanne. "Women in Architecture." House and
    Garden. 153 (March 1981), 149, 197.

Stern, Robert A.M. "Forty Under Forty." Architecture and
    Urbanism. 73 (January 1977), 96-97.

"The Town School Addition, New York, 1979; Architects R.M.
    Kliment and Frances Halsband." Architectural Record.
    167 (June 1980), 110-111.

Viladas, P. "Geometry Lesson." Progressive Architecture. 64
    (July 1983), 74-75.

"Young Women's Christian Association Addition, Kingston,
    New York; Architects, R.M. Kliment and Frances
    Halsband." Architectural Record. 167 (June 1980),
    104-107.

EXHIBITION:

Built by Women: A Guide to Architecture in the New York

Area. New York: Alliance of Women in Architecture,
1981, p. 19.

HARKNESS, SARAH PILLSBURY (1914-) :: ARCHITECT

Materials relating to Sarah P. Harkness are held in the
International Archive of Women in Architecture Collections
at Virginia Polytechnic Institute and State University in
Blacksburg, Virginia.

PRIMARY WORKS:

"The Anita Tuvin Schlechter Auditorium, Dickinson College."
    Theatre Design and Technology. 30 (October 1972),
    6-13.

and Jean B. Fletcher. "Architecture Family Style: Two Women
    Architects Look at Today's Houses, Tell How They
    Affect Family Life." House Beautiful. 92 (October
    1947), 146-149.

and James N. Groom, Jr. Building Without Barriers for the
    Disabled. New York: Whitney Library of Design, 1976.

and Walter Gropius eds. The Architects Collaborative,
    1945-1965. New York: Architectural Book Publishing
    Co., 1966.

and Leslie Horst, eds. Sustainable Design for Two Maine
    Islands. Boston: Architectural Center, 1986.

and Roland Kluver. The Practicing Architect and Societal
    Needs. Cambridge: Architects Collaborative Inc., 1976.

and others. "The Architecture of Energy." AIA Journal. 70
    (January 1981), 47-90.

SECONDARY WORKS:

"The Architects Collaborative." Arts and Architecture. 63
    (August 1946), 28-29.

The Architects Collaborative Inc. Cambridge, MA: The Firm,
    1971, brochure.

"Architectural Design: Split Down the Middle, 24th Annual
    P/A Awards." Progressive Architecture. 58 (January
    1977), 48-65.

Arnold, Diane, and Rhonda Rasmussen. "Sarah P. Harkness
    Interview." Avenu. 13 (1984), m-o.

"Bates College Library, Lewiston, Maine, 1973; architects:
    the Architects Collaborative, architect in charge:
    Sarah P. Harkness." Process Architecture. 19 (1980),
    126-129.

Berlo, J.C. "Women in Architecture: The Cambridge School."
    Feminist Art Journal. 5 (Spring 1976), 27-32.

"Buildings of 194X: Bank." Architectural Forum. 78 (May
    1943), 86-87.

Cliff, Ursula. "Three Exceptional Women." Design and
    Environment. 5 (Spring 1974), 34-37.

Cole, Doris. From Tipi to Skyscraper: A History of Women in
    Architecture. Boston: i Press, 1973, p. 93.

_____. "New England Women Architects." In: Pilgrims
    and Pioneers: New England Women in the Arts, edited by
    Alicia Faxon and Sylvia Moore. New York: Midmarch Arts
    Press, 1987, pp. 59-60.

"Duxbury House, E. Raymond and S. Pillsbury, Architects."
    Architectural Forum. 75 (December 1941), 402-403.

Gropius, Walter and others. "The Architects Collaborative:
    The Heritage Of Walter Gropius." Process Architecture.
    19 (1980), 1-163.

"Highlights of American Architecture, 1776-1976." AIA
    Journal. 65 (July 1976), 143-144.

"Johns Manville World Headquarters, Near Denver, Colorado,
    1976: Architects: the Architects Collaborative."
    Process Architecture. 19 (1980), 46-55.

"Norwell High School, Norwell, Mass. 1973, Architects: the
    Architects Collaborative." Process Architecture. 19
    (1980), 122-125.

"Partitions and Lights Work as a Modular Pair to Create
    Luminous Space: CIGNA Office Building, Bloomfield,
    Conn., Architects: the Architects Collaborative."
    Architectural Record. 171 (April 1983), 160-167.

"Portrait." Architectural Forum. 78 (May 1943), 72.

"Portrait." Pencil Points. 27 (April 1946), 18.

"Problems of Practitioners from Their Own Perspectives."
    AIA Journal. 67 (April 1978), 65.

"Proposed Academic Center, Boston University, Boston: The
    Architects Collaborative." Architectural Record. 165
    (January 1979), 47.

"Quiet Waves in the Sexual Storm." Building Design and
    Construction (September 1974), 52-55.

"Sarah Pillsbury Harkness, FAIA." Florida Architect. 29/30
    (Summer 1982), 17-18.

"Smith College Dormitory, Winning Design." Pencil Points.
    27 (April 1946), 58-59.

"Solar Section: Starting Point of Passive Design." AIA
    Journal. 70 (January 1981), 68-71.

Stevens, Mary Otis. "Struggle for Place." In: Women in
    American Architecture. New York: Whitney Library of
    Design, 1977, pp. 93-96.

"TAC: The Architects Collaborative." Macmillan Encyclopedia
    of Architects. New York: Free Press, 1982, v. 4, pp.
    210-202.

"What's Next?" AIA Journal. 69 (Mid-May 1980), 210.

"Worcester Art Museum School, Worcester, Mass., 1970;
    Architects, the Architects Collaborative: architects
    in charge: Norman C. Fletcher and Sarah P. Harkness."
    Process Architecture. 19 (1980), 98-99.

HAYDEN, SOPHIA GREGORIA (1868-1953) ⸬ ARCHITECT

Chicago Historical Society has her manuscript of the Report
to the Board of Lady Managers and other reports and plans
concerning the World's Columbian Exposition.

PRIMARY WORKS:

"Abstract of Thesis: Sophia G. Hayden, 1890." Technology
    Architectural Review. 3 (September 31, 1890), pp. 28,
    30.

"The Women's Building." In: Rand McNally & Company's A Week
    at the Fair. Chicago: Rand McNally and Co., 1893, p.
    180.

SECONDARY WORKS:

Anscombe, Isabelle. A Woman's Touch: Women in Design from
    1869 to the Present Day. New York: Viking, 1984, p.
    40.

Bancroft, Hubert H. The Book of the Fair. Chicago and San
    Francisco: 1893, pp. 257, 259, 265.

Bever, Marilynn A. The Women of MIT, 1871-1941: Who They
    Were, What They Achieved. B.S. Texas State College for
    Women, 1976, p. 38.

Darney, Virginia G. Women and World's Fairs: American
    International Expositions, 1876-1904. Ph.D. Disserta-
    tion, Emory Univ., 1982.

"Designs for Woman's Building, World's Columbian
    Exposition." Inland Architect and News Record. 18
    (September 1891), plates.

Eisen, Sylvia. "Early Heroics: Design of the Woman's
    Building at World's Columbian Exposition in 1890."
    Working Woman. 6 (December 1981), 58-59.

Elliott, Maud Howe, ed. Art and Handicraft in the Woman's
    Building of the World's Columbian Exposition. Chicago:
    Rand McNally, 1894, pp. 37ff.

"Girls as Architects." Woman's Journal. 22 (April 18, 1891), 122.

Grabenhorst-Randall, T. "The Women's Building." Heresies. 1 (Winter, 1978), 44-46.

Lobell, John. "American Women Architects." Artforum. 15 (Summer 1977), 30-31.

Millet, F.D. "The Designers of the Fair." Harper's New Monthly Magazine (November 1892), 872-883.

Paine, Judith. "Pioneer Women Architects." In: Women in American Architecture. New York: Whitney Library of Design, 1977, pp. 54-69.

_____. "Sophia Hayden and the Woman's Building Competition." In: Women in American Architecture. New York: Whitney Library of Design, 1977, pp. 70-75.

_____. "The Woman's Pavilion of 1876." Feminist Art Journal. 4 (Winter 1975-76), 5-13.

"Sophia Gregoria Hayden." Notable American Women: The Modern Period. Cambridge: Belknap Press, 1980, pp. 322-324.

Stern, Madeline. We the Women. New York: Schulte Pub. Co., 1963, 67-76.

Tallmadge, Thomas E. The Story of Architecture in America. New York: W.W. Norton, 1936, pp. 196, 212-213.

"An Unusual Opportunity for Women Architects." The Woman's Journal. 22 (February 21, 1891), 63.

Van Brunt, Henry. "Architecture at the World's Columbian Exposition, IV." Century Magazine. 44 (September 1892), 729 ff.

Weatherhead, Arthur C. The History of Collegiate Education in Architecture in the United States. Ph.D. Dissertation, Columbia University, 1941, pp. 26, 32.

Weiman, Jeanne M. The Fair Women. Chicago: Academy, 1981. References to Hayden throughout the book.

"Women in Architecture, The New Professional: Historic
    Beginnings." Progressive Architecture. 58 (March
    1977), 41.

"Women's Building." American Architect and Building News.
    32 (April 18, 1891), 45.

"The Women's Building. "American Architect and Building
    News. 38 (November 26, 1892), 134; (September 30,
    1876), 313.

Wright, Gwendolyn. "On the Fringe of the Profession: Women
    in American Architecture." In: The Architect, edited
    by Spiro Kostof. New York: Oxford University Press,
    1977, 294-295.

Yandell, Enid, and Laura Hayes. Three Girls in a Flat.
    Chicago: Knight, Leonard & Co., 1892, p. 64.

HAYES, LAURA (flourished ca. 1890's)   ARCHITECT

PRIMARY WORKS:

and Enid Yandell. Three Girls in a Flat. Chicago: Knight,
    Leonard & Co., 1892.

SECONDARY WORKS:

"Designs for Woman's Building, World's Columbian
    Exposition." Inland Architect and News Record. 18
    (September 1891), plates.

Weimann, Jeanne M. The Fair Women. Chicago: Academy, 1981,
    pp. 156-157, 159-160, 162, 163 + .

HERMANUZ, GHISLAINE   ARCHITECT

PRIMARY WORKS:

"The Struggle for Urban Design." Point. 2 (Spring 1984),
    27-31.

"Villages of the Algerian Revolution." Point. 1 (Spring
    1983), 14-15.

SECONDARY WORKS:

"Arch ou l'urbanisme contestataire." Architecture
    d'Aujourd'hui. 157 (August 1971), 77-79.

"Black Women Architects: A Blueprint for Success." Ebony.
    39 (June 1984), 58.

HICKS, MARGARET (fl. ca. 1880's)   ARCHITECT

SECONDARY WORKS:

Bell, Margaret. Women of the Wilderness. New York: Dutton,
    1938, p. 94.

"Design for a Workman's Cottage." American Architect and
    Building News. 3 (April 13, 1878), 129, illustrated
    with plans.

Hanaford, Phebe. Daughters of America. Boston: B.B.
    Russell, 1883, p. 286.

"Some Professional Roles."In: Women in American Archi-
    tecture. New York: Whitney Library of Design, 1977, p.
    69.

Wright, Gwendolyn. "On the Fringe of the Profession: Women
    in American Architecture." In: The Architect, edited
    by Spiro Kostof. New York: Oxford University Press,
    1977, pp. 292-293.

HOLMAN, EMILY ELIZABETH (fl. 1892-1915) ::   ARCHITECT

PRIMARY WORKS:

Book of Bungalows. Philadelphia: E.E. Holman, 1906.

New Picturesque Cottages. Philadelphia: E.E. Holman, 1904.

Picturesque Camps, Cabins, and Shacks. Philadelphia: E.E.
      Holman, 1908.

Picturesque Cottages. Philadelphia: E.E. Holman, 1894.

Picturesque Suburban Homes. Philadelphia: E.E. Holman,
      1907.

Picturesque Summer Cottages. 3 vols. Philadelphia: E.E.
      Holman, 1900-1903.

SECONDARY WORKS:

Tatman, Sandra L., and Roger W. Moss. Biographical
      Dictionary of Philadelphia Architects: 1700-1930.
      Boston: G.K. Hall, 1985. p. 393.

HOMSEY, VICTORINE (1900-   ) *   ARCHITECT

Historical Society of Delaware has some small house
projects by Victorine Homsey.

SECONDARY WORKS:

"Associated American Artists Galleries, New York City,
      Victorine and Samuel Homsey, Designers." Architectural
      Forum. 71 (November 1939), 347-349.

Berlo, J.C. "Women in Architecture: The Cambridge School."
      Feminist Art Journal. 5 (Spring 1976), 27-32.

"Blueprint Shop, Wilmington Blueprint Service Inc.,
      Wilmington, Delaware, Victorine and Samuel Homsey
      Architects." Architectural Forum. 70 (February 1939),
      101.

"Branch Bank in Large Shopping Center in Delaware:
      Equitable Security Trust Co., Newark, Delaware."
      Architectural Record. 119 (May 1956), 184-185.

"Brokerage Office Boosts Business and Employee Morale with

Space-Saving Modern Design, DuPont Company, Victorine and Samuel Homsey Architects." Architectural Forum. 87 (October 1947), 98-99.

"Cambridge Yacht Club, Cambridge, Maryland, Victorine and Samuel Homsey, Architects." Architectural Forum. 69 (October 1938), 254-256.

"Car Testing Station, Wilmington, Delaware, Victorine and Samuel Homsey, Architects." Architectural Review. 92 (November,1942), 117.

"Centerville, Delaware, House for H.B. Robertson; V. Homsey and S. Homsey, Architects." Architectural Forum. 68 (February 1938), 125-132.

"Children's Beach House, Lewes, Delaware, Victorine and Samuel Homsey, Architects." Architectural Forum. 69 (October 1939), 248-263.

"Community Recreation Center, Seaford, Delaware, Victorine and Samuel Homsey, Architects." Architectural Forum. 77 (July 1942), 67-70.

"Delaware School Profits from Adjoining Park, Frederick Douglass Stubbs School, Wilmington." Architectural Record. 116 (August 1954), 165-168.

"Foundations Saver, Prefabricated Parts: New House of 194X." Architectural Forum. 77 (September 1942), 71-73.

"Four Fine Fellows." AIA Journal. 52 (September 1969), 86-87.

"Friendly House Makes Room for Children, Wilmington, Delaware." House and Home. 9 (April 1956), 150-151.

"Friendly School: The Tatnall School in Wilmington, Delaware, Victorine and Samuel Homsey, Architects." Architectural Forum. 114 (March 1961), 104-105.

"Georgetown, Delaware, William C. Jason Comprehensive High School." Architectural Record. 112 (November 1952), 130-133.

"Grange, a Rural Community Structure." Beaux Arts Institute
    Design Bulletin. 28 (February 1952), 10.

Hamlin, T.F. "Modern Display for Works of Art: Galleries of
    the Associated American Artists." Pencil Points. 20
    (September 1939), 623-624.

"Hockessin Gate-House." Architectural Forum. 80 (June
    1944), 104-105.

"House for J.E. Johnson, Princeton, New Jersey."
    Architectural Record. 119 (March, 1956) 172-175.

"Maintenance Building, Greenbelt, Maryland, FPHA Region
    III." Pencil Points. 24 (March 1945), 71-72.

"The New House 1940s: Victorine and Samuel Homsey,
    Architects." Architectural Forum. 77 (September 1942),
    65-152.

"Portrait." Architectural Forum. 77 (September 1942), 71.

"Portrait." Architectural Forum. 82 (April 1945), 58.

"Portrait." Architectural Forum. 87 (October 1947), 58.

"Portrait." Architectural Record. 90 (September 1941), 69.

"A Portfolio of Recent Work by Victorine and Samuel Homsey
    of Wilmington Delaware." Architectural Forum. 73
    (September 1940), 159-172.

"Saint Barnabas Episcopal Church, Marshallton, Delaware."
    Architectural Record. 162 (July 1977), 106.

Saylor, Henry H. "Progressive Practice in the Small Office:
    Office of Victorine and Samuel Homsey, Wilmington,
    Delaware." Architectural Record. 90 (September 1941),
    69-74.

"Schools: Architectural Record's Building Types Study no.
    192." Architectural Record. 112 (November 1952),
    119-150.

"Schools: Architectural Record's Building Types Study no.
    213." Architectural Record. 116 (August 1954),

141-168.

"Seaford, Delaware Community Recreation Center." Architec-
    tural Forum. 77 (July 1942), 67-70.

Stevens, Mary Otis. "A Struggle for Place." In: Women in
    American Architecture. New York: Whitney Library of
    Design, 1977, p. 92

"Super-Multi-Purpose Area for a Junior High School,
    Wilmington, Delaware." Architectural Record. 132
    (October 1962), 176-177.

"A Thousand Women in Architecture: II" Architectural
    Record. 103 (June 1948), 109.

"Two Story Houses." Architectural Record. 119 (March 1956),
    167-183.

"Vistas Can Make a House Seem Large, Victorine and Samuel
    Homsey, Architects." House and Garden. 90 (October
    1946), 112-113.

"William W.H. Henry Comprehensive High School, Dover,
    Delaware." Architectural Forum. 98 (January 1953),
    122-125.

"Wilmington Blueprint Service, Inc., Wilmington, Delaware."
    Architectural Forum. 70 (February 1939), 101.

"Wilmington, Delaware, Automobile Testing Station,
    Victorine and Samuel Homsey, Architects."
    Architectural Forum. 77 (July 1942), 71-74.

"Zoo for Children." Beaux Arts Institute of Design
    Bulletin. 20 (October 1944), 13.

HOWE, LOIS LILLEY (1864-1964) *   ARCHITECT

MIT Archives has Howe, Manning and Almy Firm Papers; First
Firm of Women Architects in Boston and the second such firm
in the U.S.

The Daniel H. Burnham papers at the Art Institute of
Chicago include papers concerning Howe's role in the
World's Columbian Exposition.

The Schlesinger Library at Harvard University has in its
manuscript collection a biographical file on Lois Lilley
Howe.

The MIT Museum and Historical Collections maintains a file
on Howe.

PRIMARY WORKS:

An Architectural Monograph: The Colonel Robert Means House
    at Amherst, New Hampshire. New York: R.F. Whitehead,
    1927.

"The Colonel Robert Means House at Amherst, New Hampshire."
    White Pine Series of Architectural Monographs. 13
    (1927) 99-120.

"Serving Pantries in Small Houses." Architectural Review.
    14 (1907) 31-33.

with Constance Fuller. Detail from Old New England Houses.
    New York: Architectural Book Publishing Co., 1913.

SECONDARY WORKS:

"An Alumna's Architectural Career." Technology Review. 66
    (December 1963), 21, 38.

Brown, Frank C. "Boston Suburban Architecture."
    Architectural Record. 21 (April 1907), 245-280.

Cole, Doris. "New England Women Architects." In: Pilgrims
    and Pioneers: New England Women in the Arts, edited by
    Alicia Faxon and Sylvia Moore. New York: Midmarch
    Press, 1987, pp. 57-58.

"Designs for Woman's Building, World's Columbian Exposi-
    tion." Inland Architect and News Record. 18 (Septem-
    ber 1891), plates.

"House of Mrs. A.A. Burrage, Beach Road, Brookline, MA."
    American Architect and Building News. 88 (July 15,
    1905), 24 + plate.

"Lois Howe: Portrait." Architectural Forum. 101 (July
    1954), 116.

"Lois Lilley Howe." American Women, 1935-1940. Detroit:
    Gale Publishers, 1981, p. 430.

"Lois Lilley Howe: Obituary." Progressive Architecture. 45
    (October 1964), 118.

Morse, Gail. The Firm: A Study of the First Women's
    Architectural Firm in Boston: Howe, Manning and Almy.
    Boston University, B.A. Thesis, 1976.

Parks, Warren G. Mariemont Story. Cincinnati: Creative
    Writers and Pub., 1967.

Reinhardt, Elizabeth W. "Lois Lilley Howe, FAIA, 1864-
    1964." Cambridge Historical Society Publications. 43
    (1980), 153-172.

EXHIBITION:

AIA and Architectural League, New York. Architectural and
    Allied Arts Exposition. New York: AIA and Architec-
    tural League, 1925, p. 34.

HOWELL, SANDRA C. (1929-)   ENVIRONMENTAL
                                       PSYCHOLOGIST

PRIMARY WORKS:

"Behavioral Sciences in Building." Industrialization Forum.
    81, no. 1 (1977), entire issue is devoted to this
    theme.

Design Evaluation Workbook. Washington, D.C.: Gerontologi-
    cal Society, 1976.

Designing for Aging. Cambridge, MA: MIT Press, 1980.

Designing for the Elderly, Windows. Cambridge, Mass: Design
     Evaluation Project, 1976.

"Essays on Social Housing." Progressive Architecture. 65
     (July 1984), 82-87.

and others. "Applied Research Awards." Progressive
     Architecture. 64 (January 1983), 132-135, 138-139,
     142-143.

and others. "Monitoring Environment--Behavior Research in
     the Design Process." Journal of Architectural
     Research. 7 (March 1979), 12-21.

SECONDARY WORKS:

"Award for Research: Private Space, Habitability of
     Apartments for the Elderly." Progressive Architecture.
     60 (January 1979), 99.

Cliff, Ursula. "Three Exceptional Women." Design and
     Environment. 5 (Spring 1974), 34-37.

HUBBARD, THEODORA KIMBALL (1887-1935) ⋇ LIBRARIAN
                                          EDUCATOR

PRIMARY WORKS:

Founded journal, City Planning with her husband, Henry V.
Hubbard.

Edited book review section of Landscape Architecture.

American Society of Landscape Architects. Transactions of
     the American Society of Landscape Architects,
     1909-1921. edited by C. Rust Parker, Bremer W. Pond
     and Theodora Kimball. Amsterdam, New York: Recorder
     Press, 1922.

"A Brief Survey of Recent City Planning Reports in the
     United States." Landscape Architecture. 1911-
     continued on an annual basis.

Manual of Information on City Planning and Zoning.
    Cambridge: Harvard University Press, 1923.

"A Review of City Planning in the United States." National
    Municipal Review. 11 (1922), 27-33.

with Henry V. Hubbard. An Introduction to the Study of
    Landscape Design. New York: Macmillan, 1917.

with Henry V. Hubbard. Landscape Architecture. Cambridge,
    Mass: Harvard University Press, 1920.

with Henry V. Hubbard. Our Cities, Today and Tomorrow.
    Cambridge: Harvard University Press, 1929.

with Katherine McNamara. Bibliography of Planning,
    1928-1935. Cambridge: Harvard University Press, 1936.

with Katherine McNamara. Manual of Planning Information.
    Cambridge: Harvard University Press, 1928.

with Frederick Law Olmsted, editors. Forty Years of
    Landscape Architecture. Seattle: F.W. Phelps, 1928.

with Frederick Law Olmsted, editors. Frederick Law
    Olmsted, Landscape Architect,1822-1903. New York:
    Putnam, 1922.

with James Sturgis Pray. City Planning: A Comprehensive
    Analysis of the Subject Arranged for the
    Classification of Books, Plans, Photographs, Notes and
    Other Collected Material. Cambridge, MA: Harvard
    University Press, 1913.

SECONDARY WORKS:

Brown, Catherine R. Women and the Land. Baltimore: Morgan
    State University, 1979, p. [14].

"A City Planning Manual." AIA Journal. 12 (April 1924),
    205.

"H.W.S. Cleveland." Landscape Architecture. 20 (January
    1930), 91-111.

McNamara, Katherine. "Harvard's Landscape Architecture and
     City Planning Collections." Landscape Architecture. 45
     (April 1955), 159-162 + .

Palmer, Donna. An Overview of the Trends, Eras and Values
     of Landscape Architecture in America. M.L.A. North
     Carolina State University, 1976, pp. 9-11.

Theodora Kimball Hubbard." In: Public Space: Environmental
     Awareness in America During the Latter Nineteenth
     Century. Cambridge, MA: Harvard School of Design,
     1975, pp. 72-73.

"Theodora Kimball Hubbard: A Biographical Minute."
     Landscape Architecture. 26 (January 1936), 53-55.

"Theodora Kimball Hubbard: Obituary." Planning and Civic
     Comment. 2 (January-March 1936), 36.

Yarwood, George A. "History of Women in Landscape
     Architecture." ASLA Bulletin. (July 1973), [3-7].

HUTCHESON, MARTHA BROOKS (1872-1959)   LANDSCAPE ARCHITECT

PRIMARY WORKS:

The Spirit of the Garden. Boston: Atlantic Monthly Press,
     1923.

SECONDARY WORKS:

Brown, Catherine R. Women and the Land. Baltimore: Morgan
     State University, 1979, p. [15].

Fowler, Clarence. "Three Women in Landscape Architecture."
     Cambridge School of Architecture and Landscape
     Architecture, Alumnae Bulletin. 4 (1932), 7.

"Martha Brooks Hutcheson." American Women, 1935-1940.
     Detroit: Gale Publishers, 1981, p. 442.

Meade, Elizabeth. "Martha Brooks Hutcheson." Landscape
     Architecture. 50 (April 1960), 181-182.

"Martha Brooks Hutcheson: Obituary." Landscape Architecture. 50 (Spring 1960), 181-182.

Palmer, Donna. An Overview of the Trends, Eras and Values of Landscape Architecture in America. M.L.A. North Carolina State University, 1976, pp. 34-35.

EXHIBITION:

AIA and Architectural League, New York. Architectural and Allied Arts Exposition. New York: AIA and Architectural League, 1925, p. 35.

HUXTABLE, ADA LOUISE (1921-) * ARCHITECTURAL CRITIC

Wodehouse, L. Ada Louise Huxtable: An Annotated Bibliography. New York: Garland Publishing, 1981. This is a complete bibliography of works by and about Huxtable including books and periodical articles. The reader is referred to this volume for bibliographic citations previous to 1977.

PRIMARY WORKS:

Architecture, Anyone. New York: Random House, 1986.

"Architecture Today." New York Review of Books. 30 (December 8, 1983), 29 + .

"Backtalk: Office Landscapes and Inner Space." Interiors. 138 (April 1979), 99.

"Bertram Grosvenor Goodhue." New York Review of Books. 30 (December 22, 1983), 59-60.

"De Stijl, 1917-1931: Visions of Utopia." New York Review of Books. 30 (December 8, 1983), 29 + .

"Frank Lloyd Wright Letters Trilogy." New York Times Book Review. (February 15, 1987), 3.

Goodbye History, Hello Hamburger. Washington, D.C:

Preservation Press, 1986.

"High Rise, High Density." Bauwelt. 77 (September 12, 1986), 1288-1307.

"House X." New York Review of Books. 30 (December 8, 1983). 29 + .

"In the Shadow of the Architect." Blueprint. 32 (November 1986), 20-22.

"Is Modern Architecture Dead?" Architectural Record. 169 (October 1981), 100-106.
    Also: New York Review of Books. 28 (July 16, 1981), 17 + .
        Summa. 168 (November 1981), 38-45.
        CAU. 76 (December 1981), 50-63.

"James Stirling: An Architectural Design Profile." New York Review of Books. 30 (December 8, 1983), 29 + .

"Mies van der Rohe." New York Times Book Review. 90 (December 1, 1985), 1 + .

"Mirrors of Our Time: Twenty Years of Modern Building." New York Times Magazine (February 13, 1979), 82 + .

"Modern Architecture: A Critical History." New York Review of Books. 30 (December 22, 1983), 57 + .

"Modern Architecture Since 1900." New York Review of Books. 30 (December 22, 1983), 58 + .

"Moderns and Post-Moderns: The Problematic Situation of Contemporary Architecture." CAU. 66 (October 1980), 49-63.

"New York in the Eighties." New Criterion. 4 (Summer 1986), 22-27.

"A Phoenix in Barcelona." New York Times Book Review. 90 (December 1, 1985), 33-34.

The Tall Building Artistically Reconsidered. New York: Pantheon Books, 1984.

"The Tall Building Artistically Reconsidered: The Search
    for a Skyscraper Style." Architectural Record. 172
    (January 1984), 63-79.

"A Tower for Louisville: The Humana Competition." New York
    Review of Books. 30 (December 8, 1983), 29-30.

"The Troubled State of Modern Architecture." New York
    Review of Books. 27 (May 1, 1980), 22 + .
    Also : AD. 51 no. 1/2 (1981), 9-17.
            Architectural Record. 169 (January 1981),
            72-29.
            Summa. 167 (October 1981), 24-33.

"Urban Apocalypse Now? What's the Benefit of Twentieth
    Century Progress... Survey of Recent Construction and
    Development in Paris." Interiors. 139 (June 1980),
    80-81.

"What Is "Good Taste" and Who Has the Right To Say So?"
    House Beautiful. 124 (October 1982), 41 + .
    Also: Particular Passions. by Lynn Gilbert and
        Gaylen Moore.

"Where Summers Are Easy." Architectural Digest. 43 (June
    1986), 28, 33, 34.

and Hans-Gerhard Kauschke. "A New Generation of
    Skyscrapers." Bauwelt. 77 (September 1988), 1288-1307.

SECONDARY WORKS:

"Ada Louise Huxtable." Current Biography. New York: H.W.
    Wilson, 1973, pp. 196-199.

"Ada Louise Huxtable: A Question of Quality." AIA Journal.
    71 (January 1982), 54-55.

Cliff, Ursula. "New York's Better Self." Design and
    Environment. 2 (Spring 1971), 50-51.

Gilbert, Lynn and Gaylen Moore. "Ada Louise Huxtable: A
    Question of Quality." AIA Journal. 71 (January 1982),
    54-55.

Gueft, O. "Vuillard Houses and Emery Roth and Sons Palace
    Hotel." Contract Interiors. 136 (July 1977), 66-71.

"Honoured Fellows: Six New Honorary Fellows Approved by the
    RIBA Council." Architects' Journal. 179 (March 28,
    1984), 34.

Levin, E. "In Search of Lost Time." Journal of
    Architectural Education. 35 (Winter 1982), 2-7.

"More of the Met: Restaurants and Clubs." Interiors. 126
    (December 1966), 124-127.

Muschamp, Herbert. "The Good, the Bad and the Timeless Ada
    Louise Huxtable." Design Book Review (Spring 1987),
    37-42.

"The Pleasure of the Plaza: Two New Restaurants." Interior
    Design. 42 (December 1971), 66-69, 94-95.

Polledo, Eduardo. "Zero Reference." Summa. 177 (August
    1982), 67-70.

"RIBA Council Approves Six New Honorary Fellows." Building
    Design. 683 (March 30, 1984), 3.

Stephens, S. "Voices of Consequence: Four Architectural
    Critics." In: Women in American Architecture. New
    York: Whitney Library of Design, 1977 pp. 136-143.

"Times Without Huxtable: Ada Louise Huxtable in
    Perspective." Skyline (March 1982), 3.

"Winner of the 1969 Elsie de Wolfe Award: Ada Louise
    Huxtable, Architecture Critic of the New York Times."
    Interior Design. 40 (March 1969), 152-153.

EXHIBITION:

AIA, Washington, D.C. Two on Two at the Octagon.
    Washington, D.C.: the Octagon, 1979, pp. 19-20.

IREYS, ALICE RECKNAGEL (1911-) ⁝⁝ LANDSCAPE ARCHITECT

PRIMARY WORKS:

How to Plan and Plant Your Own Property. New York: William
     Morrow, 1967.

Small Gardens for City and Country. Englewood Cliffs, New
     Jersey: Prentice-Hall, 1978.

SECONDARY WORKS:

Anderson, Dorothy May. Women, Design and the Cambridge
     School. Mesa, Arizona: PDA Publishers Corp., 1980, P.
     172.

Deitz, Paula. "Designing Women." Metropolis. (December
     1982), 14-19.

Faust, Joan L. "Small Gardens for City and Country." New
     York Times Book Review. 83 (March 19, 1978) 24 +.

EXHIBITION:

Built by Women: A Guide to Architecture in the New York
     Area. New York: Alliance for Women in Architecture,
     1981. p. 19.

IRWIN, HARRIET MORRISON (1828-1897) ⁝⁝   DESIGNER

The Schlesinger Library at Harvard University has in its
manuscript collection a photographic negative of Irwin's
plan for a hexagonal building of 1869.

PRIMARY WORKS:

The Hermit of Petraea. Charlotte, North Carolina: Hill and
     Irwin, 1871.

SECONDARY WORKS:

Annual Report of the Commissioner of Patents, 1869.
    Washington, D.C.: Government Printing Office, 1871, p.
    165, 474.

Barringer, Paul B. The Natural Bent. Chapel Hill, North
    Carolina: 1949, p. 74

Brown, Mrs. Laura. Historical Sketch of the Morrison
    Family. Charlotte, North Carolina: n.p., 1919, pp.
    17-21.

Cole, Doris. From Tipi to Skyscraper: A History of Women in
    Architecture. Boston: i press, 1973 p. 35.

Fowler, Orson S. The Octagon House: A Home for All. New
    York: Dover, 1973.
    Reprint of the 1854 edition entitled, A Home for All.

"Harriet Morrison Irwin." Macmillan Encyclopedia of
    Architects. New York: Free Press, 1982, v. 2, pp.
    466-467.

Heisner, Beverly. "Harriet Morrison Irwin's Hexagonal
    House: An Invention to Improve Domestic Dwellings."
    North Carolina Historical Review. 58, no. 2 (1981),
    105-123.

Lancaster, Clay. Architectural Follies in America. Rutland,
    Vermont: Tuttle Co., 1960, pp. 130,141.

"Mrs. Irwin Dead." Charlotte Democrat (January 28, 1897),
    4.

Stern, Madeleine B. We the Women: Career Firsts of
    Nineteenth Century America. New York: Artemis, 1962,
    pp. 55-61.

Torre, Susanna. Women in American Architecture. New York:
    Whitney Library of Design, 1977, p. 55

Vare, Ethlie Ann and Greg Ptacek. Mothers of Invention. New
    York: William Morrow and Co., 1988, pp. 164-166.

JACOBS, JANE (1916-) ⚹   ARCHITECTURAL CRITIC

PRIMARY WORKS:

Canadian Cities and Sovereignty Association. Toronto:
    Canadian Broadcasting Corporation, 1980.

"Chicago's Woodlawn - Renewal by Whom?" Architectural
    Forum. 116 (May 1962), 122-124.

"A Continuing Tradition in Urban Development."
    Architectural Forum. 116 (May 1962), 107-124, 190,
    203, 206.

The Death and Life of Great American Cities. New York:
    Random House, 1961.

"Death and Life of Great American Cities: Excerpts."
    Architectural Forum. 115 (September 1961), 122-125;
    (October 1961), 144-145 + .

"Designers of Change." Interiors. 130 (November 1970),
    entire issue devoted to this theme.

"Do Not Segregate Pedestrians and Automobiles."
    Architect's Yearbook. 11 (1965), 109-110.

"Downtown Is for People." In: The Exploding Metropolis.
    compiled by the editors of Fortune Magazine. New York:
    Doubleday, 1958.

"The Dynamic of Decline." Atlantic. 253 (April 1984), 98 + .

The Economy of Cities. New York: Random House, 1969.

"Exchange between Moshe Safdie, James Rouse, and Jane
    Jacobs at the Second International Conference on Urban
    Design." Urban Design International. 2 (January-
    February 1981), 29, 38.

"Housing for the Independent Aged." Architectural Forum.
    109 (August 1958), 88-91.

"How Money Can Make or Break Our Cities." The Reporter. 25
    (October 12 1961), 38.

"Metropolitan Government." Architectural Forum. 107 (August
    1957), 124-127, 206, 208.

"The Miniature Boom." Architectural Forum. 108 (May 1958),
    106-111.

"New Heart for Baltimore." Architectural Forum. 108 (June
    1958), 88-92.

"New York's Office Boom." Architectural Forum. 106 (March
    1957), 104-113.

"Planning for Living Cities." Vogue. 139 (January 1, 1962),
    73.

"Profile." Architects' Journal. 137 (January 16, 1963),
    126-127.

"Right Way to Save Our Cities: Condensation." Reader's
    Digest. 84 (April 1964), 229.

"The Self-Generating Growth of Cities." RIBA Journal. 74
    (March 1967), 96-100.

"Social Dimensions of Design." AIA Journal. 38 (July 1962),
    29 + .

"To Repair the Social Engine, You Must Know What Makes It
    Run." Interiors. 130 (November 1970), 125.

"Washington: Twentieth Century Capital?" Architectural
    Forum. 104 (January 1958), 92-115.

"Why TVA Failed." New York Review of Books. 31 (May 10,
    1984), 41 + .

SECONDARY WORKS:

DeWolfe, I. "Death and Life of Great American Citizens:
    Discussion of a Chapter from Jane Jacobs' book."
    Architectural Review. 133 (February 1963), 91-93.

"Disturber of the Peace: Jane Jacobs." Mademoiselle. 55
    (October 1962), 142.

Freiburg, Peter. "Jane Jacobs' Old Fight Lingers On."
    Planning. 42 (January 1976), 5-6.

Gratz, Roberta Brandes. "How Westway Will Destroy New York:
    An Interview with Jane Jacobs." New York. 11
    (February 6, 1978), 30-34.

Howell, W.G. "Planning for Change: Thoughts After the Jane
    Jacobs Lecture." RIBA Journal. 74 (April 1967), 135.

Hudak, J. "Re Jane Jacobs." Landscape Architecture. 52
    (July 1962), 216.

"Jane Jacobs." In: American Women Writers. edited by Lina
    Mainiero. New York: F. Ungar Pub. Co., 1982, pp.
    383-385.

"Jane Jacobs: Against Urban Renewal, For Urban Life." New
    York Times Magazine (May 15, 1969), 34.

"Jane Jacobs in London." Werk. 54 (May 1967), 307-309.

Johnson, David A. "The City-State Revisited." Planning. 50
    (November 1984), 26-28, 30-35.

"Kind of Problem a City Is." Perspecta. 11 (1967), 222.

Klassen, David H. The Safety of Urban Neighborhoods: An
    Ecological Approach. Ph.D. Dissertation, University of
    Chicago, 1982.

Meyers, Barton, and George Baird. "Vacant Lottery...Changes
    in Urban Form and Human Interaction with the Form."
    Design Quarterly. 108 (1978), 5-52.

Moholy-Nagy, Sibyl. " In Defense of Architecture: Jane
    Jacob's Book. "Architectural Forum. 116 (April 1962),
    19.

Moses, R. "Variety of New York City Street Trees Defended."
    Landscape Architecture. 60 (October 1969), 20.

"Peter Blake, Jane Jacobs Voted Critics Awards." AIA
    Journal. 63 (March 1975), 8.

Richardson, M. "Women Theorists." AD. 45 (August 1975),
    467.

"Self Generating Growth of Cities." <u>RIBA Journal</u>. 74 (March
    1967), 95-98.

Shankland, G. "Confrontation in Boston: Jim Rouse vs. Jane
    Jacobs, Great Cities of the World Conference."
    <u>Architects' Journal</u>. 172 (November 5, 1980), 879.

Smith, Janet M. "Healthy, Wealthy and Wise." <u>Arts and
    Architecture</u>. 4 (May 1985), 19-21.

Stephens, S. "Voices of Consequence: Four Architectural
    Critics." In: <u>Women in American Architecture</u>. New
    York: Whitney Library of Design, 1977, pp. 136-143.

"Where to Locate a Bookstore in a City and Where Not to
    Locate One." <u>Publishers Weekly</u>. 181 (January 1, 1962),
    28.

"Women in Architecture: Architectural Criticism, Four
    Women." <u>Progressive Architecture</u>. 58 (March 1977),
    56-57.

JAMES, HARLEAN (1877-1969)   PLANNER
                                              WRITER

PRIMARY WORKS:

<u>American Planning and Civic Annual</u>. Washington, D.C.:
    American Civic Association, 1935-1957.

<u>The Building of Cities</u>. New York: Macmillan, 1917.

<u>City Planning Procedure</u>. Washington, D.C.: American Civic
    Association, 1926.

<u>Civic Improvement in Your Town: A Program and Plan of
    Procedure</u>. Washington., D.C.: American Civic
    Association, 1927.

ed. <u>Land Planning in the United States for City, State and
    Nation</u>. New York: Macmillan, 1921.

SECONDARY WORKS:

Brown, Catherine. Women and the Land. Batimore: Built
    Studies Environment, 1979, p. 15.

Palmer, Donna. An Overview of the Trends, Eras and Values
    of Landscape Architecture in America. M.L.A. North
    Carolina State Univ., 1976, p. 29

JOHNSTON, FRANCES BENJAMIN (1864-1952) * ARCHITECTURAL
                                          PHOTOGRAPHER

Negatives at the Huntington Library, San Marino,
California.

Some of Johnston's manuscript material and photographs are
at the Library of Congress.

PRIMARY WORKS:

The Carnegie Survey of the Architecture of the South,
    1927-1943, edited by Janet M. Gwaltney. Photographs
    by Frances Benjamin Johnston. Teaneck, New Jersey:
    Chadwyck-Healey, 1984.

Colonial Churches in Virginia. Port Washington, New York:
    Kennikat Press, 1972, text by Henry I. Brock and
    photographs by Frances Benjamin Johnston.

The Early Architecture of Georgia, with text by Frederick
    D. Nichols and photographs by Frances Benjamin
    Johnston. Chapel Hill: University of North Carolina
    Press, 1957.

The Early Architecture of North Carolina, text by Thomas T.
    Waterman and photographs by Frances Benjamin Johnston.
    Chapel Hill: University of North Carolina Press, 1941.

The Hampton Album. New York: Museum of Modern Art
    distributed by Doubleday, 1966.

Mammoth Cave By Flash Light. Washington, D.C.: Gibson
    Bros., 1893.

The Mansions of Virginia, 1706-1776, text by Thomas T.
    Waterman and photographs by Frances Benjamin Johnston.
    Chapel Hill: the University of North Carolina Press,
    1946.

Plantations of the Carolina Low Countries. text by Samuel
    G. Stoney and photographs by Frances Benjamin
    Johnston. Charleston, South Carolina: Carolina Art
    Association, 1939.

The White House. Washington, D.C.: Gibson Bros., 1893.

SECONDARY WORKS:

Alexander, Adele L. "At the American Court: Frances
    Benjamin Johnston Was an Unconventional Woman Who Took
    Her Camera to Unconventional Places." Washingtonian.
    20 (October 1984), 168 + .

_____. "Photographer Frances Benjamin
    Johnston: A Turn of the Century Chronicle of Women and
    Work." MS. 13 (April 1985), 80-84.

Andreassen, C.L. "Frances Benjamin Johnston and Her Views
    of Uncle Sam." Louisiana History (1960), 130-136.

Daniel, Pete and Raymond Smock. A Talent for Detail: The
    Photographs of Miss Frances Benjamin Johnston,
    1889-1910. New York: Harmony Books, 1974.

Doherty, A.S. "Frances Benjamin Johnston, 1864-1952."
    History of Photgraphy. 4 (April 1980), 97-111.

"Frances Benjamin Johnston." Dictionary of American
    Biography. New York: Charles Scribners Sons,
    1977, sup. 5, p. 373.

"Frances Benjamin Johnston." In: Macmillan Biographical
    Encyclopedia of Photographic Artists. New York:
    Macmillan, 1983, pp. 310-311.

"Frances Benjamin Johnston." Notable American Women: The
    Modern Period. Cambridge, Mass.: Harvard University
    Press, 1980, pp. 381-383.

"Frances Benjamin Johnston: Her Photographs of Our Old

Buildings." Magazine of Art. 30 (September 1937), 548-555.

Frances Benjamin Johnston: What a Woman Can Do with a Camera. Pudsey: Allanwood Press, 1984.

"Frances Benjamin Johnston's Photographs." AIA Journal. 8 (December 1947), 257-261.

Havice, C. "In a Class by Herself: 19th Century Images of the Woman Artist as Student." Woman's Art Journal. 2 (Spring-Summer 1981), 35-40.

"Houses of the Old South." American Architect. 147 (September 1935), 57-64.

"Johnston's Photographs at the Library of Congress." AIA Journal. 8 (December 1947), 257-258 + .

Kahan, Robert Sidney. The Antecedents of American Photo-journalism. Ph.D. Dissertation, University of Wisconsin, 1969.

Logan, Mary S. The Part Taken By Women in American History. Wilmington, Delaware: Perry-Nalle, 1912, pp. 788-789.

"Maryland's Architectural Relics: Photographs." Baltimore Museum News. 5 (December 1942), 8.

Page, Marian. "Frances Benjamin Johnston's Architectural Photographs." American Art and Antiques. 2 (July-August 1979), 64-71.

Peterson, A.E. "Crusader with a Camera." Historic Preservation. 32 (January 1980), 17-20.

Peterson, A.E. "Francis Benjamin Johnston: The Early Years, 1888-1908." Nineteenth Century. 6 (Spring 1980), 58-61.

"Photographs of Women." Camera. 51 (February 1972), 31.

Tucker, Anne. editor. "Frances Benjamin Johnston, 1864-1952." The Woman's Eye. New York: Knopf, 1973, pp. 29-43.

Vanderbilt, Paul. "Frances Benjamin Johnston, 1864-1952."
    AIA Journal. 18 (November 1952), 224-228.

Whelan, R. "Are Women Better Photographers Than Men?"
    Artnews. 79 (October 1980), 86.

EXHIBITIONS:

Baltimore Museum of Art. The Photographs of Frances
    Benjamin Johnston. Baltimore: the Museum, s.d.

California State University Art Galleries, Long Beach,
    California. Frances Benjamin Johnston: Women of Class
    and Station. Long Beach, CA: The Gallery, 1979.

Portner, D. "Women of Another Era: Art Gallery, California
    State University, Long Beach, Exhibition." Artweek. 10
    (March 3, 1979), 13.

Schmertz, R.W. "Early Southern Architecture: Photographs by
    F.B. Johnston on Exhibit." Carnegie Magazine. 17
    (February 1944), 278-279.

"Three Women Photographers." Baltimore Museum of Art
    Record. 4 (February 1974), 2.

"What a Woman Can Do with a Camera, Impressions Gallery,
    York, England." British Journal of Photography. 131
    (August 31, 1984), 916.

University of Maryland Art Gallery, College Park, Maryland.
    Women Artists in Washington Collections/Her Feminine
    Colleagues: Photographs and Letters Collected by
    Frances Benjamin Johnston in 1900. College Park, Md.:
    the Gallery and the Women's Caucus for Art, 1979.

KERBIS, GERTRUDE LEMPP (1926-) *   ARCHITECT

SECONDARY WORKS:

Miller, Nory. "Chicago Awards 1976: Five More Than We
    Needed?" Inland Architect. 11 (November 1976), 8-13.

Patterson, Anne. "Women Architects--Why So Few of Them?"
    Inland Architect. 15 (December 1971), 13-19.

"Unisex Buidlings." Progressive Architecture. 55 (June
    1974), 32 + .

Wachsman, Konrad. The Turning Point of Building: Structure
    and Design. New York: Reinhold Pub. Corp., 1961, pp.
    85, 89, 120-121, 108-109.

"Women in Architecture, Current Work: Situation Today."
    Progressive Architecture. 58 (March 1977), 50.

EXHIBITION:

Art Institute of Chicago. Chicago Architects Design: A
    Century of Architectural Drawings from the Art
    Institute of Design. New York and Chicago: Rizzoli
    Pubs., 1982, p. 93.

Chicago Women in Architecture. Chicago Women Architects:
    Contemporary Direction. Chicago: Chicago Women in
    Architecture, 1978.

Chicago Historical Society. "Chicago Women in Architecture:
    Progress and Evolution, 1979-1984." In: Inland
    Architect. 28 (November-December 1984), p. 16.

KING, LOUISA YEOMANS 1863-1948) WRITER ON LANDSCAPE
                            ARCHITECTURE

PRIMARY WORKS:

The Beginners Garden. New York: Charles Scribner's Sons,
    1927.

Chronicles of the Garden. New York: Charles Scribner's,
    1925.

The Flower Garden Day by Day. New York: Stokes Co., 1927.

From a New Garden. New York: A. Knopf, 1930.

The Gardener's Colour Book. New York: A. Knopf, 1929.

The Little Garden. New York: Atlantic Monthly Press, 1921.

Pages from a Garden Notebook. New York: Charles Scribner's,
    1921.

Rohde, Eleanor S. The Story of the Garden. London: The
    Medici Society, 1932.
    Contains a chapter on American Gardens by King.

Variety in the Little Garden. New York: Atlantic Monthly
    Press, 1923.

The Well Considered Garden. New York: Charles Scribner's
    Sons, 1915.

SECONDARY WORKS:

Brown, Catherine R. Women and the Land. Baltimore: Morgan
    State University, 1979, p. [16].

"Louisa King, Obituary." Flower Grower. 35 (April 1948),
    330.

"Louisa Yeomans King." American Women, 1935-1940. Detroit:
    Gale Publishers, 1981, p. 487.

"Louisa Yeomans King." American Women Writers, edited by
    Lina Mainiero. New York: F. Ungar Pub. Co., 1982, pp.
    459-460.

Massingham, B. A Century of Gardeners. London: Faber and
    Faber, 1982, pp. 139-149.

Massingham, B. "Taste Maker in American Gardening: Louisa
    King's Work and Ideas." Country Life. 164 (October 12,
    1978), 1141-1142.

"Mrs. Francis King: Gardener's Guide and Friend." In: Her
    Garden Was Her Delight, by Buckner Hollingsworth. New
    York: Macmillan, 1962, pp. 143-154.

Seaton, Beverly. "Louisa Yeomans King." IN: American Women
    Writers. vol. 2 (1980), pp. 459-460.

KRESS, JERRILY (1945 -) ⁂   ARCHITECT

SECONDARY WORKS:

"Jerrily Kress: Kress/Cox Associates." Washingtonian. (May
      1985), 147-149.

"Kress Sets Energetic Pace in Business of Architecture."
      Board of Trade News (March 1987), 11.

LEERS, ANDREA (1942-) ⁂   ARCHITECT

PRIMARY WORKS:

"Child Care Center." Architecture and Urbanism. 193
      (October 1986), 52-53.

"MIT Martin Center for Design, Cambridge, Massachusetts."
      Architecture + Urbanism. 185 (February 1986), 101-103.

"Narrow Extension Gains Presence with a Distinctive Face,
      Tokyo University Museum." Architecture. 73 (September
      1984), 128-131.

"Professor Shinohara at Yale: Cesar Pelli Interviewed by
      Andrea Leers." Japan Architect. 60 (July 1985), 44-47.

"Western Influences and Japanese Traditions in Three Recent
      Works by Fumihiko Maki." Japan Architect. 58 (March
      1983), 46-48.

and Herashi Watanabe and Jacqueline Keslenbaum. "Japan."
      Architecture. 73 (September 1984), 128-147.

SECONDARY WORKS:

Dean, Andrea Oppenheim. "Women in Architecture: Individual
      Profiles and Discussion of Issues." AIA Journal. 71
      (January 1982), 42-51.

Dixon, J. M. "Crow's Nest Refeathered: Rehabilitation of
      Tobin Bridge Administration Building, Boston."
      Progressive Architecture. 63 (May 1982), 156-157.

"Works: Andrea Leers Associates." <u>Architecture and
     Urbanism</u>. 2 (February 1985), 95-106.

LIN, MAYA YING (1960? -) *   ARCHITECT

SECONDARY WORKS:

"AIA Awards: No Duds, No Surprises." <u>Progressive
     Architecture</u>. 65 (May 1984), 22-24.

"Beauty and the Bank." <u>New Republic</u> (December 23, 1985)
     25-29.

Blum, Shirley N. "The National Vietnam War Memorial." <u>Arts
     Magazine</u>. 59 (December 1984), 124-128.

Campbell, Robert. "Emotive Place Apart: Vietnam Veterans
     Memorial." <u>AIA Journal</u>. 72 (May 1983), 150-151.

_____. "The Sixth Annual Review of New American
     Architecture. "<u>AIA Journal</u>. 72 (May 1983), 149-359.

Capasso, Nicholas J. "Vietnam Veterans Memorial." In:
     <u>Critical Edge</u>. Cambridge, MA: MIT Press, 1985, pp.
     188-202.

Davis, Lorraine. "And The Winner Is... Young Woman Wins
     Design Competition for Vietnam Veterans Memorial."
     <u>Vogue</u>. 171 (September 1981), 115-116.

Freeman, Allen. "An Extraordinary Competition." <u>AIA
     Journal</u>. 70 (August 1981), 47-53.

Hess, E. "Tale of Two Memorials: The Debate over the Design
     for a Vietnam Veterans Memorial." <u>Art in America</u>. 71
     (April 1983), 120-127.

Howett, Catherine M. "The Vietnam Veterans Memorial: Public
     Art and Politics." <u>Landscape</u>. 28, no. 2 (1985), 1-9.

Kelley, J. "Maya Ying Lin, Vietnam Veterans Memorial, The
     Mall, Washington, D.C." <u>Artforum</u>. 21 (April 1983),
     76-77.

Lewis, Maggie. "Vietnam War Memorial." <u>Christian Science
     Monitor</u> (August 18, 1981), B9.

Ridley, Richard. "No Peace for Vietnam Memorial." New Art
    Examiner. 9 (Summer 1982), 1, 6-7.

"Vietnam Memorial: America Remembers." National Geographic
    (May 1985) 552-557.

"Vietnam War Memorial." Artnews. 82 (January 1983), 11-12.

von Eckardt, Wolf. "Of Heart and Mind: Serene Grace of the
    Vietnam Memorial." Washington Post (May 16, 1981),
    B1 + .

LOBELL, MIMI (1942-) ⁎   ARCHITECT
                                             EDUCATOR

PRIMARY WORKS:

Architecture for Women: Some Notes. Brooklyn: Pratt
    Institute, 1975 [pamphlet].

"Postscript: Kahn, Pann and the Philadelphia School."
    Oppositions. 4 (October 1974), 63-64.

"Temples of the Great Goddess." Heresies. 2 (Spring 1978),
    32-39.

and John Lobell. "A Conversation with John Hejduk." Pratt
    Journal of Architecture. 1 (Fall 1985), 46-49.

SECONDARY WORKS:

Orenstein, Gloria F. "The Reemergence of the Archtype of
    the Great Goddess in Art by Contemporary Women."
    Heresies, (Spring 1978), 74-84.

"Women in Architecture, Current Work: Situation Today."
    Progressive Architecture. 58 (March 1988), 53.

EXHIBITION:

Built by Women: A Guide to Architecture in the New York
    Area. New York: Alliance of Women in Architecture,

1981, p. 25.

LOW, JUDITH ELEANOR GILCHRIST   EDUCATOR

SECONDARY WORKS:

Brown, Catherine. Women and the Land. Baltimore: Built
    Studies Environment, 1979, p. 18

Brown, Catherine and Celia Maddox. "Women and the Land: A
    Suitable Profession." Landscape Architecture. 72 (May
    1982), 65-69.

"Judith Gilchrist Low." House and Garden. 47 (March 1925),
    100.

"Judith Gilchrist Low." Public Space. Cambridge: Harvard
    University Graduate School of Design, 1975, p. 71.

Nevins, Deborah. "The Triumph of Flora: Women and the
    American Landscape 1890-1935." Antiques. 127 (April
    1985), 904-922.

Palmer, Donna. An Overview of the Trends, Eras and Values
    of Landscape Architecture in America. M.L.A. North
    Carolina State University, 1976, p. 5.

Yarwood, George A. "History of Women in Landscape
    Architecture." ASLA Bulletin, (July 1973), [3-7].

LUKENS, HELENA AUGUSTA (1881-1979)   ARCHITECT

Lukens' papers are at the Athenaeum of Philadelphia.

SECONDARY WORKS:

Drexel Institute of Technology. Recipients of Certificates,
    Diplomas and Degrees, 1893-1948. Philadelphia: the
    Institute, 1948, p. 62.

Tatman, Sandra L. and Roger W. Moss. Biographical

Dictionary of Philadelphia Architects: 1700-1930.
Boston: G.K. Hall, 1985, p. 494.

LUSCOMB, FLORENCE HOPE (1887-1985)   REFORMER

The Schlesinger Library at Harvard University has in its
manuscript collection material on the Women's Rights
Collection ca. 1633-1958.

PRIMARY WORKS:

Oral History Interview with Florence Luscomb, Women's Trade
    Union League. Ann Arbor, Mich.: Program on Women and
    Work, 1978.

SECONDARY WORKS:

Cole, Doris. From Tipi to Skyscraper: A History of Women in
    Architecture. Boston: i Press, 1973, p. 112.

"Personality, Miss Luscomb Takes a Stand." Time (April 26,
    1971), 20.

MCCOY, ESTHER ⁂   ARCHITECTURAL CRITIC

PRIMARY WORKS:

"A. Quincy Jones and Frederick E. Emmons." Arts and
    Architecture. 83 (May 1966), 8-13.

"An Affection for Objects: Interior Design, The Charles
    Eames Office." Progressive Architecture. 54 (August
    1973), 64-67.

"Architecture in Mexico." Arts and Architecture. 68 (August
    1951), 27 +.

"Architecture West." Progressive Architecture.52 (April
    1971), 53; (June 1971), 47; (August 1971), 43; 54
    (July 1973), 52; (October 1973) 52; 55 (February

1974), 38; (March 1974), 44; 55 (May 1974), 38 + .

"Arts and Architecture Case Study Houses." Perspecta. 15
    (1975), 54-73.

"Before the Silvers." Progressive Architecture. 57 (October
    1976), 66-69.

"Books." Arts and Architecture. 75 (March 1958), 9; (April
    1958), 30-31.

"Bruce Goff." Arts and Architecture. 2, no. 3 (1983),
    44-47.

"Charles Greene's Presence." SAH Southern California
    Chapter. Review. 1 (Spring 1982), 1-2.

"Concrete Shell Forms: Felix Candela." Arts and
    Architecture. 74 (May 1957), 16-19 + .

"The Death of Juan O'Gorman." Arts and Architecture. 1, no.
    3 (1982), 36-40.

"Designing for a Dry Climate." Progressive Architecture. 52
    (August 1971), 50-57.

"Dr. Salk Talks About His Institute." Architectural Forum.
    127 (December 1967), 27-35.

"Eames House, Santa Monica, California: On Attaining a
    Certain Age." Progressive Architecture. 58 (October
    1977), 80-83.

"XI Triennale." Arts and Architecture. 75 (January 1958),
    28-29 + .

"The Envelope, The Show, the Eye Opener." Arts and
    Architecture. 2, no. 1 (1983), 25.

"Everyman's Casa: Villas Florestas, Tijuana, Mexico."
    Progressive Architecture. 59 (July 1978), 76-79.

"Exhibition in Como." Arts and Architecture. 74 (October
    1957), 33-35.

Five California Architects. New York: Reinhold, 1960.

"Five California Architects: Excerpts." Progressive
    Architecture. 41 (July 1960), 129-136.

"Four Schindler Houses of the 1920's." Arts and
    Architecture. 70 (September 1953), 12-14 + .

"Gio Ponti, 1891-1979." LA Architect. 5 (November 1979), 1.

"The Greenhouse: Architects, Milica Dedijer-Mihich." Arts
    and Architecture. 1, no. 3 (1982), 45-40.

"Health Center with Muscles." Architectural Forum. 130
    (March 1969), 60-63.

"Irving Gill." Arts and Architecture. 75 (October 1958),
    28-29.

"Irving Gill, Architect." Historic Preservation. 24 (April
    1972), 8-11.

"Italian Building Materials." Arts and Architecture. 81
    (May 1964), 20-25 +.

"Italian Designs." Arts and Architecture. 80 (May 1963),
    26-27.

"Italian Exhibitions." Arts and Architecture. 75 (December
    1958), 22-23 +.

"Konrad Wachsmann, 1901-1980." International Architect. 1,
    no. 5 (1981), 3.

"Letters Between R.M. Schindler and Richard Neutra."
    Society of Architectural Historians Journal. 33
    (October 1974), 219-224.

"Lloyd Wright." Arts and Architecture. 83 (October 1966),
    22-26.

"Mexico: Mayan Art and Architecture." Arts and Architec-
    ture. 81 (February 1964), 14-17.

"Mexico: Mosaics of Juan O'Gorman." Arts and Architecture.
    81 (February 1964), 18-20 + .

"Mexico Revisited." Zodiac. 12 (1963), 106-131.

Modern California Houses. New York: Reinhold, 1962.

"Neutra in California." *Zodiac*. 8 (1961), 58-63.

"New University City of Mexico." *Arts and Architecture*. 69
(August 1952), 20-37 + .

"Notes on Greene and Greene." *Arts and Architecture*. 70
(July 1953), 27 + .

"Of Chairs and Architects." *Richard Neutra*. New York: G.
Braziller, 1960.

"On Attaining a Certain Age: Charles Eames's House in Santa
Monica, Built in 1949." *Progressive Architecture*. 58
(October 1977), 80-83.

"Pierre Koenig." *Zodiac*. 5 (1960), 156-163.

"Planned for Change: Cesar Pelli Designs an Adapable
Electronics Plant." *Architectural Forum*. 129 (July
1968), 102-107.

"Post Mies Architecture di Anthony J. Lumsden." *Domus*. 552
(November 1975), 1-8.

"Remodeling Portfolio: Horatio West Court." *Progressive
Architecture*. 57 (November 1976), 68-69.

"Report From Guanajuato." *Progressive Architecture*. 55
(September 1974), 28.

"Report from London." *Progressive Architecture*. 56 (January
1975), 34.

"Report from Malibu." *Progressive Architecture*. 55 (July
1974), 35.

"Report from Malibu Hills: House for Artist Ron Davis."
Progressive Architecture. 55 (December 1974), 40.

"Retreats in Venice, California: Cube Addition Resting on
the Garage and Service Area." *Progressive Architecture*. 63 (March 1982), 80-83.

"Retrospect: Gregory Ain's Social Housing." *Arts and*

Architecture. 1, no.2 (1981), 66-70.

"Retrospect: Konrad Wachsmann." Arts and Architecture. 1, no. 1 (1981), 62-66.

"Roots of California Contemporary Architecture." Arts and Architecture. 73 (October 1958), 14-17 + .

"San Bernadino City Hall: High Tech Images." Progressive Architecture. 55 (February 1974), 66-71.

The Second Generation. Salt Lake City: G.M. Smith, 1984.

"Something to Wrap the Herring In: Santa Monica's La Mesa Drive." Progressive Architecture. 67 (February 1986), 25.

Ten Italian Architects. Los Angeles: Los Angeles County Museum, 1967.

"Tribute to Sardinia." Arts and Architecture. 79 (November 1962), 26-27 + .

"Un Reformatore in California, Irving Gill." Architettura. 5 (December 1959), 555-559; (January 1960), 627-631; (February 1960), 693-697; (March 1960), 771-775.

"Vast Hall Full of Light." Arts and Architecture. 70 (April 1953), 20-21 + .

Vienna to Los Angeles. Santa Monica, CA: Arts and Architecture Press,   1979.

"West Coast Architects: William Wilson Wurster, Victor Gruen." Arts and Architecture. 81 (July 1964), 20-25 + (October 1964), 26-30.

"Young Architects: The Small Office." Arts and Architecture. 83 (February 1966), 28-33.

"Young Architects in the United States: 1963." Zodiac. 13 (1964), 164-197.

and Garrett Eckbo. "Garrett Eckbo: Early Years." Arts and Architecture. 1 no. 4 (1982), 39-44.

and Barbara Goldstein. <u>Guide to U.S. Architecture, 1940–1980</u>. Santa Monica, CA: Arts and Architecture Press, 1982.

and others. "John Entenza: Reminiscences and Photographs." <u>Arts and Architecture</u>. 3 no. 3 (1984), 28–33.

SECONDARY WORKS:

Banham, Reyner. "The Founding Mother: On Esther McCoy and the Origins of California's Architectural Style." <u>California Magazine</u>. 10 (March 1985), 104–108.

Crosbie, Michael J. "Ten To Be Honored by AIA for Distinguished Achievements." <u>Architecture</u>. 74 (April 1985), 15, 18, 24.

Goldstein, Michael J. "Tinseltown Honors Doyenne of Architectural Writing." <u>Progressive Architecture</u>. 66 (April 1985), 32.

MCFAUL, IRENE MARGARET (fl. 1920-30's)   ARCHITECT

SECONDARY WORKS:

"Irene Margaret McFaul." <u>American Women, 1935-1940</u>. Detroit: Gale Pub., 1981, p. 591.

"Santa Ana House for M.J. Poppett, I. McFaul, Architect." <u>California Arts and Architecture</u>. 57 (September 1940), 37.

"A Thousand Women in Architecture: II." <u>Architectural Record</u>. 103 (June 1948), 115.

MANNING (O'CONNOR), ELEANOR (1884-1973) ⁑   ARCHITECT

MIT Archives has Howe, Manning and Almy firm papers; they were the first firm of women architects in Boston and the second such firm in the U.S.

PRIMARY WORKS:

"Architecture as a Profession for Women." Simmons Review
     (April 1934), 71-75.

SECONDARY WORKS:

Cole, Doris. From Tipi to Skyscraper: A History of Women in
     Architecture. Boston: i Press, 1973, p. 110-111.

Cole, Doris. "New England Women Architects." In: Pilgrims
     and Pioneers: New England Women in the Arts, edited by
     Alicia Faxon and Sylvia Moore. New York: Midmarch Arts
     Press, 1987, pp. 57-58

"Eleanor Manning." Macmillan Encyclopedia of Architects.
     New York: Free Press, 1982, v. 3, pp. 91-92.

"Eleanor Manning O'Connor." American Women, 1935-1940.
     Detroit: Gale Publishers, 1981, p. 669.

Morse, Gail. The Firm: A Study of the First Women's
     Architectural Firm in Boston: Howe, Manning and Almy.
     Boston University, B.A. Thesis, 1976.

Paine, Judith. "Pioneer Women Architects" In: Women in
     American Architecture. New York: Whitney Library of
     Design, 1977, pp. 66,73.

Parks, Warren W. Mariemont Story. Cincinnati: Creative
     Writers and Publishers, 1967.

Prather-Moses, Alice I. compiler. The International
     Dictionary of Women Workers in the Decorative Arts.
     Metuchen, N.J.: Scarecrow Press, 1981, p. 107.

EXHIBITION:

AIA and Architectural League of New York. Architectural and
     Applied Arts Exposition. New York: AIA and Architec-
     tural League, 1925, p. 34.

MATHEWS, LUCIA KLEINHAUS (1870-1955)   FURNITURE DESIGN
                                        ARCHITECTURAL DECORATION

SECONDARY WORKS:

Anscombe, Isabella. A Woman's Touch: Women in Design from
    1860 to the Present Day. New York: Viking, 1984, pp.
    49-50.

Jones, H.L. Mathews: Masterpieces of the California
    Decorative Style. Santa Barbara, CA: Peregrine Smith,
    1980.

"Lucia Kleinhaus Mathews." Artists of the American West by
    Doris O. Dawdy. Chicago: Swallow Press, 1974, p. 156

Prather-Moses, Alice I., compiler. The International
    Dictionary of Women Workers in the Decorative Arts.
    Metuchen, N.J.: Scarecrow Press, 1981, p. 110.

EXHIBITION:

"Mathews: Masterpieces of the California Decorative Style,
    Oakland, Museum Exhibit." Craft Horizons. 32 (August
    1972), 49.

MEAD, MARCIA (1879-1967) ⋇   ARCHITECT

PRIMARY WORKS:

with Daniel P. Higgins. Homes of Character. New York: Dodd,
    Mead and Co., 1926.

"The Architecture of the Small House as Influenced by Our
    Modern Industrial Communities." Architecture. 37 (June
    1918), 145-154.

SECONDARY WORKS:

"The Bridgeport Housing Development." American Architect.
    113 (February 6, 1918), 129-148.

"Connecticut Development--Bridgeport Housing Co."
    Architectural Record. 44 (October 1918), 303-304.

"Marcia Mead." American Women, 1935-1940. Detroit: Gale
    Publishers, 1981, p. 603.

"More Women Architects." Architect and Engineer. (April
    1914), 116.

Paine, Judith. "Pioneer Women Architects." In: Women in
    American Architecture. New York: Whitney Library of
    Design, 1977, p. 67.

Prather-Moses, Alice I. compiler. The International
    Dictionary of Women Workers in the Decorative Arts.
    Metuchen, N.J.: Scarecrow Press, 1981, p. 110.

"Women at Columbia: A Century of Change." Progressive
    Architecture. 63 (June 1982), 22-23.

Women of Achievement. New York: House of Field, 1940, p.
    201.

EXHIBITION:

AIA & Architectural League, New York. Architecture and
    Allied Arts Exposition. New York: AIA & Architectural
    League, 1925, p. 46.

Built by Women: A Guide to Architecture in the New York
    Area. New York: Alliance of Women in Architecture,
    1981, p. 29.

MOCK, ELIZABETH BAUER (1911 -)   CURATOR
                                         WRITER

PRIMARY WORKS:

The Architecture of Bridges. New York: Museum of Modern

Art, 1949.

Built in the U.S.A., 1932-1944. edited by Elizabeth Mock.
    New York: Museum of Modern Art, 1944.

If You Want To Build a House. New York: Museum of Modern
    Art, 1946.

"Le Corbusier's Swiss Pavilion." American Magazine of Art.
    27 (January 1934), 18-19.

"Modern Houses, How to Look at Them." House and Garden. 90
    (August 1946), 30-47.

"Taliesin West." House and Garden. 94 (August 1948), 52-55.

and others. Are Clothes Modern? Chicago: Paul Theobold and
    Co., 1947.

SECONDARY WORKS:

"Industrial Arts." Magazine of Arts. 33 (June 1940),
    350-355.

"Paris Exposition." Magazine of Art. 30 (May 1937),
    267-273.

"Portrait." Architectural Forum. 82 (March 1945), 7.

"Portrait." Museum of Modern Art Bulletin. 13 (February
    1946), 18.

"Rain on the Roof." Architectural Record. 124 (September
    1958), 197-204.

"Water and Architecture." Architectural Record. 123 (June
    1958), 137-152.

"Water Inside and Out." Architectural Record. 125 (June
    1959), 163-174.

"Why Water?" Architectural Record. 125 (May 1959), 189-196.

MOHOLY-NAGY, SIBYL (1903-1971) ※ ARCHITECTURAL CRITIC

The Archives of American Art has correspondence, papers and photos of Moholy-Nagy.

PRIMARY WORKS:

"The Achievement of Le Corbusier." Arts Magazine. 40 (November 1965), 40-45.

"The Aging of Modern Architecture." Arkitekten. 7/8 (1967), 19-20.

"Architects Without Architecture." Progressive Architecture. 47 (April 1966), 234-236, 240, 246, 258.

"Architectural History and the Student Architect: A Symposium." Society of Architectural Historians Journal. 26 (October 1967), 178-199.

"L'Architecture Americaine prend une nouvelle orientation." Architecture d'Aujourd'hui. 35 (April-May 1964), 82-95.

"Architecture and the Moon Age." Architectural Forum. 118 (February 1963), 90-92.

"Architecture's Young and the Real Reality." AIA Journal. 52 (October 1969), 53-54.

"The Arcology of Paolo Soleri." Architectural Forum. 132 (May 1970), 70-75.

"El Arquitecto en la Historia." Cuadernos de Arquitectura. 6 (Fall 1966), 6-8.

"The Bauhaus-Weimar Dessau Berlin, Chicago." Architectural Forum. 132 (January-February 1970), 19-21.

Carlos Raul Villanueva and the Architecture of Venezuela. New York: Praeger, 1964.

"Cesar Pelli: Public Architect." Architectural Forum. 132 (March 1970), 42-47.

"Changing Concepts in Architectural Space." Structurist. 8
     (1968), 35-37.

"Chicago Circle: Grossstaft Campus der Universitat
     Illinois." Baumeister. 63 (May 1966), 525-536.

"City Planning and the Historical Perspective." Arts and
     Architecture. 81 (December 1964), 22-23, 35-36.

"Constructivism from Kasimir Malevitch to Laszlo
     Moholy-Nagy." Arts and Architecture. 83 (June 1966),
     24-28.

"The Diaspora." Society of Architectural Historians
     Journal. 24 (March 1965), 24-26.

"Environment and Anonymous Architecture." Perspecta. 3
     (1955), 2-7, 77.

"An Exchange of Letters Between Howard Dearstyne and Sibyl
     Moholy-Nagy." Society of Architectural Historians
     Journal. 24 (October 1965), 254-256.

"Expo '67." Bauwelt. 58 (July 17, 1967), 687-696.

"Expo '67 Montreal." Architecture d'Aujourd'hui. 38
     (September 1967), ix-xi.

"Formation-Fonction-Position." Architecture, Formes, and
     Fonctions. 15 (1969), 9-78.

"Formgliederung - Urprinzip der Architektur." Der
     Baumeister. 62 (December 1965), 1409-1422.

"The Four Environments of Man." Landscape. 16 (Winter
     1966-67), 3-9.

"Frank Lloyd Wright and the Aging of Modern Architecture."
     Perspective (1959), 40-45.
     Also: Progressive Architecture. 40 (May 1959),
          136-142.

"The Future of the Future." Architectural Forum. 132 (April
     1970), 90-92.

"The Future of the Past." Perspecta. 7 (1961), 65-76.

"Has 'Less Is More' Become 'Less Is Nothing'?" Columbia
    University School of Architecture Bulletin (1961),
    118-123.

"The Heritage of Cezanne." Progressive Architecture. 33
    (August 1952), 104, 136-137, 139-149, 142, 144, 148,

"History and Psyche: A Reply to A.E. Parr." Arts and
    Architecture. 88 (May 1966), 17.

"Hitler's Revenge: The Grand Central Tower Project." Art in
    America. 56 (September-October 1968), 42-43.

"The Ideas." Architecture, Formes, Fonctions. 16 (1971),
    1-240.

"In Barcelona, An Architectural Heritage Is Transformed
    Into a Modern Tradition." Architectural Forum. 123
    (July-August 1965), 52-57.

"In Defense of Architecture." Architectural Forum. 116
    (April 1962), 19.

"Intelecto Arquitectonico." Venezuela Universidad Central,
    Caracas. Centro de Investigaciones Historicas y
    Esteticas Boletin. 1 (January 1964), 43-50.

"Maass for Measure." Society of Architectural Historians
    Journal. 29 (March 1970), 60-61.

"The Making of Non-Architects." Architectural Record. 146
    (October 1969), 149-152.

Matrix of Man. New York: Praeger, 1963.

"Mexican Critique." Progressive Architecture. 54 (November
    1953), 109, 170, 172, 175-178.

Moholy-Nagy Experiment in Totality. New York: Harper, 1950.

Native Genius in Anonymous Architecture in North America.
    New York: Horizon Press, 1957.

"New Cities in the Twentieth Century." AIA Journal. 35
    (March 1961), 104-109.

"On the Environmental Brink." Landscape. 127 (Spring 1968),
    3-6.

"The Origin and Destiny of Abstraction." Royal Architec-
    tural Institute of Canada Journal. 36 (July 1959),
    247-249.

Philip C. Johnson, Holabird and Roche, Early Virginia
    Architecture. Charlottesville: University Press of
    Virginia for the American Association of Architectural
    Bibliographers, 1966.

"The Rear End of the Xerox or How I Learned to Love That
    Library." Architectural Forum. 124 (May 1966), 60-61.

"Situacion de la historiografia de la arquitecture
    Latinoamericana." Venezuela Universidad Central
    Caracas. Centro de Investigaciones Historicsy
    Esteticas Boletin. 9 (April 1968), entire issue.

"Some Aspects of South American Architecture." Progressive
    Architecture. 41 (April 1960), 135-140.

"Some Aspects of South American Planning." Progressive
    Architecture. 41 (February 1960), 136-142.

"Squared Paper and the SAH Assailed." Society of Archi-
    tectural Historians Journal. 22 (May 1963), 107.

"Style and Materials." Progressive Architecture. 35
    (October 1954), 93-97.

"Take a Second Look." Charette. 45 (March 1965), 20-22.

"U.S.A." Architecture, Formes, Fonctions. 16 (1971).
    333-341.

"Washington--A Critique of 'The Plan for the Year 2000'."
    Architectural Forum. 115 (December 1961), 126-131

"Yale's School of Art and Architecture." Architectural
    Forum. 120 (February 1964), 76.

and John Johansen. "Architecture Through Improvisation?"
    Architectural Forum. 131 (September 1969), 44.

and others. "What's Wrong with Architectural Education?"
   Architectural Forum. 129 (July-August 1968), 54-59.

PRIMARY WORKS:

"Aufregung in Braunschweig." Der Baumeister. 62 (July
   1965), 713.

"Awarding of A.I.A. Critic's Medal Ends Notable Career of
   Sibyl Moholy-Nagy." AIA Journal. 55 (February 1971),
   8.

Burns, James T. "Sibyl Moholy-Nagy, 1903-1971." Design and
   Environment. 2 (Spring 1971), 4-5.

Collins, Peter. "Sibyl Moholy-Nagy." Architecture Canada.
   48 (March 15, 1971), 3.

Paine, J. "Sibyl Moholy-Nagy: A Complete Life." Archives of
   American Art Journal. 15 (1975), 11-16.

Parr, A.E. "History and Other Diversions: A Reply to Sibyl
   Moholy-Nagy." Arts and Architecture. 83 (June 1966),
   17.

Rudolph, Paul. "Sibyl Moholy-Nagy." Architectural Forum.
   134 (June 1971), 29.

"Sibyl Moholy-Nagy Is Dead: Leading Architecture Critic."
   Washington Post (January 10, 1971), D14.

Stephens, S. "Voices of Consequence: Four Architectural
   Critics." In: Women in American Architecture. New
   York: Whitney Library of Design, 1977, pp. 136-143.

MORGAN, JULIA (1872-1957) ::   ARCHITECT

Julia Morgan Architectural History Project is at the
Schlesinger Library, Radcliffe College, Cambridge, Mass.

Letter to J.M. Hearst and some drawings by Morgan are at
the Bancroft Library, University of California at Berkeley.

Some of Morgan's personal and professional papers are at
California Polytechnic State University.

SECONDARY WORKS:

Entire issue of Architect and Engineer of California,
    November 1918, is devoted to her work.

Aidala, Thomas K. Hearst Castle: San Simeon. New York:
    Hudson Hills Press, 1981.

Armstrong, June. "Woman Architect Who Helped Build the
    Fairmount Hotel." Architect and Engineer of
    California. (October 1907), 69-71.

Boutelle, Sara H. "Julia Morgan." In: Women in American
    Architecture. New York: Whitney Library of Design,
    1977, pp. 79-87.

_____. "Julia Morgan: A Synthesis of Tradition."
    Architecture California. 7 (January-February 1985),
    30-31.

_____. "The Long Distance Dreamer Who Altered
    the Look of California." California Monthly (April
    1976), 12-14, 23.

_____. "Women's Networks: Julia Morgan and her
    Clients." Heresies. 3 (March 1981), 91-94.

Burke, Margaret. "Santa Maria de Ovila: Its History in the
    Twentieth Century in Spain and California." Studies in
    Cistercian Art and Architecture. 1 (1982), 78-82.

"California Polytechnic Receives Gift." Wilson Library
    Bulletin. 55 (January 1981), 331-332.

"California Polytechnic State University's Robert E.
    Kennedy Library." American Libraries. 12 (April 1981),
    227-228.

Clements, Robert M. "William Randolph Hearst's Monastery."
    American Heritage. 32 (April-May 1981), 50-60.

Cole, Doris. From Tipi to Skyscraper: A History of Women in

Architecture. Boston: i Press, 1973, p. 113.

"Covered Walkway for an Uncloistered Complex: Student-
Faculty Center for Mills College." Interiors. 130
(January 1971), 86-89.

Davis, D. "Designing Women." Newsweek. 89 (March 7, 1977),
79-80.

Everett, Edith. "Old Features of California Architecture."
Keith's Magazine. (April 1910), 263-265.

Failing, Patricia. "She Was America's Most Successful Woman
Architect and Hardly Anybody Knows Her Name." Art
News. 80 (January 1981), 66-71.

_____. "William Randolph Hearst's Enchanted
Hill." Artnews. 78 (January 1979), 54-55.

"Julia Morgan." American Women 1935-1940. Detroit: Gale
Publishers, 1981, p. 1163.

"Julia Morgan." A Companion to California.   Berkeley:
University of California Press, 1987, p. 283.

"Julia Morgan." Dictionary of American Biography. New York:
Charles Scribner's, 1980, sup. 6, pp. 462-464.

"Julia Morgan." Macmillan Encyclopedia of Architects. New
York: Free Press, 1982, v. 3, p.238.

"Julia Morgan." National Cyclopedia of American Biography.
New York: J.T. White, 1946, pp. 151-152.

"Julia Morgan." Notable American Women: The Modern Period.
Cambridge: Belknap Press, 1980, pp. 499-501.

"Julia Morgan." Who's Who in California, 1928-1929. San
Francisco: Who's Who Publishing Co., 1929.

"Julia Morgan: Obituary." AIA Journal. 28 (May 1957), 28.

Lewis, Oscar. Fabulous San Simeon. San Francisco:
California Historical Society, 1958.

Lobell, John. "American Women Architects." Artforum. 15

(Summer 1977), 31.

Longstreth, Richard W. Julia Morgan, Architect. Berkeley:
    Architectural Heritage Association, 1977.

_____. "Julia Morgan: Some Introductory
    Notes." Perspecta. 15 (1975), 74-86.

McKinley, Cameron C. "Yesterday Now: Echoes of the San
    Francisco Past." Architectural Digest. 38 (July 1981),
    60-66.

Maddex, Diane, editor. Master Builders. Washington, D.C:
    Preservation Press, 1985, pp. 132-135.

Marvin, Betty. Residential Work in Berkeley of Five Women
    Architects. Berkeley: Architectural Heritage
    Association, 1984, pp. 9-13.

"Merchants of Frisco." Architect. 122 (October 1976),
    46-47.

Mesic, Julian C. "Berkeley City Woman's Club." Architect
    and Engineer (April 1931), 25-27.

Molten, Philip L. "Asilomar: One of the Best Preserved
    Works of Julia Morgan, California's Pioneer Woman
    Architect." Architectural Review. 157 (February
    1975), 123-124.

Morrow, Irving. "Reflections on Houses." Architect and
    Engineer. 73 (April 1973), 51-86.

Moulten, Robert. "Housing for Women War Workers."
    Architectural Record. 37 (November 1918), 422-429.

Murray, Ken. The Golden Days of San Simeon. New York:
    Doubleday, 1971.

Olson, Lynne. "A Tycoon's Home Was His Petite Architect's
    Castle." Smithsonian. 16 (December 1985), 60-70.

Osman, Mary E. "Julia Morgan of California: A Passion for
    Quality and Anonymity." AIA Journal. 65 (June 1976),
    44-48.

"Refectory at La Cuesta Encantada Estate of W.R. Hearst,
    San Simeon, California, J. Morgan Architect." American
    Architect. 145 (September 1934), 37-42.

"Rich Interiors Restored in San Francisco." Progressive
    Architecture. 57 (March 1976), 22-23.

Richey, Elinor. Eminent Women of the West. Berkeley, CA:
    Howell-North Books, 1975, pp. 237-263.

Riess, Suzanne. ed. The Julia Morgan Architectural History
    Project. 2 vols. University of California: Regional
    Oral History, Bancroft Library, 1976.

Rochlin, Harriet. " Distinguished Generation of Women
    Architects in California." AIA Journal. 66 (August
    1977), 38-39.

_____. "Westways Women: Designed by Julia
    Morgan." Westways. 68 (March 1976), 26-29, 75-80.

Scharlach, Bernice. "The Legacy of Julia Morgan." San
    Francisco Sunday Examiner and Chronicle (May 24,
    1975), 24-31.

Steilberg, Walter. "Some Examples of the Work of Julia
    Morgan." Architect and Engineer of California. 55
    (1918), 34-107.

Sumner, Charles K. "Some Neglected Aspects of School
    Architecture." Architect and Engineer. 64 (March
    1921), 46-52.

Thompson, E.K. "Early Domestic Architecture of the San
    Francisco Bay Region." Society of Architectural
    Historians Journal. 10 (October 1951), 19-20.

Winslow, Carelton. The Enchanted Hill. Milbrae, California:
    Celestial Arts, 1980.

"Women in Architecture: the New Professional, Coming of
    Age." Progressive Architecture. 58 (March 1977), 42 +

Woodbridge, Sally B. "Preservation: St. John's." Architec-
     tural Forum. 139 (September 1973), 18.

Wright, Gwendolyn. "On the Fringe of the Profession: Women
     in American Architecture." In: The Architect. New
     York: Oxford University Press, 1977, pp. 287-288.

Ziflinski, Ann S. "Santa Maria de Ovila: Two Reconstruc-
     tions." Melangesa la Memoire du Pere Anselme Dimier. 3
     (1982), 781-792.

EXHIBITION:

Oakland Museum. Julia Morgan: Architectural Drawings by
     Julia Morgan. Oakland: Oakland Museum Art Department
     and the Council on Architecture, 1976.

MUIR, EDLA (1906-1971) ※   ARCHITECT

University of California at Santa Barbara's Art Museum has
a collection of Edla Muir's architectural drawings.

SECONDARY WORKS:

"Azusa, California: Residence of W. Chase; J. Byers and E.
     Muir, Architects." California Arts and Architecture. 5
     (March 1939), 20-21.

"Brentwood Park House for A.M. Chaggey; J. Byers and E.
     Muir, Architects." California Arts and Architecture.
     58 (January 1941), 24.

"Building for Tomorrow." Travel. 81 (June 1943), 26-30 + .

A Catalogue of the Architectural Drawings Collection. Santa
     Barbara: University Art Museum, 1985, pp. 458-506.

"Four Houses with Excellent Sites." Architectural Record.
     111 (March 1952), 172-178.

"Honor Award: Residence for Z. Hall." Arts and
     Architecture. 69 (June 1952), 29.

"House for L. Crabbe; J. Byers and E. Muir." California
     Arts and Architecture. 57 (September 1940), 35.

"House in Santa Monica, California." Architectural Forum. 9
     (August 1943), 90-91.

"Los Angeles Residence of Mrs. Z. Hall." Architectural
     Record. 111 (March 1952), 172-175.

"Mandeville Canyon Residence of H.B. Martin; J. Byers and
     E. Muir, Architects." California Arts and
     Architecture. 57 (June 1940), 30.

Newton, D. "Home of R.G. Karshner; J. Byers and E. Muir."
     Arts and Decoration. 50 (May 1939), 32-34.

"Paddock Pool Building." Architect and Engineer. 172
     (February 1948), 28-29.

Rochlin, Harriet. "Distinguished Generation of Women
     Architects in California." AIA Journal. 66 (August
     1977), 41.

"Santa Monica Canyon House." Architectural Forum. 79
     (August 1943), 90-91.

Shearer, Marva. "The Little House That Moved." House
     Beautiful. 107 (September 1965), 158-160, 190.

Stevens, Mary Otis, "Struggle for Place." In: Women in
     American Architecture. New York: Whitney Library of
     Design, 1977, p. 96.

"A Thousand Women in Architecture." Architectural Record.
     103 (March 1948), 109.

EXHIBITION:

A Catalogue of the Architectural Drawing Collection. Santa
     Barbara: University Art Museum, 1983. pp. 458-506.

NESKI, BARBARA (1928-) *   ARCHITECT

PRIMARY WORKS:

and Julian Neski. "German House, Amagansett, New York."
    Architectural Record. 145 (Mid-May 1969), 54-57.

SECONDARY WORKS:

"A Barn with a Spirit All Its Own." House Beautiful. 113
    (May 1971), 86-89.

"Bruce Kaplan House, Sagoponack, New York, 1978-1980." GA
    Houses. Tokyo: A.D.A. Edita, 1983, pp. 46-51.

"The Chiaraviglio House, Eastern Long Island."
    Architectural Record. 170 (May 15, 1982), 108-110.

"Chiaraviglio Residence, Amagansett, New York, 1980-1981."
    GA Houses. Tokyo: A.D.A. Edita, 1983, pp. 52-57.

Flanagan, Barbara. "Women in Architecture." Newsday
    (October 10, 1985), 10, 13.

"The Foundation Center, Neski Associates Convert a Lower
    Fifth Avenue Loft into Expanded Facilities for a
    Philanthropic Organization." Interior Design. 56
    (September 1985), 270-273.

"Frisch House, Ashley Falls, Massachusetts." Architectural
    Record. 157 (Mid-May 1975), 62-65.

"Kaplan House, East Hampton, New York." Architectural
    Record. 151 (Mid-May 1972), 26-29.

"New Angled Country House on Long Island." House Beautiful.
    110 (September 1968), 119-123.

"New York Chapter of A.I.A. Announces Seven Winners of 1972
    Residential Design Awards." New York Times (January
    28, 1973), 50.

"Nine Award-Winning Custom Houses." House and Home. 42
     (August 1972), 74-87.

"Novel Slant on a Seaside House." House Beautiful. 108
     (February 1966), 104-105.

"Plastic Surgery Offices for Dr. George Berakha."
     Architectural Record. 168 (August 1980), 94-95.

"Sable House, Bridgehampton, New York." Architectural
     Record. 149 (Mid-May 1971), 22-25.

"Savage House, Amagansett, New York, 1981-1982." GA Houses.
     13 (March 1983), 58-61.

"Simon House, Remsenburg, New York." Architectural Record.
     153 (Mid-May 1973), 46-49.

"Surrounded by Neighbors: A Very Private House." House
     Beautiful. 112 (August 1970), 54-57.

"Two Surgeons' Offices: Interiors Ease Operations for
     Doctors and Patients Alike." Architectural Record. 168
     (August 1980), 90 + .

"Vacation Houses: Far-Out Design Finds Eager Market." House
     and Home. 36 (October 1969), 82-93.

"Women in Architecture, Current Work: Situation Today."
     Progressive Architecture. 58 (March 1977), 53.

Yamashita, Kazumasa and Gunther Feuerstein. "Residential
     Design." Architecture and Urbanism. 4 (April 1983),
     31-114.

EXHIBITION:

Built by Women: A Guide to Architecture in the New York
     Area. New York: Alliance of Women in Architecture,
     1981, p. 27.

HISTORY

OF

ARCHITECTURE,

FROM

THE EARLIEST TIMES;

ITS PRESENT CONDITION

IN EUROPE AND THE UNITED STATES;

WITH

𝕬 𝕭iography of 𝕰minent 𝕬rchitects,

AND A GLOSSARY OF ARCHITECTURAL TERMS.

BY MRS. L. C. TUTHILL.

WITH NUMEROUS ILLUSTRATIONS.

"Behold those broken arches, that oriel all unglazed,
That crippled line of columns bleaching in the sun,
The delicate shaft stricken midway, and the flying buttress
Idly stretching forth to hold up tufted ivy."
M. F. TUPPER.

"Some pretend to judge of an individual by his handwriting; but I would
rather say, 'show me his house.'"—LONDON ARCHITECTURAL MAGAZINE.

PHILADELPHIA:

LINDSAY AND BLAKISTON.

1848.

Louisa C. Tuthill's title page from *History of Architecture*.

Eleanor Raymond.
Solar House.

Museum of Design, Cul...

Leslie Armstrong.
Grand Opera House Restoration, Wilmington, Delaware.

Lavone Dickensheets Andrews.
Knappogue Castle, County Clare, Ireland.

Elizabeth Close. Duff House, Minneapolis, Minnesota.

Doris Cole.
Hoberkorn Residence Renovation, Weston, Mass.
Photo Credit: Herb Englesberg.

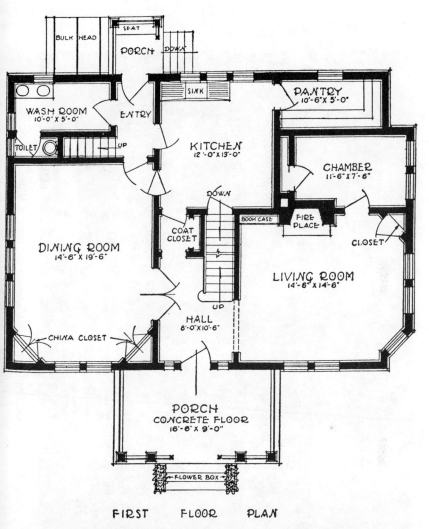

FIRST FLOOR PLAN

Greta Gray. Farm House Plan. *House and Home*, 1923.

Judith Edelman. Goddard Riverside Community Center & Elder Housing, New York City.

Frances Halsband.
Computer Science Building, Columbia University, New York City.
Photo Credit: Cervin Robinson.

WORKMAN'S COTTAGE.
MISS MARGARET HICKS.
Cornell University. DESIGNER.

Margaret Hicks.
Workman's Cottage.
American Architect and Building News, 1878.

Sarah P. Harkness. Olin Arts Center, Bates College, Lewiston, Maine.

Jerrily Kress. Colorado Building. Washington, D.C.

Julia Morgan.
Detail of the Berkeley Women's Club, Berkeley, California
Photo credit: Images of North American Living, Washington, D.C.

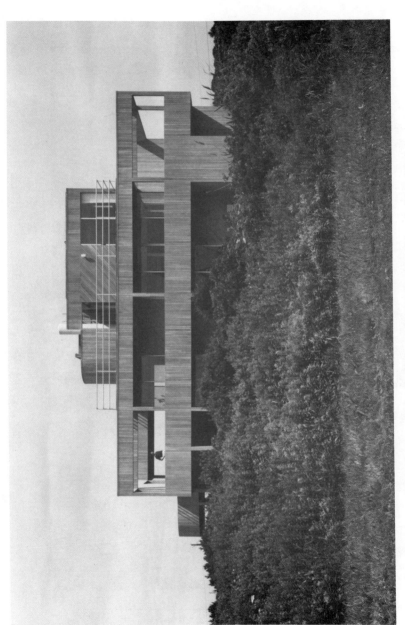

Barbara Neski. Bruce Kaplan Residence, Sagoponack, New York.

Cathy Simon. Primate Discovery Center, San Francisco, Calif.
Photo Credit: Kirk Gittings

Chloethiel Woodard Smith.
Harbour Square, Washington, D.C.

Mary Otis Stevens.
Pool Pavilion, Chestnut Hill, Mass.
Photo Credit: Fitzgerald, O'Reilly, Jones.

Susana Torre.
Fire Station Five. Columbus, Indiana.
Photo Credit: Timothy Hursley, The Arkansas Office.

Cynthia Weese.
House in the Woods, Sheboygan, Wisconsin.

Beverly Willis. San Francisco Ballet Building,
San Francisco.

NICHOLS, MINERVA PARKER (1863-1949) ::   ARCHITECT

Schlesinger Library at Radcliffe College has a small
collection of Mrs. Nichols' architectural drawings and
plans.

The Delaware Historical Society has some drawings by
Nichols.

PRIMARY WORKS:

"A Woman on the Woman's Building." American Architect and
    Building News. 38 (December 10, 1892) 170.

SECONDARY WORKS:

Cole, Doris. From Tipi to Skyscraper: A History of Women in
    Architecture. Boston: i Press, 1973, p. 73.

Croly, Janice C. History of the Women's Club Movement in
    America. New York: Allen and Co., 1898, pp. 332-334,
    1021-1027.

"House at Cynwyd, Pennsylvania." American Architect and
    Building News. 39 (February 11, 1893), 95 + plate.

Livermore, Francis, and Mary Livermore. A Woman of the
    Century. New York: Charles Wells Moulton, 1893, pp.
    536-537.

Logan, Mary S. The Part Taken by Women in American History.
    Wilmington, Delaware: Perry-Nalle, 1912, pp. 786-787.

"Minerva Parker Nichols." Notable American Women. Camb-
    ridge, MA: Harvard University Press, 1971, pp. 629-630

"Minerva Parker Nichols: Obituary." New York Times
    (November 20, 1949), 94.

Paine, Judith. "Pioneer Women Architects." In: Women in
    American Architecture. New York: Whitney Library of
    Design, 1977, pp. 62, 64 +.

Prather-Moses, Alice I., compiler. The International
    Dictionary of Women Workers in the Decorative Arts.
    Metuchen, N.J.: Scarecrow Press, 1981, p. 122.

"Representative Women: Minerva Parker Nichols." Woman's
    Progress. 1 (May 1893), 57-58.

Tatman, Sandra L., and Roger W. Moss. Biographical
    Dictionary of Philadelphia Architects: 1700-1930.
    Boston: G.K. Hall, 1985, pp. 573-575.

"Victorian Career Woman Inspires Gothic Novel." Victorian
    Homes. (Spring 1982), 59-60.

EXHIBITION:

Art Club. Catalogue of the Annual Exhibition. Philadelphia:
    The Association, 1892, p. 26.

Weiman, Jeanne M. The Fair Women. Chicago: Academy, 1981,
    pp. 60, 66, 146, 148.

OSTERTAG, BLANCHE (flourished ca. 1890-1915) DESIGNER
                                                ILLUSTRATOR

PRIMARY WORKS (decorated by Ostertag):

Burt, Mary E. Poems That Every Child Should Know. New York:
    Doubleday, 1913.

Fairy Tales Every Child Should Know. New York: Doubleday,
    1906.

World-Famed Stories and Legends. New York: Christian
    Herald, 1908.

SECONDARY WORKS:

"Blanche Ostertag." Childhood in Poetry. by John M. Shaw.
    Detroit: Gale Pub., 1976.

Love, J. "Blanche Ostertag: Another Wright Collaborator."
    Frank Lloyd Wright Newsletter. 4 pt. 2 (1982), 11-16.

Waters, Clara E.C. Women in the Fine Arts From the 7th
    Century B.C. to the 20th Century A.D.. New York:

Houghton Mifflin, 1904, p. 262.

PEDDLE, JULIET (1899-1979) ∗   ARCHITECT

SECONDARY WORKS:

Cole, Doris. From Tipi to Skyscraper: A History of Women in
     Architecture. Boston: i Press, 1973, p. 108.

Goff, Alice C. Women Can Be Engineers. Youngstown, Ohio:
     the author, 1946, pp. 173-176.

Stevens, Mary Otis. "Struggle for Place: Women in
     Architecture, 1920-1960." In: Women in American
     Architecture. New York: Whitney Library of Design,
     1977, p. 89.

PERKINS, RUTH H. (1899-)   ARCHITECT

SECONDARY WORKS:

Cole, Doris. From Tipi to Skyscraper: A History of Women in
     Architecture. Boston: i Press, 1973, p. 115.

"Portrait." Pencil Points. 11 (January 1930), 47.

Stevens, Mary Otis. "Struggle for Place: Women in
     Architecture, 1920-1960." In: Women in American
     Architecture. New York: Whitney Library of Design,
     1977, p. 89.

RAPORT, LUCILLE BRYANT (1914 -)   ARCHITECT

PRIMARY WORKS:

Cole, Doris. From Tipi to Skyscraper: A History of Women in
     Architecture. Boston: i Pres, 1973, p. 108.

"Guest House for a Mountain Site for Mr. and Mrs. John

Lockheed, Lake Arrowhead, California: Lucille Bryant Raport, Architect." Architectural Record. 103 (February 1948), 102-105.

"How to Merchandise a Model House, Sherman Oaks, California." House and Home. 4 (November 1953), 154-157.

"NAHB-Forum Competition: Kitchen Planning Awards." Architectural Forum. 94 (March 1951), 160.

Stevens, Mary Otis. "Struggle for Place: Women in Architecture 1920-1960." In: Women in American Architecture. New York: Whitney Library of Design, 1977, p. 96.

"A Thousand Women in Architecture: I ." Architectural Record. 103 (March 1948), 112.

RAYMOND, ELEANOR (1887-   ) ☼   ARCHITECT

Harvard's Loeb Library, Graduate School of Design has archival collections of her plans, drawings, projects, correspondence etc.

PRIMARY WORKS:

Early Domestic Architecture of Pennsylvania. New York: William Helburn, 1931.

SECONDARY WORKS:

Anderson, Dorothy M. Women Design and the Cambridge School. West Lafayette, Indiana: DPA Publishing Co., 1980.
        References to Raymond throughout the book.

Belmont House for T.T. Miller, E. Raymond, Architect." Architectural Forum. 72 (February 1941), 112-113.

Berlo, J.C. "Women in Architecture: the Cambridge School."

Feminist Art Journal. 5 (Spring 1976), 27-32.

"Biographical Sketch." Architectural Record. 103 (March 1948), 111.

Campbell, Robert. "Eleanor Raymond: Early and Indomitable, Her Early Houses Were Made of 'Human Perfections'." AIA Journal. 71 (January 1982), 52-53.

"Chestnut Hill House, E. Raymond, Architect." Architectural Forum. 72 (February 1941), 108.

Cole, Doris. "Eleanor Raymond." In: Women in American Architecture. New York: Whitney Library of Design, 1977, pp. 103-107.

_____. Eleanor Raymond, Architect. New Jersey and London and Toronto: Associated University Presses for Art Alliance Press, 1981.

_____. From Tipi to Skyscraper: History of Women in Architecture. Boston: i Press 1973, pp. 87-90.

_____. "New England Women Architects." In: Pilgrims and Pioneers: New England Women in the Arts, edited by Alicia Faxon and Sylvia Moore. New York: Midmarch Arts Press, 1987, p. 59.

"Designing Women." Newsweek (March 7, 1977), 79-80.

"Duxbury House: E. Raymond and S. Pillsbury, Architects." Architectural Forum. 75 (December 1941), 402-403.

"Economy Still Favored Two Story Type." Architectural Record. 103 (June 1948), 103-106.

"Economy Still Favors Two Stories: Three Post War Designs." Architectural Record. 97 (May 1945), 96-97.

"Eleanor Raymond." American Women, 1935-1940. Detroit: Gale Pub., 1981, p. 740.

"Eleanor Raymond '09 Builds Houses." Wellesley Alumni Magazine (March 1953), 164.

Frost, Henry A., and Sears, William R. Women in Architec-

ture and Landscape Architecture (Institute for the
Coordination of Women's Interests, Publication no. 7),
Northampton, MA: Smith College, 1928.

Greely, Rose. "An Architect's Garden in the City." House
Beautiful (November 1926), 557.

"Haddam Remodeled House of Mrs. D.R. Ellis; Haverhill
Remodeled House of F. Barnes, E. Raymond Architect."
Architectural Record. 76 (October 1934), 298-304.

"House in Duxbury, MA, Eleanor Raymond Architect."
Architectural Forum. 75 (December 1941), 402-403.

"House in Weston, Massachusetts." Architectural Forum. 79
(November 1943), 82-83.

"House in Wincester, Massachusetts." Architectural Record.
103 (June 1948), 103-105.

"Newton Center House with Office, E. Raymond Architect."
Architectural Forum. 74 (May 1941), 356.

Power, Ethel B. "A Beacon Hill Renovation." House Beautiful
(November 1924), 462-463.

_____. The Smaller American House. Boston: Little,
Brown and Co., 1927.

"Remodeled House of Frank Barnes, Haverhill,
Massachusetts." Architectural Record. 76 (October
1934) 300-302.

"Sculptor's Studio, Dover, Massachusetts, E. Raymond
Architect." Architectural Forum. 67 (July 1937),
36-37.

"Small and Medium Cost Houses." Architectural Record. 74
(August 1933), 121-141.

Smith, Mary B. "Two Houses from One." House Beautiful
(September 1928), 243.

Soo, Lydia M. "Eleanor Raymond, Architect." Society of
Architectural Historians Journal. 63 (March 1984),
89-90.

"A Suburban House, Milton, Massachusetts." Architectural
    Record. 72 (November 1932), 316-317.

"A Test House Heated Only by Solar Heat." Architectural
    Record. 105 (March 1949), 136-137.

"A Thousand Women in Architecture: I." Architectural
    Record. 103 (March 1948), 111.

"Two Houses in One." House Beautiful (October 1928), 383.

Vare, Ethlie Ann and Greg Ptacek. Mothers of Invention. New
    York: William Morrow and Co., 1988, pp. 14, 160-161.

"Weekend Residence of R. L. Pope, Smith's Point,
    Manchester-by-the-Sea, Massachusetts." Architectural
    Record. 113 (January 1953), 137-139.

"Weston House." Architectural Forum. 79 (November 1943),
    82-83.

"Women in Architecture: The New Professional, Coming of
    Age." Progressive Architecture. 58 (March 1977), 47.

Wright, Gwendolyn. "On the Fringe of the Profession: Women
    in American Architecture." In: The Architect. New
    York: Oxford University Press, 1977, pp. 272-293.

EXHIBITION:

Constantine, Eleni. "Eleanor Raymond in Boston." Skyline
    (December 1981), 15.

"Eleanor Raymond: A Lifetime's Work at the Institute of
    Contemporary Art in Boston." Architectural Record. 169
    (November 1981), 32.

Gabor, Andrea. "Eleanor Raymond: One of the Country's First
    Women Architects." Architectural Record. 169 (November
    1981), 37-38.

Institute of Contemporary Art, Boston. Eleanor Raymond:
    Architectural Projects, 1919-1973. Boston: The
    Institute, 1981.

Kay, Jane H. "Eleanor Raymond: A Book, an Exhibition."
    Christian Science Monitor (October 2, 1981), 15.

RENSHAW, LARCH (1906-) ⁑   ARCHITECT

PRIMARY WORKS:

"Household Closets." Architectural Record. 94 (November
    1943), 83-86; 95 (May 1944), 105-110; 96 (September
    1944), 113-114; (December 1944), 103-104.

"The Household Laundry." Architectural Record. 97 (May
    1945), 111-117; (July 1945), 109 +.

SECONDARY WORKS:

"A Thousand Women in Architecture: I." Architectural
    Record. 103 (March 1948), 113.

RENSSELAER, MARIANA VAN (1851-1934) ⁑ ARCHITECTURAL CRITIC

PRIMARY WORKS:

"American Country Dwellings." Century Magazine (May 1886),
    3-20; (June 1886), 206-220; (July 1886), 421-434.

"The Architectural League of New York." Century. 11
    (November 1888), 157-158.

"Architecture as a Profession." Chautauquan. 7 (May 1887),
    451-454.

"Art and Architecture in Berlin." American Architect and
    Building News. 8 (October 16, 1880), 184-185.

"An Art Critic's Pen Picture." In: A Week at the Fair.
    Chicago: Rand McNally and Co., 1893, pp. 72-78.

Art Out-of-Doors: Hints on Good Taste in Gardening. New
    York: Charles Scribner's Sons, 1893.

"Berlin and New York." <u>American Architect and Building News</u>. 18 (July 18, 1885), 27-29; (July 25, 1885), 40-42.

"Canterbury Cathedral." <u>Century</u>. 11 (April 1887), 819-838.

"The Cathedral Churches of England." <u>Century</u>. 11 (March 1887), 724-735.

"The Cathedral of LePuy." <u>Century</u>. 36 (September 1899), 722-735.

"The Churches of Auvergne." <u>Century</u>. 36 (August 1899), 568-575.

"The Churches of Perigueux and Angouleme." <u>Century</u>. 29 (April 1896), 918-931.

"The Churches of Poitiers and Caen." <u>Century</u>. 32 (July 1897), 421-439.

"The Churches of Provence." <u>Century</u>. 27 (November 1894), 117-135.

"Client and Architect." <u>North American Review</u>. 151 (September 1890), 319-328.

"Color in Rural Buildings." <u>Garden and Forest</u>. 5 (March 30, 1892), 146-147.

"The Competition in Wall Paper Designs." <u>American Architect and Building News</u>. 10 (November 26, 1881), 251-253.

"The Development of American Homes." <u>The Forum</u>. 12 (January 1892), 667-676.

"Durham Cathedral." <u>Century</u>. 13 (December 1887), 226-243.

"Eleventh Annual Exhibition of the Architectural League of New York." <u>Garden and Forest</u>. 9 (February 26, 1896), 88-89.

"Ely Cathedral." <u>Century</u>. 12 (October 1887), 803-818.

<u>English Cathedrals: Canterbury, Peterborough, Durham, Salisbury, Lichfield, Lincoln, Ely, Wells, Winchester,</u>

Gloucester, York, London. New York: The Century
    Company, 1892.

"Explorations in Samothrace." American Architect and
    Building News. 3 (May 25, 1878), 181-182.

"Gloucester Cathedral." Century. 17 (March 1890), 680-697.

"The Grant Monument or Riverside Park." Garden and Forest.
    4 (January 21, 1891), 27-28.

Handbook of English Cathedrals. New York: Century Co.,
    1893.

Henry Hobson Richardson, and His Works with a Portrait and
    Illustrations of the Architect's Designs. Boston and
    New York: Houghton Mifflin and Company, 1888.

History of the City of New York in the Seventeenth Century.
    New York: Macmillan Company, 1909.

"Lincoln Cathedral." Century. 14 (August 1888), 583-599.

"Litchfield Cathedral." Century. 14 (July 1888), 379-392.

"Madison Square Garden." Century. 25 (March 1894), 732-747.

"The Metropolitan Opera House, New York." American
    Architect and Building News. 15 (February 16, 1884),
    76-77; (February 23, 1884), 86-89.

"Midsummer in New York City." Century. 40 (August 1901),
    483-501.

"Mr. Fiske and the History of New York." North American
    Review. 173 (August 1901), 171-189.

"Mr. St. Gaudens's Statue of General Farragut in New York."
    American Architect and Building News. 10 (September
    10, 1881), 119-120.

"The New Public Library in Boston: Its Artistic Aspects."
    Century. 28 (June 1895), 260-264.

"The New York Produce Exchange Competition." American
    Architect and Building News. 9 (March 12, 1881),

123-124.

"Optical Illusions as Affecting Architecture." American
    Architect and Building News. 1 (May 27, 1876),
    174-175.

"Painters' Architecture." Scribner's Magazine. 73 (May
    1923), 635-640.

"Peterborough Cathedral." Century. 12 (June 1887), 163-175.

"Places in New York City." Century. 31 (February 1897),
    501-516.

"The Portal of the Old Palace Chapel, Dresden." American
    Architect and Building News. 2 (August 18, 1877),
    263-265.

"Recent Pictures in New York." American Architect and
    Building News. 5 (March 22, 1879), 93-94.

"Recent Architecture in America, I: Public Buidings."
    Century. 6 (May 1884), 48-67.

"Recent Architecture in America, II: Public Buidings."
    Century. 6 (July 1884), 323-334.

"Recent Architecture in America, III: Commercial
    Buildings." Century. 6 (August 1884), 511-523.

"Recent Architecture in America, IV: Churches." Century.
    7 (January 1885), 323-338.

"Recent Architecture in America: City Dwellings." Century.
    9 (March 1886), 677-687.

"Recent Architecture in America: Country Dwellings."
    Century. 10 (May 1886), 3-20.

"The Restorations at Goslar." American Architect and
    Building News. 3 (April 6, 1878), 120-121.

"St. Paul's Cathedral, London." Century. 21 (March 1892),
    643-665.

"Salisbury Cathedral." Century. 13 (March 1888), 693-707.

"A Suburban Country Place." Century. 32 (May 1897), 3-17.

"Taste and the Mind's Eye." Unpartisan Review. 15 (January 1921), 132-142.

"War Memorials." American Magazine of Art. 10 (May 1919), 170-175.

"Wells Cathedral." Century. 18 (September 1890), 724-743.

"Winchester Cathedral." Century. 16 (July 1889), 323-340.

"York Cathedral." Century. 15 (March 1889), 718-736.

PRIMARY WORKS ON LANDSCAPE ARCHITECTURE:

"Alexander Pope and the Gardener's Art." Garden and Forest. 1 (June 27, 1888), 207-208.

"The Beauty of Orchids." Garden and Forest. 7 (February 21, 1894), 78-79.

"The Choice of a National Flower." Garden and Forest. 2 (July 10, 1889), 333-335.

"Down the Rhone." Garden and Forest. 3 (January 8, 1890), 14-15; (January 15, 1890), 27-28.

"Early Autumn Near Cape Cod." Garden and Forest. 5 (September 28, 1892), 465-466.

"Flowers in Town." Garden and Forest. 5 (April 27, 1892), 195-196.

"Frederick Law Olmstead." Century. 24 (October 1893), 860-867.

"Glimpse of Nantucket." Garden and Forest. 1 (November 14, 1888), 447-448.

"Great Hill: A New American Country-Seat." Garden and Forest. 4 (October 21, 1891), 494-495; (October 28, 1891), 506-507.

"Ivy in an Old French Garden." Garden and Forest. 4 (May

27, 1891), 242.

"Japanese Gardening." Garden and Forest. 2 (January 30, 1889), 51-52; (February 6, 1889), 63-64.

"John Brown's Grave." Garden and Forest. 9 (January 29, 1896), 47.

"July on the Shores of Buzzard's Bay." Garden and Forest. 1 (September 5, 1888), 327.

"Landscape Gardening." American Architect and Building News. 22 (October 1, 1887), 157-159; (December 3, 1887), 263-264; 23 (January 7, 1888), 3-5.

"Landscape Gardening: A Definition." Garden and Forest. 2 (February 29, 1888), 2.

"The Mountain Maple." Garden and Forest. 6 (July 26, 1893), 318.

"Native Plants for Ornamental Planting." Garden and Forest. 10 (September 22, 1897), 376.

"Newport." Garden and Forest. 1 (November 28, 1888), 470-471; (December 5, 1888), 482-483.

"Pine Bank." Garden and Forest. 5 (September 21, 1892), 446-447.

"The Rattlesnake Plantain as a Window Plant." Garden and Forest. 4 (May 13, 1891), 227.

"Sir Christopher Wren as a Gardener." Garden and Forest. 4 (June 3, 1891), 254-255.

"Some Questions of Color." Garden and Forest. 10 (October 20, 1897), 416.

"A Twin Tree." Garden and Forest. 6 (August 9, 1983), 339.

"Wild Flowers of Early September." Garden and Forest. 10 (September 15, 1897), 359-361.

"Wood Roads on Cape Cod." Garden and Forest. 5 (November 30, 1892), 574-575.

SECONDARY WORKS:

Adelman, Joseph. _Famous Women_. New York: Ellis M. Lonow,
    1926, p. 248.

Brown, Catherine R. _Women and the Land_. Baltimore: Morgan
    State University, 1979, p. [26].

Dinnerstein, Lois. _Opulence and Ocular Light, Splendor and
    Squalor: Critical Writings in Art and Architecture by
    Marianna Griswold van Rensselaer_. Ph.D. Dissertation,
    City University of New York, 1979.

Gilder, Joseph B. "An Eminent New Yorker: The Late Mrs.
    Schuyler Van Rensselaer Was a Distinguished Author."
    New York Times (January 26, 1934), 16.

"Henry Hobson Richardson and His Works. "_American Architect
    and Building News_. 24 (July 7, 1888), 10-11

Kinnard, C.D. _The Life and Works of Mariana Griswold Van
    Rensselaer American Art Critic_. Ph.D. Dissertation,
    Johns Hopkins University, 1977.

"Mariana Alley Griswold Van Rensselaer." _Notable American
    Women_. Cambridge, MA: Belknap Press, 1971 pp. 511-
    513.

"Mariana Griswold Van Rensselaer." _Dictionary of American
    Biography_. New York: Charles Scribner's Sons,
    1928-1937, v. XIX, pp. 207-208.

"Mrs. M. Van Rensselaer." _New Brunswick Daily Home News_.
    (January 22, 1934), 2.

"Mrs. Schuyler Van Rensselaer." _Landscape Architecture_. 24
    (April 1934), 168.

"Mrs. Van Rensselaer, Art Authority, Dies." _New York
    Times_ (January 21, 1934), 29.

"Mrs. Van Rensselaer Dead." _Art Digest_. 8 (February 1,
    1934), 9.

"Mrs. Van Rensselaer Dies: Descendant of Pioneer New York
    Family." _New York Herald Tribune_ (January 21, 1934),

18; (January 23, 1934), 14.

Moore, Helen. "A Great Democrat: The Late Mrs. Van Rensselaer Was a Teacher Beloved by Her Pupils." New York Times (February 8, 1934), 18.

Mumford, Lewis. Roots of Contemporary American Architecture. New York: Reinhold Pub. Corp., 1952, p. 429.

O'Gorman, James F. "Henry Hobson Richardson and Frank Lloyd Wright." Art Quarterly. 32 (Autumn 1969), 292-315.

Placzek, Adolf K. "Henry Hobston Richardson and His Works by Mariana Schuyler Van Rensselaer." Prairie School Review. 5, no. 3 (1968), 48.

Spooner, Walter W., ed. Historic Families of America. 3 vols. New York: Historic Families Pub. Asso., 1908.

Warshaver, Gerald E. Psycho-Geographic Traditions of City Folk in the 1890's as Revealed in Writings by Mariana Van Rensselaer, H.C. Bunner, and Stephen Crane. Ph.D. Dissertation, Indiana University, 1979.

"Woman Art Critic Left $215,958: Mrs. Mariana Van Rensselaer Gave Her Paintings, Drawings and Books to Museums." New York Times (August 16, 1934), 20.

Zaitzevsky, Cynthia. "The Olmsted Firm and the Structures of the Boston Park System." Society of Architectural Historians Journal. 32 (May 1973), 167-174.

RICE, LILIAN JEANETTE (1888-1938) * ARCHITECT

San Diego Historical Society Library and Manuscript Collection has the papers and sketchbooks of Lilian Rice.

PRIMARY WORKS:

"Architecture: A Common Asset." Architect and Engineer. 94 (July 1928), 43-45.

"Rancho Santa Fe--A Vision." The Modern Clubwoman.

(January-February 1930), 5.

"Valenciana Apartments Rancho Santa Fe, California."
    Architectural Record. 67 (March 1930), 246-247.

SECONDARY WORKS:

Blue and Gold Yearbook. Univ. of Ca. Berkeley, 1911, p. 88

Eddy, Lucinda L. "Lilian Jenette Rice: Search for a
    Regional Ideal, The Development of Rancho Santa Fe."
    Journal of San Diego History. 29, no. 4 (1983),
    262-285.

"Lilian Jeanette Rice." American Women, 1935-1940. Detroit:
    Gale Pub., 1981, p. 752.

Olten, Carol. "Lillian Rice Set Rancho Santa Fe's
    Architectural Style." San Diego Union (March 2,
    1986), F6, F13, F17.

"Our Little Ranch in the West: L. Rice, Architect."
    California Arts and Architecture. 48 (October 1935),
    24-25 +.

Paine, J. "Lilian Rice." In: Women in American
    Architecture. New York: Whitney Library of Design,
    1977, pp. 108-111.

Rochlin, Harriet. "Distinguished Generation of Women
    Architects in California." AIA Journal. 66 (August
    1977), 40.

Withey, Henry F., and Elsie R. Withey. Biographical
    Dictionary of American Architects. Los Angeles:
    Hennessey and Ingalls Inc., 1970, p. 505.

"Zlac Rowing Club, Pacific Beach, California; L.J. Rice
    Architect." California Arts and Architecture. 48
    (August 1935), 27.

RIDDLE, THEODATE POPE (1868-1946) *   ARCHITECT

Theodate Pope Riddle's diaries are part of the Archival
Collection of the Hillstead Museum in Farmington, Conn.

PRIMARY WORKS:

A Letter. Paris: s.n., 1924.
    Private signed edition of twenty-five numbered copies.

"Sinking of the Lusitania." American Heritage. 26 (April
    1975), 98-101.

SECONDARY WORKS:

"Avon Old Farms: A School for Boys." American Architecture.
    128 (November 5, 1925), 391-394.

Cameron, Roderick. "Hill-Stead: The Legacy of the
    Pioneering Woman Architect Theodate Pope Riddle."
    House and Garden. 157 (April 1985), 186-196.

Cunningham, Phyllis P. My Godmother, Theodate Pope Riddle:
    A Reminiscence of Creativity. Canaan, New Hampshire:
    s.n., 1983.

Emeny, Brooks. Avon Old Farms. privately printed.

Ferree, Barr. "Notable American Homes: Hill Stead."
    American Homes and Gardens. 7 (February 1910), 45-51.

Flanagan, Henry. The Educational Ideals of Theodate Pope
    Riddle. Ph.D. Dissertation, University of Michigan,
    1976.

Gandee, Charles K. "A Lesson in Deportment: Additions to
    Westover School, Middlebury, Conn." Architectural
    Record. 173 (February 1985), 125-133.

Kahn, D.M. "The Theodore Roosevelt Birthplace in New York
    City." Antiques. 116 (July 1979), 176-181.

LaRoche, N. "Hill-Stead Museum: A Victory of the Muses."
    Art News. 74 (December 1975), 70 + .

"Mr. Alfred A. Pope's House." Architectural Record. 20
    (August 1906), 122-129.

Paine, Judith. "Avon Old Farms School: The Architecture of
     Theodate Pope Riddle." Perspecta. 18 (1982), 42-49.

_____. "Pioneer Women Architects." In: Women in
     American Architecture. New York: Whitney Library of
     Design, 1977, pp. 54-69.

_____. Theodate Pope Riddle: Her Life and Work.
     Washington, D.C.: National Park Service, 1979.

Powers, Barbara A. The Educational Architecture of Theodate
     Pope. M.A. Thesis, University of Virginia, 1980.

Ramsay, Gordon Clark. Aspiration and Perserverance: The
     History of Avon Old Farms School. Conn: the School,
     1984.

"Residence of J. P. Chamberlain, Esq." Architectural
     Record. 46 (November 1919), 408-409.

Simpson, Babs. "Hill Stead." House and Garden. (April
     1985), 189-196.

Stern, Robert A.M. "Guest Speaker: Robert A.M. Stern on
     Hill-Stead, Hollyhock House and Others." Architectural
     Digest. 43 (April 1986), 30 + .

"Theodate Pope Riddle." Biographical Cyclopedia of American
     Women. New York: Halvord Pub., 1924, v. 1, p. 310.

"Theodate Pope Riddle." Macmillan Encyclopedia of
     Architects. New York: Free Press, 1982, v. 3, pp.
     577-578.

Trowbridge, S.B. "Architecture of the Small College."
     American Architect and Building News. 119 (June 8,
     1921), 614.

Withey, Henry F. and Elsie R. Withey. Biographical
     Dictionary of American Architects. Los Angeles:
     Hennessey and Ingalls Inc., 1970, p. 512.

EXHIBITION:

A.I.A. & Architectural League, New York. Architectural and

Allied Arts Exposition. New York: A.I.A. & Architectural League, 1925, p. 52.

Built by Women: A Guide to Architecture in the New York Area. New York: Alliance of Women in Architecture, 1981, p. 7.

RIGGS, LUTAH MARIA (1896-1984) *   ARCHITECT

The Schlesinger Library at Harvard University has in its manuscript collection a biographical file on Lutah Maria Riggs.

The University of California at Santa Barbara has correspondence and drawings of Lutah Riggs in its architectural drawing collection.

SECONDARY WORKS:

"California Doctor's Office." Architectural Record. 113 (May 1953), 184.

"Commercial Buildings: Architectural Record's Building Types Study no. 198." Architectural Record. 113 (May 1953), 162-186.

"Estate of Mr. and Mrs. Allen Breed Walker, Montecito, California, Lutah Maria Riggs, Architect." Country Life. 70 (July 1936), 58-60.

"Glass Tent, a Santa Barbara House." House and Home. 2 (September 1952), 114-119.

"A House Full of Adaptable Ideas." House and Garden. 122 (November 1962), 220-225, 269, 270.

"House to Take Full Advantage of Your Site." House Beautiful. 103 (May 1961), 102-109, 160, 163-164.

"Lutah Maria Riggs, Obituary." Architecture. 73 (May 1984), 378.

McCoy, Esther. "A Walk with Lutah Riggs." L.A.Architect. 5
    (July 1979), 3.

"Montecito Weekend Home of K.K. Parrot: L.M. Riggs,
    Architect." California Arts and Architecture. 55
    (February 1939), 18.

"New Fellows of the AIA." AIA Journal. 33 (June 1960), 55.

"Project for a House in Santa Barbara." Arts and
    Architecture. 66 (March 1949), 26-29.

Rochlin, Harriet. "All In a Day's Work." Ms. 5 (December
    1976), 16.

_____. "Distinguished Generation of Women
    Architects in California." AIA Journal. 66 (August
    1977), 41-42.

"Santa Barbara Project for a House." Arts and Architecture.
    62 (March 1949), 26-29.

ROBERTSON, JAQUELIN TAYLOR (1933-   )   ARCHITECT

PRIMARY WORKS:

"Peter Eisenman and Jaquelin Robertson." In: American
    Architecture Now II. New York: Rizzoli, 1983, pp.
    72-81.

SECONDARY WORKS:

"Jaquelin Taylor Robertson." In: Contemporary Architects.
    New York: St. Martin's Press, 1980, pp. 676-677.

"Lufkin House, Southampton, New York." Progressive
    Architecture. 62 (January 1981), 124-125.

"Private House, East Hampton, New York." Architectural
    Record. 169 (Mid-May 1981), 78-81.

Stephens, Suzanne. "Role-models: The Gamesman, Jaquelin
    Robertson." Progressive Architecture. 58 (May 1977),

66-67.

ROBINSON, FLORENCE BELL (fl. ca. 1930's-40's) LANDSCAPE
                                              ARCHITECT

Robinson's notes, typescripts, photos, sketches and papers
are at the University of Illinois Archives, Urbana
Champaign.

PRIMARY WORKS:

"Astronomical Observatory in Peking." Art and Archaeology.
      30 (July 1930), 36-43.

"Five Fundamentals of Art." Landscape Architecture. 25
      (October 1934), 19-25.

"Fundamental Principles of Garden Design." American
      Landscape Architect. 2 (March 1930), 26-28 + .

"Impressions of the Conference by a Participant." Landscape
      Architecture. 39 (January 1949), 75-79.

Landscape Planting for Airports. Urbana: University of
      Illinois, 1948.

"New Approach to Planting Design." American Landscape
      Architect. 6 (April 1932), 26-30

Palette of Plants. Champaign, Illinois: Garrard Press,
      1950.

Planting Design. New York: McGraw-Hill Book Co., 1940.

"Shrubs in the Landscape." American Landscape Architect. 6
      (January 1932), 18-21.

Tabular Keys for the Identification of Woody Plants.
      Champaign, Ill: Garrard Press, 1941.

Useful Trees and Shrubs. Champaign, Ill: Garrard Press,
      1938.

"Walls and Walks in China." Landscape Architecture. 20

(July 1930), 339-350.

SECONDARY WORKS:

"Florence Bell Robinson." American Women, 1935-1940.
    Detroit: Gale Publishers, 1981, p. 765.

Hamblin, S.F. "Tabular Keys for the Identification of Woody
    Plants." Landscape Architecture. 32 (January 1942),
    85.

Palmer, Donna. An Overview of the Trends, Eras and Values
    of Landscape Architecture in America. MLA North
    Carolina State University, 1976, p. 39

Strong, W.A. "Planting Design." Landscape Architecture. 30
    (July 1940), 198.

Yarwood, George A. "History of Women in Landscape
    Architecture." ASLA Bulletin. (July 1973), [3-7].

RYAN, IDA ANNAH (1873-1950) ⁙   ARCHITECT

SECONDARY WORKS:

Bever, Marilynn A. The Women of MIT, 1871-1941: Who They
    Were, What They Achieved. B.S. Thesis, MIT, 1976, p.
    38.

"Ida Annah Ryan." American Women, 1935-1940. Detroit: Gale
    Pub., 1981, p. 784.

Paine, Judith. "Some Professional Roles." In: Women in
    American Architecture. New York: Whitney Library of
    Design, 1977, p. 66.

Smith, Marcia F. "Amherst Worth Saving to Honor an Orlando
    Pioneer." Orlando Sentinel (October 31, 1985), 3.

SAWYER, GERTRUDE (1895-) ⚹   ARCHITECT

SECONDARY WORKS:

Anderson, Dorothy May. "Woman's Breakthrough Via the
     Cambridge School." Landscape Architecture. 68 (March
     1978), 145-148.

"Art Deco Designs by Woman Architect To Be Preserved Near
     Dupont Circle." Trans-Lux. 4 (Winter 1986), 3.

Clark, Wayne E. "Archeology Along the Chesapeake Bay."
     Place (May 1985), 6-8.

Cole, Doris. From Tipi to Skyscraper: A History of Women in
     Architecture. Boston: i Press, 1973, p. 96.

Dean, Ruth. "For the Seabees: Woman Architect Came to Their
     Aid." Washington Star (March 25, 1956), D10.

"Gertrude Elizabeth Sawyer." American Women 1935-1940.
     Detroit: Gale Pub., 1981, p. 792.

"Its Past Was Victorian: A Nineteenth Century Remodeled
     House in Washington, D.C." House and Garden. 92
     (September 1947), 118-119.

Leiner, Glen B. "Small Comeback at Dupont Circle."
     Trans-Lux. 4 (Spring 1986), 8-9.

"A Thousand Women in Architecture: II" Architectural
     Record. 103 (June 1958), 110.

"Three Houses in Colony Hill, Washington, D.C." American
     Architect. 142 (November 1932), 59-65.

SCHENCK, ANNA P. (?-1915) ⚹   ARCHITECT

SECONDARY WORKS:

"The Bridgeport Housing Development." American Architect.
     113 (February 6, 1918,) 129-148.

"Connecticut Development--Bridgeport Housing Co."
     Architectural Record. 44 (October 1918), 303-304.

174   Architecture and Women

"More Women Architects." Architect and Engineer. 36 (April
    1914), 116.

Paine, Judith. "Some Professional Roles." In: Women in
    American Architecture. New York: Whitney Library of
    Design, 1977, p. 68.

Prather-Moses, Alice I., compiler. The International
    Dictionary of Women Workers in the Decorative Arts.
    Metuchen, N.J.: Scarecrow Press, 1981, p. 146.

Withey, Henry F., and Elsie R. Withey. Biographical
    Dictionary of American Architects. Los Angeles:
    Hennessey and Ingalls Inc., 1970, pp. 538-539.

SCHMERTZ, MILDRED FLOYD (1925-) *   ARCHITECT
                                        CRITIC

PRIMARY WORKS:

"Administration and Visitors Center, Botanic Garden of
    Chicago Horticultural Society, Glencoe, Illinois."
    Architectural Record. 166 (July 1979), 89-96.

"Affording the Best: The King Khaled International Airport,
    Riyadh, Saudi Arabia." Architectural Record. 173
    (October 1985), 152-157.

"AIA Headquarters." Architectural Record. 153 (May 1973),
    131.

"AIA Votes Yes on the National Policy Task Force Report."
    Architectural Record. 151 (June 1972), 42-43.

"Analysis of Excellence: The New York State University
    Construction Fund--a Notable Record of Enlightened and
    Effective Organization for Good Campus Design."
    Architectural Record. 149 (January 1971), 105.

Apartments, Townhouses and Condominiums. New York: McGraw-
    Hill, 1981.

"Architectural Drawing for Printing by Half-tone." Archi-
    tectural Record. 133 (June 1963), 133-140.

"Architectural Drawing for Printing Processes." Architectural Record. 133 (February 1963), 137-144.

"Architecture at the New York World's Fair." Architectural Record. 136 (July 1964), 143-150.

"Architecture USSR." Architectural Record. 153 (February 1973), 91-102.

"Art for Art's Sake: The Hult Center for the Performing Arts, Eugene, Oregon." Architectural Record. 171 (May 1983), 120-133.

"Boxes Are Black: Four Low Cost Houses in the Hamptons." Architectural Record. 155 (May 1974), 123.

"Building a New Corporate Image: Building Types Study 605." Architectural Record. 172 (September 1984), 103-119.

"Building for the Art of the Twentieth Century: Building Types Study no, 584, a Museum." Architectural Record. 171 (February 1983), 79-91.

"Building Types Study 529: Buildings for the Performing Arts." Architectural Record. 165 (April 1979), 125-140.

"Building Types Study 538: College Buildings." Architectural Record. 177 (November 1979), 87-102.

"Buried Treasure: Two New Museums for the Smithsonian Institution, Washington, D.C." Architectural Record. 172 (February 1984), 112-121.

"Campus Architecture." Architectural Record. 157 (January 1975), 123-124.

Campus Planning and Design. New York: McGraw-Hill, 1972.

"Canadians Build an Office Complex by Mies van der Rohe in Toronto." Architectural Record. 149 (March 1971), 105-114.

"Chapel for Tuskegee: Paul Rudolph and Fry & Welch, Architects." Architectural Record. 146 (November 1969), 117-126.

"The Charleston Museum: A Competition Winner Built."
    Architectural Record. 169 (July 1981), 94-99.

"Choosing a Style for a Desert Campus: King Saud
    University, Saudi Arabia." Architectural Record. 174
    (April 1986), 126-135.

"Citicorp Center: If You Don't Like Its Crown, Look at Its
    Base." Architectural Record. 163 (June 1978), 107-116.

"Conservatory for a Botanic Garden." Architectural Record.
    166 (July 1979), 89-96.

"Conserving a Rich Architectural Heritage: Building Types
    Study 593." Architectural Record. 171 (September
    1983), 67-85.

"Coping with Cairo: A Study in Urban Decline." Architec-
    tural Record. 173 (May 1985), 91-93.

"County Government Center by Paul Rudolph." Architectural
    Record. 150 (August 1971), 83.

"Crowell House, Eastern Shore, Long Island." Architectural
    Record. 173 (Mid-April 1985), 116-121.

"Crown Center, Kansas City Grey Area." Architectural
    Record. 154 (October 1973), 113.

"Design Alternative for Low-to-Moderate Income Urban
    Housing." Architectural Record. 160 (August 1976),
    101.

"Design Distilled: The Seagrams Museum, Waterloo, Ontario,
    Canada." Architectural Record. 173 (April 1985),
    138-145.

"Design for a Variety of Campus Life Styles." Architectural
    Record. 151 (January 1972), 115.

"Design for Diplomacy: Diplomatic Reception Rooms, U.S.
    Department of State, Washington, D.C." Architectural
    Record. 173 (October 1985), 152-159.

"Design for Learning: Work of Hardy Holzman Pfeiffer
    Associates." Architectural Record. 151 (April 1972),

109.

"Design for Leisure: Two Urban Hotels, a Riverboat and a Recreational Village." Architectural Record. 162 (October 1977), 109.

"Design for the 1970's: A New Professional Conscience." Architectural Record. 148 (October 1970), 118-127.

"Design in the Miesian Tradition: The Current Work of C.F. Murphy Associates." Architectural Record. 149 (May 1971), 95.

"Design in the Spirit of Islam: The Aga Kahn Award for Excellence." Architectural Record. 165 (March 1979), 117-124.

"Designing a Learning Environment for Children." Architectural Record. 156 (October 1974), 113.

"Designing the Campus as One Big Building." Architectural Record. 166 (November 1979), 87-102.

"Designing the Urban Landscape: New Projects by M. Paul Friedberg and Associates." Architectural Record. 151 (March 1972), 97-105.

"Designs for the Campus." Architectural Record. 147 (February 1970), 101.

"Distinguished Architecture for a State University." Architectural Record. 139 (May 1966), 165-172.

"Evoking the Spirit of 1876 for a Display of Victoriana." Architectural Record. 160 (November 1976), 89-94.

"Expo '70." Architectural Record. 147 (June 1970), 115-128.

"Facing Some Environmental Issues in House Design." Architectural Record. 170 (November 1982), 114-121.

"Fin de Siecle: An Exhibition." Architectural Record. 173 (September 1985), 104-113.

"Finding New Functions to Save a Landmark." Architectural Record. 172 (September 1984), 134-139.

"Form and Figure: THe Portland Museum of Art."
    Architectural Record. 171 (November 1983), 108-119.

"From Slum to Community, From Despair to Hope: Upgrading
    the Slum and Squatter Settlements." Architectural
    Record. 159 (August 1975), 67.

"A Gathering of Fragments: Robert O. Anderson Building, Los
    Angeles." Architectural Record. 175 (February 1987),
    110-119.

"Getting Ready for John F. Kennedy Library: Not Everyone
    Wants to Make It Go Away." Architectural Record. 156
    (December 1974), 98-105.

"Hardy Holzman Pfeiffer Re-establish the Formal Themes of a
    Great Beaux Arts Building." Architectural Record. 164
    (October 1978), 85-96.

"High Density Design for Undergraduate Science at Land-
    Starved Harvard." Architectural Record. 155 (March
    1974), 111-118.

"Homage to Catalonia." Architectural Record. 161 (March
    1977), 85.

"Housing." Architectural Record. 163 (February 1978),
    79-94.

"Housing in Islam." Architectural Record. 166 (August
    1979), 87-92.

"In Deference to Its Environment, Pusey Library was Built
    Beneath Harvard Yard." Architectural Record. 160
    (September 1976), 97-102.

"In Praise of the Unexciting Old Concepts Which Inspire the
    Work of Edward Larrabee Barnes for the College at
    Potsdam." Architectural Record. 152 (August 1972), 81.

"Inventing the Ideal Environment for Scientific Research."
    Architectural Record. 170 (October 1982), 108-115.

"Islamic Architecture and Rural Dwellings from Beijing to
    Kashi." Architectural Record. 170 (May 1982), 92-101.

"Jerusalem." Architectural Record. 163 (April 1978),
    103-114.

"Johns Manville World Headquarters Building--A Winner for
    J-M and TAC." Architectural Record. 162 (September
    1977), 89 + .

"Julliard School." Architectural Record. 147 (January
    1970), 121-130.

"Kennedy School of Government: A Purposefully Non-Heroic
    New Gateway to Harvard." Architectural Record. 165
    (June 1969), 99-106.

"La Cite." Architectural Record. 163 (January 1978),
    111-116.

"Last Work of Walter Gropius." Architectural Record. 146
    (September 1969), 131-150.

"Learning from Denise: The Role in Architecture of Denise
    Scott Brown. "Architectural Record. 170 (July 1982),
    102-107.

"Licensure of Landscape Architects: An Interdisciplinary
    Debate." Architectural Record. 173 (November 1985), 9.

"Lobby for a Landmark: Ohio Theatre Expansion and Arts
    Pavilion, Columbus, Ohio." Architectural Record. 173
    (September 1985), 114-119.

"Long Wait for the Renaissance: Report on Planning and
    Redevelopment in Philadelphia." Architectural Record.
    138 (July 1965), 119-132.

"Low Income Housing: a Lesson from Amsterdam."
    Architectural Record. 173 (January 1985), 134-143.

"Low Profile for IBM: World Trade Americas." Architectural
    Record. 161 (January 1977), 141.

"Madison Civic Center, Madison, Wisconsin." Architectural
    Record. 168 (July 1980), 77-87.

"Mix and Match: Two Small Shops in Pre-Classical Free-
    Style." Architectural Record. 171 (March 1983),

122-127.

"Museums for Today." Architectural Record. 152 (July 1972), 97.

"Neo Richardson Romanesque Cathedral by Edward L. Barnes." Architectural Record. 165 (January 1979), 129-136.

"New Architecture for the Changing Church?" Architectural Record. 142 (November 1967), 129.

"New Architecture of Florence." Architectural Record. 155 (February 1974), 95 + .

"New Boston City Hall: Kallmann, McKinnell and Knowles." Architectural Record. 145 (February 1969), 133-144.

"New Developments in Japanese Architecture." Architectural Record. 148 (September 1970), 109.

"New Directions for Downtown and Suburban Shopping Centers." Architectural Record. 155 (April 1974), 137-152.

"New Directions for Gunnar Birkerts." Architectural Record. 150 (October 1971), 97.

"New Hopes, New Options, But No Money. Whatever Happened to the Title VII?" Architectural Record. 154 (December 1973), 86-87.

"A New House for the American Academy of Arts and Sciences." Architectural Record. 169 (November 1981), 79-87.

New Life for Old Buildings. New York: McGraw-Hill, 1982.

"New Life for Old Buildings: Three Additions by SBR&A." Architectural Record. 158 (July 1975), 89 + .

"New Madison Civic Center by Hardy Holzman Pfeiffer Associates." Architectural Record. 168 (July 1980), 77-86.

"New MOMA: Expansion and Renovation of the Museum of Modern Art, New York City." Architectural Record. 172

(October 1984), 164-177.

"New Museum by Walter Nesch of SOM Given Order by His Field
    Theory." Architectural Record. 167 (January 1980),
    111-120.

"The 1980 Winners in the First Aga Khan Award for
    Architecture." Architectural Record. 168 (November
    1980), 104-127.

"Oakland Museum." Architectural Record. 147 (April 1970),
    115.

Office Building Design. New York: McGraw-Hill, 1975.

"An Old Brewery Born Again as the San Antonio Museum of
    Art." Architectural Record. 169 (June 1981), 92-99.

"Open Plan Elementary School." Architectural Record. 154
    (September 1973), 121-128.

"Open Space for People." Architectural Record. 152 (July
    1972), 131-40.

"Paul Rudolph: Boston State Service Center." Architectural
    Record. 154 (July 1973), 105.

"Paul Rudolph: Work in Progress." Architectural Record. 148
    (November 1970), 89.

"Philadelphia Report: A Long Wait for the Renaissance."
    Architectural Record. 138 (July 1965), 119-132.

"Prep School Athletics Building: Controlled, Concentrated,
    Balances and Alive with Distilled Energy."
    Architectural Record. 149 (June 1971), 97.

"Present and Future Trends in Library Design and Planning:
    Communications Technology and Its Implications for
    Library Design." Architectural Record. 153 (April
    1973), 119-136.

"Problem of Pan Am." Architectural Record. 133 (May 1963),
    151-158.

"Product Reports 1987." Architectural Record. 174 (December

1986), 31-215.

"Prometheus Rebounded: Rockefeller Center Promenade
     Restaurants, New York City." Architectural Record. 174
     (September 1986), 126-131.

"Recycling 'Main': A Landmark At Vassar." Architectural
     Record. 162 (July 1977), 73.

"Rehabilitation and Re-use." Architectural Record. 158
     (August 1975), 67.

"A Report from Australia: The Environmental Crisis Down
     Under." Architectural Record. 151 (May 1972), 105-108.

"Resort Hotels and Condominiums Designed for Romantics in
     Search of Just the Right Ambiance." Architectural
     Record. 150 (November 1971), 95, 113.

"The Right Look for Now: Linda Dresner, New York City."
     Architectural Record. 178 (August 1985), 114-117.

"Round Table: Housing and Community Design for Changing
     Family Needs." Architectural Record. 166 (October
     1979), 97-104.

"School for the Dance by Gunnar Birkerts." Architectural
     Record. 161 (February 1977), 85.

"Search for Meaning in the Architecture of Islam."
     Architectural Record. 168 (August 1980), 86-89.

"Shaping the Community in an Era of Dynamic Social Change."
     Architectural Record. 140 (July 1966), 189-206.

"Skyscraper in Context: IBM, 590 Madison Avenue, New York
     City." Architectural Record. 172 (May 1984), 146-153.

"Some Thoughts on Education by a Thoughtful Architect."
     Architectural Record. 148 (December 1970), 10.

"Spaces for Anthropological Art." Architectural Record. 161
     (May 1977), 103.

"XIII UIA World Congress." Architectural Record. 165
     (January 1979), 38-40.

"Three Precast Buildings From the Office of Marcel Breuer
    and Associates." Architectural Record. 153 (March
    1973), 117.

"Two College Libraries." Architectural Record. 156 (August
    1974), 97-108.

"Two Houses By Charles Moore." Architectural Record. 161
    (June 1977), 109-111.

"Two Libraries." Architectural Record. 157 (June 1975),
    91 + .

"Underground Church for Benedictine Monks." Architectural
    Record. 153 (January 1973), 105-110.

"Upgrading Barns to be Inhabited by People." Architectural
    Record. 155 (June 1974), 117.

"Vest Pocket Housing Brings a New Scale to the Bronx."
    Architectural Record. 153 (June 1973), 121.

"Walter Gropius, 1883-1969." Architectural Record. 146
    (August 1969), 9-10.

"Weese (Ben) versus Mies (Tigerman): Two Buildings, Two
    Architects, Two Points of View." Architectural Record.
    157 (April 1975), 83-90.

"Where the Money Is." Architectural Record. 160 (December
    1976), 124-128.

"Wish You Were Here: Hotel Lenado, Aspen, Colorado."
    Architectural Record. 173 (July 1985), 116-121.

"Yale University Is Preserving Its Great Late 19th Century
    Architecture by Remodeling the Old Campus."
    Architectural Record. 161 (March 1977), 93-100.

and Robert E. Fischer. "Denver's Boettcher Concert Hall."
    Architectural Record. 165 (March 1979), 99-110.

SECONDARY WORKS:

Beatty, Paul B. "Our New Editor: Mildred F. Schmertz,

FAIA." <u>Architectural Record</u>. 173 (September 1985), 9 +

SHIPMAN, ELLEN BIDDLE *   LANDSCAPE ARCHITECT

Ellen Shipman's Papers are at Cornell University, Ithaca,
New York.

SECONDARY WORKS:

Anderson, Dorothy May. "Women's Breakthrough Via the
    Cambridge School." <u>Landscape Architecture</u>. 68 (March
    1968), 145-148.

Brown, Catherine. <u>Women and the Land</u>. Baltimore: Built
    Environment Studies, 1979, p. 23.

_____, and Celia Maddox. "Women and the Land: A
    Suitable Profession." <u>Landscape Architecture</u>. 72 (May
    1982), 65-69.

Deitz, Paula. "Designing Women." <u>Metropolis</u> (December
    1982), 14-19.

"House and Garden's Own Hall of Fame." <u>House and Garden</u>. 63
    (June 1933), 50.

Nevins, Deborah. "The Triumph of Flora: Women and the
    American Landscape, 1890-1935." <u>Antiques</u>. 127 (April
    1985), 904-922.

Palmer, Donna. <u>An Overview of the Trends, Eras and Values
    of Landscape Architecture in America</u>. M.L.A. North
    Carolina State University, 1976, p. 32.

EXHIBITION:

AIA & Architectural League, New York. <u>Architectural and
    Allied Arts Exposition</u>. New York: AIA & Architectural
    League, 1925, p. 57.

SIMON, CATHY (1943-   ) *   ARCHITECT

PRIMARY WORKS:

"Commodore Sloat Elementary School in San Francisco;
     Architects Marquis Associates, Project Architects
     Cathy Simon and Peter Winkelstein." Baumeister. 75
     (September 1978), 772-775.

"Do You See New Directions?" Architecture. 74 (May 1985),
     242-243.

"Looking for the Future." Architecture. 76 (May 1987), 121.

"We Have Witnessed a Rekindled Interest in Materials."
     Architecture. 74 (May 1985), 242-243.

and Marquis, Robert. "New Directions for an Established
     Firm in a Time of Change." Architectural Record. 164
     (November 1978), 93-102.

SECONDARY WORKS:

Canty, Donald. "Soaring Simian Conservatory." Architecture.
     74 (June 1985), 42-49.

Dean, Andrea O. "Women in Architecture: Individual Profiles
     and a Discussion of Issues." AIA Journal. 71 (January
     1982), 42-51.

SKLAREK, NORMA (1928-) *   ARCHITECT

SECONDARY WORKS:

"Black Women Architects: A Blueprint for Success." Ebony.
     39 (June 1984), 55-56.

"Conversation: Norma Sklarek, FAIA." Architecture
     California. 7 (January-February 1985), 22-23.

SMITH, ALICE ORME (1888-1980)   LANDSCAPE ARCHITECT

Smith College Archives has some of Alice Orme Smith's
papers.

SECONDARY WORKS:

Anderson, Dorothy May. Women Design and the Cambridge
    School. Mesa, Arizona: PDA Pub., 1980, p. 165.

Palmer, Donna. An Overview of the Trends, Eras and Values
    of Landscape Architecture in America. M.L.A. North
    Carolina State University, 1976, p. 39

SMITH, CHLOETHIEL WOODARD (1910-   ) ::   ARCHITECT

PRIMARY WORKS:

"Argentina: Survey of Contemporary Architecture."
    Architectural Forum. 86 (February 1947), 103-114.

"Cities in Search of Form." AIA Journal. 35 (March 1961),
    74-78.

"Forum's Correspondent Reports on Columbia and Venezuela."
    Architectural Forum. 85 (November 1946), 106-115.

"The New Town: Philosophy and Reality." Building Research.
    3 (January-February 1966), 9-34.

and Associate Architects. Architecture, Urban Design,
    Planning. brochure prepared by the firm.

SECONDARY WORKS:

"Apartments: Harbour Square, Washington, D.C."
    Architectural Record. 134 (September 1963), 202-204.

Berkeley, Ellen P. "LaClede Town: The Most Vital Town in
    Town." Architectural Forum. 129 (November 1968),
    57-61.

"The Blithe Spirit of St. Louis." Fortune. 73 (January
    1966), 175.

Breathnach, Sarah B. "Chloethiel Woodard Smith: Building
    Blocks." Washington Post Magazine. (February 25,
    1979), 31.

"Chloethiel Woodard Smith." Macmillan Encyclopedia of
    Architects. New York: Free Press, 1982, v. 4, p. 87.

"Esthetic Lion-Taming in the City." AIA Journal. 38
    (November 1962), 36-38.

Forgey, Benjamin. "The Work of an Architect Is a
    Compromise." Washington Star (February 2, 1977),
    C1-C2.

"Fresh Idea for Hillsides: Here Is How It Works, House in
    Washington, D.C." House and Home. 14 (November 1958),
    92-95.

"Good Design Makes This a Handsome Split from Any Angle."
    House and Home. 10 (October 1956), 120-123.

"Highlights of American Architecture, 1776-1976." AIA
    Journal. 65 (July 1976), 93-94.

"House for R.W. Komer, Fairfax County, Virginia."
    Architectural Record. 119 (March 1956), 176-179.

"Large Living in Small Space." House and Garden. 102
    (August 1952), 22-54, 78, 83.

McGroarty, J. "New Professsional Identities: Four Women in
    the Sixties." In: Women in American Architecture. New
    York: Whitney Library of Design, 1977, pp. 115-131.

McLendon, Winzola. "Architect Designs No Ivory Towers."
    Washington Post (July 30, 1967), E1 + .

Miller, Robert L. "Architects' Favorite Rooms."
    Washingtonian (February 1986), 170.

Poole, Daniel. "What Creates a Beautiful City?" The Evening
    Star (March 12, 1965), D1, D3.

"Portrait." Architectural Forum. 86 (February 1947), 56.

"Public Works." AIA Journal. 39 (January 1963), 99-103.

"Recent South American Building." Architects' Yearbook. 3
    (1949). 87-98.

Rochlin, Harriet. "All In a Day's Work." Ms. 5 (December
    1976), 16.

Stern, Robert A.M. New Directions in American Architecture.
    New York: Braziller, 1977, pp. 83, 86 and figures
    89-91.

"Two Story House Gives Flexibility for Big Families." House
    and Home. 8 (October 1955), 169.

"Washington Efficiency: Capitol Park Apartments."
    Architectural Record. 125 (June 1959), 212-213.

Whyte, William H. Cluster Development. New York: American
    Conservation Asso., 1964, pp. 47, 63, 87.

"Women in Architecture, the New Professional: Coming of
    Age." Progressive Architecture. 58 (March 1977), 48.

EXHIBITION:

AIA, Washington, D.C. Two On Two At the Octagon.
    Washington, D.C.: the Octagon, 1979, pp. 5-10.

Built by Women: A Guide to Architecture in the New York
    Area. New York: Alliance of Women in Architecture,
    1981, p. 11.

SPEAR, LAURINDA (1950-) ∺   ARCHITECT

PRIMARY WORKS:

and others. "Arquitectonica: Interview and Recent Works
    and Projects." GA Document. 7 (August 1983), 4-67.

and others. "What Counts: Experts Discuss Your Clothes,
    Your Looks, Your House, and Show How Health Is Basic
    to Balance." Vogue. 169 (June 1979), 186 +.

SECONDARY WORKS:

Architectural League of New York. Emerging Voices. New
    York: Princeton Architectural Press, 1986, pp. 30-31.

"Arquitectonica: Some Projects." Architectural Design. 49,
    no. 7 (1979), 186-189.

"Arquitectonica Fragmenta." Domus. 641 (July-August 1983),
    2-8.

"Award: House on the Waterfront, Southern Florida."
    Progressive Architecture. 56 (January 1975), 46-47.

Dixon, John M. "Layers of Meaning: Spear House, Miami,
    Florida; Architects, Arquitectonica, Bernardo
    Fort-Brescia and Laurinda Spear." Progressive
    Architecture. 60 (December 1979), 66-71.

"Doctor's Office and Apartment Complex, Miami, Florida,
    Architects; Arquitectonica, Bernardo Fort-Brescia and
    Laurinda Spear." Architectural Record. 169 (January
    1981), 80-81.

Dumaine, Brian. "Architects for the 1990's." Fortune (June
    22, 1987), 152-163.

Filler, Martin. "Harbingers: Ten Architects." Art in
    America. 69 (Summer 1981), 114-223.

_____. "High-Rise Hotshots." House and Garden. 155
    (June 1983), 120-129, 175.

Flanagan, Barbara. "Women in Architecture." Newsday
    (October 10, 1985), 1, 10.

Gandee, Charles K. "Making It in Miami...The Work of
    Arquitectonica." Architectural Record. 170 (August
    1982), 112-121.

Gutterman, Scott. "Architect Designed Tableware." Art and
    Design. 1 (July 1985), 10-11.

Jodidio, P. "Risk Anything/Tout Oser." Connaissance des
    Arts. 379 (September 1983), 80-87.

"Portfolio of Recent Works: Arquitectonica. Project
     Designers: Bernardo Fort Brescia, Hervin Romney,
     Laurinda Spear." Perspecta. 18 (1982), 170-179.

Stephens, Suzanne. "Women in Architecture." House and
     Garden. 153 (March 1981), 146, 196.

Wechsler, Susan. "The New American Ceramics." Industrial
     Design. 32 (May-June 1985), 22-27 + .

STEPHENS, SUZANNE (1942-)   CRITIC

PRIMARY WORKS:

"Adventure in Style." House and Garden. 158 (November
     1985), 138-147.

"Adventures of Harry Barber in OPEC Land." Progressive
     Architecture. 57 (October 1976), 56-65.

"Architect: Preston Phillips." House and Garden. 157
     (January 1985), 128-133.

"Architectural Artifact." New York. 10 (September 19,
     1977), 46-48.

"Architectural Journalism Analyzed: Reflections on a Half
     Century." Progressive Architecture. 51 (June 1970),
     132-139.

"Architecture Unadorned." Progressive Architecture. 58
     (September 1977), 68-69.

"Architecture Cross-Examined." Progressive Architecture. 58
     (July 1977), 43-54.

"As Troy Turns: Uncle Sam Atrium, Troy, New York."
     Progressive Architecture. 62 (July 1981), 90-93.

"At MOMA: Mondrian's Milieu." Progressive Architecture. 64
     (September 1983), 52.

"At the Core of the Apple: The Market at Citicorp, New York
     City." Progressive Architecture. 59 (December 1978),

54-59.

"BEA Offices, Citicorp Building, New York City."
    Progressive Architecture. 60 (September 1979),
    156-159.

"Basic Bauhaus: Linda Hopp Store, SOHO District, New York."
    Progressive Architecture. 61 (August 1980), 74-77.

"Bathhouse Revisited: Cooper Field Bathhouse, Trenton, New
    Jersey." Progressive Architecture. 60 (June 1979),
    70-73.

"Before the Virgin Met the Dynamo: Vernacular Architec-
    ture." Architectural Forum. 139 (July 1973), 76-78.

"Beneath the Halls of Ivy: Avery Library Extension,
    Columbia University. New York City." Progressive
    Architecture. 59 (March 1978), 60-61.

"Beyond Fragments." Progressive Architecture. 60 (December
    1979), 88-89.

"Beyond Modernism: Book of Lists." Progressive
    Architecture. 60 (December 1979), 56-59.

"Big Deals and Bitter Endings: The Hirshhorn Museum and
    Sculpture Garden." Artforum. 13 (February 1975),
    56-62.

Building the New Museum, editor. Princeton: Princeton
    Architectural Press, 1987.

"California Redwood Association Offices, One Lombard Street
    Building, San Francisco, California." Progressive
    Architecture. 60 (September 1979), 160-161.

"Calvin Klein Showroom and Apartment, New York:
    Monochromed and Minimal." Progressive Architecture. 58
    (September 1977), 60-65.

"Campus Architecture." Progressive Architecture. 59 (March
    1978), 53-75.

"Casa Moderna: Kislevitz House, Long Island, New York."
    Progressive Architecture. 59 (July 1978), 72-75.

"Cash on the Line." Progressive Architecture. 61 (November
    1980), 100-105.

"Casino Qua Non: A Hotel-Casino Project in Atlantic City,
    New Jersey." Progressive Architecture. 58 (October
    1977), 67-69.

"Cheap Trix: Exposing Marc Treib." Print. 27 (May 1973),
    61-66.

"Chicago Frame-Up: Illinois Center." Architectural Forum.
    140 (January 1974), 75-79.

"City Report: New York: Zoning for Context." Skyline.
    (December 1981), 6.

"City Under Sod: Minnesota High Security Correctional
    Facility." Progressive Architecture. 61 (April 1980),
    156-157.

"Columbia Architecture at 100: Exhibition Review of 'The
    Making of an Architect'." Skyline (January 1982),
    16-17.

"Compromised Ideal: Marcus Garvey Park Village Housing,
    Brooklyn, New York." Progressive Architecture. 60
    (October 1979), 50-53.

"Conversion to a Candy Factory, Henry Street Studios,
    Brooklyn." Progressive Architecture. 58 (November
    1977), 66-67.

"Cool School: Gloria Floyd Elementary School, Miami,
    Florida 1979." Progressive Architecture. 61 (April
    1980), 166-169.

"Corporate Form Givers: IBM, New York; AT&T Headquarters,
    New York; Philip Morris Headquarter, New York."
    Progressive Architecture. 60 (July 1979), 55-59.

"Corrigan's Cabinet of Unearthly Delights." Print. 26 (May
    1972), 55-61.

"Cultural Overlay: Karme-Choling Meditation Center, Barnet,
    Vermont." Progressive Architecture. 59 (November
    1978), 88-91.

"Culture as Consumption." Architectural Forum. 139
     (December 1973), 46-47.

"Dance Studio and Music Performance Hall, Saint Paul's
     School, Concord, New Hampshire." Progressive
     Architecture. 62 (February 1981), 74-77.

"De-institutionalizing for the Blind: Life Learning Center
     for the Blind, Retarded Boston." Progressive
     Architecture. 59 (April 1978), 92-93.

"Design and Planning." Progressive Architecture. 58
     (December 1977), 33-49.

"Design Deformed." Artforum. 15 (January 1977), 44-47.

"Emblematic Edifice: the Atheneum, New Harmony, Indiana."
     Progressive Architecture. 61 (February 1980), 67-75.

"An Equitable Relationship." Art in America. 74 (May 1986),
     116-123.

"Firm Profile: Hammond, Beeby and Babka." Progressive
     Architecture. 61 (June 1980), 84-93.

"Firm Profile: SOM at Midlife." Progressive Architecture.
     62 (May 1981), 138-149.

"First Village, Santa Fe, New Mexico: Living Proof, a
     Laboratory for Living with Solar Heat." Progressive
     Architecture. 60 (April 1979), 110-115.

"Foiled Again." Progressive Architecture. 61 (November
     1980), 96-99.

"Formal Dynamics: The Implications of Energy Use on Form."
     Progressive Architecture. 60 (April 1979), 116-119.

"Foster Associates: Technical Effects." Progressive
     Architecture. 60 (February 1979), 59-64.

"Frame by Frame: Richard Meier's Museum for Decorative
     Arts." Progressive Architecture. 66 (June 1985),
     81-91.

"Frank O. Gehry and Associates Inc., Where Categories

Collide." Progressive Architecture. 59 (September
    1978), 74-77.

"Franklin Court." Progressive Architecture. 57 (April
    1976), 69-70.

"The Future of Architecture." Progressive Architecture. 58
    (May 1977), 49-96.

"Future Past: Physical Mise-en-scene: Centre Pompidou."
    Progressive Architecture. 58 (May 1977), 84-89.

"Gillette Apartment, New York: In the Nature of Fake
    Materials." Progressive Architecture. 58 (September
    1977), 92-93.

"Going Solar in the City." Progressive Architecture. 61
    (April 1980), 113-116.

"Green Residence: Standing by the Twentieth Century Brick."
    Progressive Architecture. 55 (October 1974), 78-83.

"Hidden Barriers: The Social, Psychological and
    Physiological Factors Which Impinge upon the Awareness
    of the Handicapped, the Elderly and the Rest of
    Society in Experiencing Architecture." Progressive
    Architecture. 59 (April 1978), 94-97.

"High Density on the Dunes: Resort Condominium, Ocean City,
    Maryland." Progressive Architecture. 57 (September
    1976), 64-67.

"High Rise Housing." Progressive Architecture. 57 (March
    1976), 58-63.

"Higher Level of Concern: Foley Square Courthouse Annex,
    New York City." Progressive Architecture. 57 (July
    1976), 60-65.

"The Historicist Vision: The Shingle Style Genre." Skyline
    (July 1982), 13-19.

"Hotel-Casino Project, Atlantic City, New Jersey: Casino
    Qua Non." Progressive Architecture. 58 (October 1977),
    67-69.

"Housing as Matrix: Dundas-Sherbourne Housing, Toronto."
     Progressive Architecture. 58 (December 1977), 40-45.

"How the West Village Was Won." New York. 11 (April 17,
     1978), 56-58.

"Imagery and Integration: English Architecture."
     Progressive Architecture. 60 (August 1979), 66-67.

"Images for Education: Wharton Graduate Center, University
     of Pennsylvania." Progressive Architecture. 56 (April
     1975), 60-65.

"Impeccably Park Avenue." Progressive Architecture. 58
     (September 1977), 84-85.

"Inside 'Our Town', River Hills Plantation, South
     Carolina." Progressive Architecture. 59 (June 1978),
     56-59.

"Introduction: Beds of Academe." Progressive Architecture.
     56 (August 1975), 35-36.

"Introduction: Campus Architecture, the New College."
     Progressive Architecture. 59 (March 1978), 53.

"Introduction: Common Grounds." Progressive Architecture.
     58 (December 1977), 33.

"Introduction: The Future of Architecture." Progressive
     Architecture. 58 (May 1977), 49.

"Introduction: Leaving the Natural Behind." Progressive
     Architecture. 59 (February 1978), 45.

"Introduction: Shopping Malls, Introversion and the Urban
     Context." Progressive Architecture. 59 (December
     1978), 49-53.

"Introduction: Taste in America, The Architects Taste and
     The Public Taste." Progressive Architecture. 59 (June
     1978), 49-51.

"Introduction: Urban Waterfronts." Progressive Architec-
     ture. 56 (June 1975), 41-42.

"Is There a New Architecture?: Theories from New England and the U.S." House and Garden. 159 (December 1986), 74-80.

"It's Not Graphic Design Exactly nor Is It Architecture and It Probably Isn't Art. What Is It? Graphitecture." Print. 26 (November 1972), 23-31.

"J51 Conversions in New York: Many Commercial and Hotel Structures in New York Are Being Converted into Multiple Dwellings." Progressive Architecture. 58 (November 1977), 68-71.

"Judicious Juxtapositions: Hampshire College Recreational Facility." Progressive Architecture. 56 (October 1975), 86-91.

"Kalamazoo Center, Kalamazoo, Michigan: Urbanity Comes to Kalamazoo." Progressive Architecture. 57 (May 1976), 64-69.

"Knoll International Showroom, New York." Progressive Architecture. 61 (July 1980), 74-77.

"Law Courts and Robson Square Complex, Vancouver." Progressive Architecture. 62 (March 1981), 82-87.

"Let the Sunshine In: Mary Medina Health and Social Services Centre in Taos, New Mexico." Progressive Architecture. 60 (April 1979), 128-131.

"Living in a Work of Art: Synderman House, Fort Wayne, Indiana." Progressive Architecture. 59 (March 1978), 80-87.

"Looking Back at Modern Architecture: The International Style Turns 50." Skyline (February 1982), 18-27.

"Los Angeles: Two for the Show." Art in America. 75 (May 1967), 146-161.

"Magnificent Intentions: AIA Headquarters." Architectural Forum. 139 (October 1973), 36-43.

"Main Street Revisited: A Young Firm of Architects Working With Developers Has Taken a Look at Some Dying

Downtowns." Architectural Forum. 139 (November 1973), · 56-65.

"Material Connections: Steuart Building, St. Albans School, Washington, D.C.: Architects, Keyes Condon and Florance." Progressive Architecture. 61 (July 1980), 64-65.

"Maurice Tidy Hair Salon, New York: Impeccably Park Avenue." Progressive Architecture. 58 (September 1977), 84-85.

"Minnesota High Security Correctional Facility Project, Oak Park Heights, Minnesota." Progressive Architecture. 61 (April 1980), 156-157.

"Mixed-Use Buildings: Microcosms of Urbanity." Progressive Architecture. 56 (December 1975), 37-38.

"Modernism and the Monolith: National Air and Space Museum, Washington, D.C." Progressive Architecture. 57 (July 1976), 70-75.

"Modernism Reconstituted: Sainsbury Centre for the Visual Arts, Norwich." Progressive Architecture. 60 (February 1979), 49-58.

"Modernist Recall: Lancaster Neighborhood Center, Lancaster, PA" Progressive Architecture. 58 (May 1977), 72-75.

"Modified Modernism: BEA Offices, New York." Progressive Architecture. 60 (September 1979), 156-159.

"MOMA's Castle in the Air." Artforum. 14 (June 1976), 28-31.

"Monochromed and Minimal." Progressive Architecture. 58 (September 1977), 60-65.

"Monumental Main Street: Pennsylvania Avenue, Washington, D.C." Progressive Architecture. 60 (May 1979), 110-113.

110-113.

"More Than Skin Deep: Architect Franklin D. Israel
     Restructures the New York Loft of Make-Up Artist
     Francis R. Gillette." House and Garden. 158 (January
     1986), 80-89, 177.

"Mummer's Museum." Progressive Architecture. 57 (April
     1976), 70-71.

"Museum as Monument: Hirshhorn Museum and Sculpture Garden,
     Washington, D.C." Progressive Architecture. 56 (March
     1975), 42-47.

"National Center for the Performing Arts, Bombay, India."
     Progressive Architecture. 62 (March 1981), 76-81.

"The New Gray Neighbor: Woolf House, San Francisco,
     California." Progressive Architecture. 62 (August
     1981), 72-75.

"The New York Knoll Showroom: Architects, Venturi, Rauch
     and Scott Brown." Progressive Architecture. 61 (July
     1980), 74-77.

"New York City Waterfront: A Fear of Filling?" Progressive
     Architecture. 56 (June 1975), 48-49.

"Niagara Rises: Rainbow Center Mall and Winter Garden,
     Niagara Falls, New York." Progressive Architecture. 59
     (August 1978), 72-81.

"No Set Style." House and Garden. 157 (May 1985), 110-114.

"Nostalgie du Chateau: Pavillon Soixante-dix, St. Sauveur,
     Quebec." Progressive Architecture. 60 (March 1979),
     70-75.

"Of Nature and Modernity: Native American Center,
     Minneapolis, Minn." Progressive Architecture. 56
     (October 1975), 66-69.

"On Style II: Gwathmey Siegel's Beach House Discussed at
     IAUS." Skyline. (March 1983), 8-9.

"1199 Plaza, New York. New York: High Rise in Harlem."

Progressive Architecture. 57 (March 1976), 64-69.

"Out of the Rage for Order: Frank Gehry House." Progressive Architecture. 61 (March 1980), 81-85.

"P/A On Pei: Roundtable on a Trapezoid, East Building, National Gallery of Art, Washington, D.C." Progressive Architecture. 59 (October 1978), 49 + .

"Pattern on Pattern: Philip Mayberry Loft, New York City." Progressive Architecture. 62 (September 1981), 165-167.

"Perceptual Factors: Hidden Barriers." Progressive Architecture. 59 (April 1978), 94-97.

"Plane on Plain: Recreational Facilities Building, Southern Illinois University, Carbondale." Progressive Architecture. 61 (May 1980), 122-125.

"Playing with a Full Decade." Progressive Architecture. 60 (December 1979), 49-55.

"Purveyors of Taste." Progressive Architecture. 59 (June 1978), 80-85.

"Quaker Meeting House, Brooklyn, New York: Appropriately Unadorned." Progressive Architecture. 58 (September 1977), 68-69.

"R/UDAT Redux, Regional Urban Design Assistance Teams." Progressive Architecture. 60 (October 1979), 72-75.

"Realization of Symbols." Progressive Architecture. 58 (October 1977), 49-69.

"Reconstructing Rice." Skyline (November 1981), 19-20.

"Regional Urban Design Assistance Teams." Progressive Architecture. 60 (October 1979), 72-75.

"Residence, Westchester County, New York: Grand Illusions." Progressive Architecture. 58 (February 1977), 58-63.

"Restoration and Remodeling." Progressive Architecture. 58 (November 1977), 51-84.

"Return of the Megastructure: A One-Building Campus."
    Architectural Forum. 139 (September 1973), 40-47.

"Revitalization: Main Streets, Nostalgie de la Rue."
    Progressive Architecture. 57 (November 1976), 70-75.

"Richard the Famous: The J. Paul Getty Trust Awards
    Architect Meier the Commission of the Decade." House
    and Garden. 157 (February 1985), 54, 60.

"Richardson on the Half Shell." Progressive Architecture.
    61 (November 1981), 92-95.

"Role-models: the Gamesman, Jacquelin Robertson."
    Progressive Architecture. 58 (May 1977), 66-67.

"Role-models: The Individual, Richard Meier." Progressive
    Architecture. 58 (May 1977), 60-62.

"Role-models: Polemicist Theorist." Progressive
    Architecture. 58 (May 1977), 68.

"Roosevelt Island Housing Competition: This Side of
    Habitat." Progressive Architect. 56 (July 1975),
    58-59.

"Rust City: Brockport College Apartments, Brockport, N.Y."
    Progressive Architecture. 56 (August 1975), 42-47.

"Saavy About Steel, Game with Glass." Progressive
    Architecture. 55 (September 1974), 78-83.

"Saving Traces: Hogan Hall, Columbia University, New York."
    Progressive Architecture. 59 (March 1978), 62-63.

"Score for a Loft." House and Garden. 157 (January 1985),
    128-134.

"Semantic Distinctions: Two House Additions, Princeton, New
    Jersey." Progressive Architecture. 56 (April 1975),
    88-91.

"Shopping Malls." Progressive Architecture. 59 (December
    1978), 49-69.

"Showroom Design: Kohler, New York." Interior Design. 57

(January 1986), 264-269.

"Simply Sensuous: Southern Alleghenies Museum of Art,
    Loretto, PA." Progressive Architecture. 59 (May
    1978), 90-93.

"The Sky Is Not the Limit: Midtown Zoning." Skyline.
    (October 1981), 5-7.

"Sleek Revival: Yves Saint Laurent Enterprises Office, New
    York." Progressive Architecture. 60 (September 1979),
    162-163.

"Stephen Kiviat-James Rappoport: Big Time on 57th Street."
    Progressive Architecture. 59 (September 1978), 94-97.

"Street Smarts: Arts for Living Center: Henry Street
    Settlement, New York." Progressive Architecture. 56
    (November 1975), 64-70.

"The Strength of Tradition." House and Garden. 158 (July
    1986), 72-79, 155.

"Such Good Intentions: Architecture for the Arts at
    Purchase." Artforum. 14 (January 1976), 26-31.

"Taking to the Waterfront." Horizon. 21, no. 10 (1978),
    30-37.

"Tigerman Private Residence, Chicago Suburb." Progressive
    Architecture. 57 (August 1976), 42-45.

"Tight Fit: Sartogo and Schwarting's redesign of FIT
    Block." Skyline (March 1983), 6-7.

"Too Little from Tange: Minneapolis Institute of Arts."
    Progressive Architecture. 56 (May 1975), 114.

"Tradition of the New." Skyline (December 1981), 4-5.

"Twenty-five Years After the Chinese Wall: Philadelphia
    Urban Design and Planning." Progressive Architecture.
    57 (April 1976), 46-51.

"Two Buildings from Mitchell/Giurgola Associates."
    Progressive Architecture. 55 (December 1974), 54-67.

"Ward Bennett: Keeeping It Clean." <u>Progressive
    Architecture</u>. 59 (September 1978), 82-85.

"West Village Houses, New York, New York: Low Rise Lemon."
    <u>Progressive Architecture</u>. 57 (March 1976), 54-57.

"What Becomes a Monument Most?" <u>Progressive Architecture</u>.
    60 (May 1979), 87-89.

"Within the Walls of Modernism: Nilsson House, Los
    Angeles." <u>Progressive Architecture</u>. 60 (December
    1979), 60-65.

"Women in Architecture: Breaking New Ground." <u>House and
    Garden</u>. 153 (March 1981), 146-149.

"Women in Architecture: Introduction, The Woman Behind the
    T Square." <u>Progressive Architecture</u>. 58 (March 1977),
    37-38.

"World Trade Center 2023." <u>Architectural Forum</u>. 138 (April
    1973), 56-61.

"Writing on the Walls: On an Architectural Palimpsest,
    Henry Smith-Miller Creates a New Environment for
    Fashion Designer Neil Bieff." <u>House and Garden</u>. 158
    (February 1986), 172-176, 216.

and J.M. Dixon. "Apres le denouement: Hopeful Reviews for
    the Future of Architecture." <u>Progressive Architecture</u>.
    58 (May 1977), 95-96.

and J.M. Dixon. "Netsch: Netsch House, Chicago, Illinois."
    <u>Progressive Architecture</u>. 57 (August 1976), 54-57.

and J.M. Dixon. "Plot Line: Scenarios Without End."
    <u>Progressive Architecture</u>. 58 (May 1977), 50-53.

and Sheila Metzner. "Fifties Style on the Hudson." <u>House
    and Garden</u>. 157 (September 1985), 196-202.

and Don Raney. "Operation Breakthrough: Operation P/R."
    <u>Progressive Architecture</u>. 51 (April 1970), 120-133.

and others. <u>Building the New Museum</u>. Princeton:
    Princeton Architectural Press, 1986.

and others. "Critics Discuss State of the Press." <u>Texas</u>
    <u>Architect</u>. 34 (March-April 1984), 30-31, 33.

and others. "Critics on Criticism." <u>Metropolis</u>. 5 (November
    1985), 28-31, 39-41.

and others. "Edmonton City Hall Competition." <u>Trace</u>. 1
    (July-September 1981), 27-41.

and others. "Firm Profile: Frank O. Gehry and Associates."
    <u>Progressive Architecture</u>. 61 (March 1980), 69-85.

SECONDARY WORKS:

"Senior Editor Named." <u>Progressive Architecture</u>. 55 (August
    1974), 26.

STEVENS, MARY OTIS (1928-) ⁎   ARCHITECT

PRIMARY WORKS:

"Struggle for Place, Women in American Architecture:
    1920-1960." In: <u>Women in American Architecture</u>. New
    York: Whitney Library of Design, 1977, pp 88-102.

and Thomas F. McNulty. <u>World of Variation</u>. New York: G.
    Braziller, 1970.

SECONDARY WORKS:

"Casa a Beaver Pond, Presso Boston." <u>Architettura</u>. 11
    (March 1966), 740-741.

"Concavo e convesso: una Casa a Lincoln, Massachusetts."
    <u>Domus</u>. 443 (October 1966), 25-29.

"Eigenes Haus in Lincoln, Massachusetts, U.S.A." <u>Deutsche</u>
    <u>Bauzeitung</u>. 11 (November 1966), 918-922.

"Habitation des architects McNulty a Lincoln,

Massachusetts." <u>Architecture d'Aujourd'hui</u>. 36
(February 1966), 6.

"Honor: Pool Pavilion." <u>Remodeling</u>. (February–March 1987),
64.

"McNulty House in Lincoln, Mass." <u>Architectural Forum</u>. 123
(November 1965), 30–35.

McGroarty, J. "New Professional Identities: Four Women in
the Sixties." In: <u>Women in American Architecture</u>. New
York: Whitney Library of Design, 1977, pp. 115–131.

Stern, Robert A.M. "Forty Under Forty." <u>Architecture and
Urbanism</u>. 73 (January 1977), 44.

STRANG, ELIZABETH LEONARD (1886–1948) LANDSCAPE ARCHITECT

SECONDARY WORKS:

Brown, Catherine. <u>Women and the Land</u>. Baltimore: Built
Studies Environment, 1979, p. 24.

"Elizabeth Leonard Strang." <u>Landscape Architecture</u>. 39
(July 1949), 194.

Palmer, Donna. <u>An Overview of the Trends, Eras and Values
of Landscape Architecture in America</u>. M.L.A. North
Carolina State University, 1976, p. 33–34.

SUTTON, SHARON E. ∗   ARCHITECT

PRIMARY WORKS:

"Architectural Education: Should Behavioral Studies be
Integrated into the Design Studio?" <u>Architectural
Record</u>. 172 (July 1984), 43, 45–47.

"The Human Contribution to Architectural Space." <u>Faith and
Form</u>. 19 (Spring 1986), 17–20.

<u>Learning Through the Built Environment</u>. New York: Irvington
    Pub., 1985.

SECONDARY WORKS:

"Black Women Architects: A Blueprint for Success." <u>Ebony</u>.
    39 (June 1984), 56.

"Sharon Sutton." <u>Printworld Directory</u>. Bala Cynwyd, Pa.:
    Printworld Inc., 1985, pp. 580-581.

EXHIBITION:

<u>Built by Women: A Guide to Architecture in the New York
    Area</u>. New York: Alliance of Women in Architecture,
    1981, p. 23.

SWANN, PATRICIA ⁕   ARCHITECT

SECONDARY WORKS:

Rochlin, Harriet. "All in a Day's Work." <u>Ms.</u> 5 (December
    1976), 10.

EXHIBITION:

<u>Built by Women: A Guide to Architecture in the New York
    Area</u>. New York: Alliance of Women in Architecture,
    1981, p. 13, 19.

TORRE, SUSANA (1944-) ⁕   ARCHITECT

PRIMARY WORKS:

"Space as Matrix." <u>Heresies</u>. 3, no. 3 (1981), 51-52.

(editor). <u>Women in American Architecture</u>. New York: Whitney
    Library of Design, 1977.

and Martin Filler. "Rooms." Design Quarterly. 69 (September
    1980), 62-69.

and others. "The Appropriation of the House: Changes in
    House Design and Concepts of Domesticity." In: New
    Space for Women, edited by Gerda Wekerle and others.
    Boulder: Westview Press, 1980, pp. 83-100.

and others. "Rethinking Closets, Kitchens, and Other
    Forgotten Spaces." Ms. (December 1977), 54.

SECONDARY WORKS:

Abercrombie, Stanley. "Rooms for the Federal Design
    Assembly: Using Stock Materials, Some Non-stock
    Solutions." Interiors. 138 (January 1979), 90-95.

_____. "Samplings of the Work of an Emergent
    Dozen." AIA Journal. 69 (September 1980), 68-69.

Architectural League of New York. Emerging Voices.
    Princeton: Princeton Architectural Press, 1986, pp.
    34-35.

"Architecture with People." Design Quarterly. 109 (1979)
    16-31.

"Bach House, Pound Ridge, New York, 1978-1979; Architect
    Susana Torre. "Architecture and Urbanism. 3 (March
    1981), 40-41.

"Bach House, Pound Ridge, New York 1979; Architect Susana
    Torre with Richard Velsor." GA Houses. 11 (1982),
    130-131.

Boles, Daralice D. "Teaching Architecture." Progressive
    Architecture. 67 (September 1986), 128-131.

"Clark House, Southampton, Long Island, New York,
    1979-1980; Architect, Susana Torre." GA Houses. 11
    (1982), 132-137.

"Consulate of the Ivory Coast, New York, New York;
     Architect Susana Torre." Architecture and Urbanism. 3
     (March 1981), 67-73.

Davey, Peter. "Interior Dilemmas." Architectural Review.
     172 (November 1982), 26-30.

Drimer, M. "Speaking Freely." Residential Interiors. 4
     (September 1979), 96-97.

"Entretien avec Susana Torre: une approche de
     l'enseignement de l'architecture." Architecture/
     Quebec. 24 (April 1985), 19-21.

Filler, Martin. "Between Dream and Memory: Remodeling of
     1900 Carriage House; Architect for Remodeling, Susana
     Torre." House and Garden. 154 (January 1982), 112-116.

_____. "Harbingers: Ten Architects." Art in
     America. 69 (Summer 1981), 114-123.

_____. "Rooms for Improvement." Progressive
     Architecture. 59 (December 1978), 76-77.

Flanagan, Barbara. "Women in Architecture." Newsday
     (October 10, 1985), 10, 13.

"The Future of Architecture." Progressive Architecture. 58
     (May 1977), 49-9.

Hoyt, Charles. "Consular and Financial Offices of the
     Embassy of the Ivory Coast, New York, New York;
     Architect Susana Torre." Architectural Record. 167
     (May 1980), 85-89.

_____. "Do New Family Concepts Call for a New
     Housing Type?" Architectural Record. 168 (September
     1980), 98-101.

"Law Offices/Studio Legals." Domus. 572 (July 1977),
     34-35.

Lippard, Lucy R. "Complexes: Architectural Sculpture in

Nature." Art in America. 67 (January-February 1979), 86-88.

Morton, D. "For More Complexity: Law Offices." Progressive Architecture. 58 (May 1977), 76-79.

_____. "Role Models: Neotypes." Progressive Architecture. 58 (May 1977), 69.

"Remodeled Carriage House, Eastern Long Island; Architect Susana Torre." Architectural Record. 170 (Mid-May 1982), 112-115.

Smith, H.L. "Two Interiors by Torre: An Office and a Restaurant." Architectural Record. 170 (August 1982), 128-131.

Stephens, Suzanne. "Women in Architecture. House and Garden. 153 (March 1981), 148, 196.

Stern, Robert A.M. "America Now: Drawing Towards a More Modern Architecture." Architectural Design. 47 (June 1977), entire issue.

_____. "Forty Under Forty." Architecture and Urbanism. 73 (January 1977), 131.

EXHIBITION:

Bletter, R.H. "Collaboration: Artists and Architects, New York Historical Society, New York Traveling Exhibit." Art Journal. 41 (Winter 1981), 383.

Built by Women: A Guide to Architecture in the New York Area. New York: Alliance of Women in Architecture, 1981. p. 13.

Castle, Frederick T. "Ronald Feldman Fine Arts, New York." Art in America. 73 (May 1985), 178.

Phillips, Patricia C. "Susana Torre, Allan Wexler: Ronald Feldman Fine Arts, New York." Artforum. 23 (April 1985), 95.

TUTHILL, LOUISA C. (1800-1879)   WRITER

The Bancroft Library at the University of California at
Berkeley has several of Tuthill's letters.

The Historical Society of Philadelphia's Library also has
some of Mrs. Tuthill's papers.

PRIMARY WORKS:

Ancient Architecture. New York: Babcock, 1830.

History of Architecture. Philadelphia: Lindsay and
     Blakiston, 1848.

SECONDARY WORKS:

Adams, Oscar Fay. "Louisa C. Tuthill." In: A Dictionary of
     American Authors. Boston: Longwood Press, 1897, p.
     292.

"Louisa C.H. Tuthill." In: Appleton's Cyclopaedia of
     American Biography. New York: D. Appleton and Co.,
     1889, p. 189.

"Louisa Tuthill." In: Notable American Women, 1607-1950.
     Cambridge, MA: Belknap Press, 1971, pp. 487-488.

TYNG, ANNE GRISWOLD (1920-) ⁑   ARCHITECT

Architectural Archives at the University of Pennsylvania
has drawings by Anne Griswold Tyng.

PRIMARY WORKS:

"Architecture Is My Touchstone." Radcliffe Quarterly
     (September 1984), 5-7.

"The Energy of Abstraction in Architecture: A Theory of
     Creativity." Pratt Journal of Architecture. 1 (Fall
     1985), 32-38.

"An Exploration of a 20th Century Matrix." Visionary
    Drawings of Architecture and Planning. edited by
    George R. Collins. Cambridge, MA: MIT Press, 1979.

"Geometric Extensions of Consciousness." Zodiac. 19 (1969),
    130-173.

"Industrialized Buildings." RAIC Journal. 45 (November
    1968), entire issue devoted to this theme.

Israel Museum, Jerusalem. Zvi Hecker: Polyhedric
    Architecture. Jerusalem: the Museum, 1976.

"Resonance Between Eye and Archtype." Via. 6 (1983), 47-67.

"Seeing Order: Systems and Symbols." In: Hypergraphics,
    edited by David W. Bresson. s.n.: American Association
    for the Advancement of Science, 1978, pp. 71-108.

Simultaneous Randomness and Order: The Fibonacci-Divine
    Proportion as a Universal Forming Principle. Ph.D.
    Dissertation, University of Pennsylvania, 1975.

"Urban Space Systems as Living Form." Architecture Canada.
    45 (November 1968), 45-48; (December 1968), 43-45; 46
    (January 1969) 52-56.

and Louis I. Kahn. "Toward a Plan for Midtown Philadel-
    phia." Perspecta. 2 (Fall 1953), 23-27.

and others. International Congress of Women Architects,
    Proceedings. The Crisis of Identity in Architecture.
    Ramsar, Iran: Ministry of Housing and Urban
    Development, 1976, pp. 107-130.

and others. Mill Creek Redevelopment Area Plan.
    Philadelphia, PA: Philadelphia City Planning
    Association, 1954.

SECONDARY WORKS:

"Anne Griswold Tyng." Macmillan Encyclopedia of Architects.
    New York: Free Press, 1982, v. 4, p. 232.

"Anne Griswold Tyng: Architectural Works." Zodiac. 19

(1974), 163-172.

Buttolph, Suzanne, and others. "Digressions on the
    Architectural Model." North Carolina State University.
    Student Publication of the School of Design. 27
    (1978), 1-95.

McGroarty, J. "New Professional Identities: Four Women in
    the Sixties." In: Women in American Architecture. New
    York: Whitney Library of Design, 1977, pp. 115-131.

Sky, Alison, and Michelle Stone. Unbuilt America. New
    York: McGraw-Hill, 1976, pp. 246-247.

"Tyng Toy." Everyday Art Quarterly. 8 (1948), 5.

"Women in Architecture, the New Professional: Coming of
    Age." Progressive Architecture. 58 (March 1977), 48.

EXHIBITION:

AIA, Washington, D.C. Two on Two at the Octagon.
    Washington, D.C.: the Octagon, 1979, pp. 11-16.

Drawing Center, New York. Visionary Drawings of
    Architecture and Planning. New York: Drawing Center
    for SITES, 1979.

VIGNELLI, LELLA   DESIGNER

SECONDARY WORKS:

Ambasz, Emilio. Design: Vignelli. New York: Rizzoli, 1980.

"Annual Design Review." Industrial Design. 30 (October
    1983), 56-57, 62-63, 86, 100.

"Artemide's Showrooms in Milan and Los Angeles." Abitare.
    222 (March 1984), 5.

"Chiesa nel Citicorp Center: A Multipurpose Church." Domus.
    584 (July 1978), 36-37.

Constantine, E.M. "Casa Vignelli: A Showcase of Modern
    Design." Architectural Record. 168 (July 1980),
    104-109.

Deitsch, D. "Special Award Winner: Los Angeles Hauserman
    Showroom." Interiors. 142 (January 1983), 110-111.

"E.F. Hauserman Showroom, Pacific Design Center, Los
    Angeles." Architectural Record. 170 (July 1982),
    120-123.

"Hauserman Showroom, Pacific Design Center, Los Angeles."
    Architectural Review. 172 (November 1982), 58-59.

"Italcenter, Chicago." Architectural Record. 170 (September
    1982), 102-105.

"Italcenter Debuts During NEOCON." International Design. 53
    (November 1982), 266.

"Italcenter Showroom: Merchandise Mart, Chicago."
    Architectural Review. 172 (November 1982), 30-32.

Katzumie, M. "Massimo and Lella Vignelli--A Husband-Wife
    Team from Milan." Graphic Design. 80 (December 1980),
    31-38.

"Lella and Massimo Vignelli." In: Interior Design in the
    20th Century. New York: Harper and Row, 1986, pp.
    212-215.

"Lella and Massimo Vignelli." Progressive Architecture. 59
    (September 1978), 102.

"Light Show: Artemide Show Room, Los Angeles." Architec-
    tural Record. 171 (September 1983), 138-139.

"Light Show: The Hauserman Showroom in the Pacific Design
    Center, Los Angeles." Interior Design. 53 (July 1982),
    46-53.

"Massimo and Lella Vignelli." In: Contemporary Designers.
    Detroit: Gale, 1984, pp. 610-611.

"Programma ARA." Casabella. 396 (1974), 60.

"Rejuvenated Houses--American Anonymous." Abitare. 243
    (April 1986), 181-191.

Slavin, M. "With Characteristic Understatement and
    Elegance, Lella Vignelli's Own Office Functions as a
    Testing Ground for Vignelli Associates." Interiors.
    140 (May 1981), 162.

Sparke, P. "American Graffiti." Design. 396 (December
    1981), 25.

Stephens, Suzanne. "Women in Architecture." House and
    Garden. 153 (March 1981), 146, 149, 196.

EXHIBITION:

"All That Glitters: Knoll International's Recent
    Exhibition." Industrial Design. 19 (April 1972),
    62-67.

Built by Women: A Guide to Architecture in the New York
    Area. New York: Alliance of Women in Architecture,
    1981, p. 13.

"Designing Couple: Parsons School of Design, New York."
    AFF. 119 (Spring 1980), 80-81.

Dorfles, G. "PAC, Milan: Exhibit." Domus. 615 (March 1981),
    40.

"Knoll au Louvre." Interiors. 131 (April 1972), 136-139 +.

"Massimo and Lella Vignelli: Their Work Shown at Parsons."
    Interior Design. 51 (May 1980), 48-49.

"Modernizing Antiquity: Knoll Designs." Architectural
    Forum. 136 (March 1972), 5.

Pile, J. "Vignelli at Parsons Gallery, New York." Interior
    Design. 27 (May-June 1980), 10.

Slavin, M. "Total Design Experience: Parsons School of
    Design, New York." Interiors. 139 (May 1980), 130-
    131 + .

VINCIARELLI, LAURETTA   DESIGNER

SECONDARY WORKS:

Architectural League of New York. <u>Emerging Voices</u>.
    Princeton: Princeton Architectural Press, 1986, pp.
    26-27.

Stephens, Suzanne. "Women in Architecture." <u>House and
    Garden</u>. 153 (March 1981), 146-149, 196-197.

WARNER, ANNA (1827-1915)   WRITER ON LANDSCAPE

PRIMARY WORKS:

<u>Gardening by Myself</u>. New York: Randolph and Co., 1872.

<u>Miss Tiller's Vegetable Garden and the Money She Made by
    It</u>. New York: A.D.F. Randolph and Co., 1873.

SECONDARY WORKS:

"Anna Bartlett Warner." <u>American Women Writers</u>, edited by
    Lina Mainiero New York: F. Ungar Pub. Co., 1982, pp.
    332-333.

"Anna Warner." <u>Dictionary of American Biography</u>. New York:
    Charles Scribner's Sons, 1943, v. 19, p. 461.

"Anna Warner: Glad Hands and Good Little Flowers." In: <u>Her
    Garden Was Her Delight</u>, by Buckner Hollingsworth. New
    York: Macmillan, 1962, pp. 91-101.

Hanaford, Phoebe. <u>Daughters of America</u>. Augusta, Maine:
    True and Co., 1882, pp. 315-316.

Stokes, Olivia E. <u>Letters and Memories of Susan and Anna
    Bartlett Warner</u>. New York and London: G.P. Putnam's
    Sons, 1925.

WASHINGTON, ROBERTA   ARCHITECT

SECONDARY WORKS:

"Black Women Architects: A Blueprint for Success." <u>Ebony</u>.
    39 (June 1984), 55.

Yilma, Meseret. "Roberta Washington: A Struggle for
    Individuality." <u>Point</u> (Spring 1984), 9.

WATERMAN, HAZEL WOOD (1865-1948) ::   ARCHITECT

Her correspondence notebooks, working drawings and papers
are held at the San Diego Historical Society Library and
Manuscript Collections.

SECONDARY WORKS:

Rochlin, Harriet. "Distinguished Generation of Women
    Architects in California." <u>AIA Journal</u>. 66 (August
    1977), 39-40.

WEESE, CYNTHIA (1940-)   ARCHITECT

PRIMARY WORKS:

"Corn Crib Barn Converted to House, 1976-1977." <u>GA Houses</u>.
    28 (February 1979), 90-95.

"Eileen Gray, Architect Designer." <u>Inland Architect</u>. 24
    (May 1980), 25-27.

and Benjamain Weese. "From the Boards of Weese, Seegers
    Hickey and Weese." <u>Inland Architect</u>. 21 (December
    1977), 16-19.

SECONDARY WORKS:

Benson, Mary Ellen. "Cynthia Weese: Working in an
    All-Encompassing Profession." <u>Architecture News</u>
    (February 1985), 3.

"Chestnut Place Apartments, Chicago, Illinois."
    Architectural Record. 171 (July 1983), 96-97.

"Chicago AIA Makes Awards to a Bridge and Fourteen
    Buildings." Architectural Record. 163 (January 1978),
    40-41.

Gordon, B. "Kunz Residence, St. Charles, Illinois."
    Architectural Record. 169 (November 1981), 96-101.

"Grenier a Mais: maison de week-end, centre Illinois."
    Architecture d' Aujhourd'hui. 194 (December 1977),
    xiv.

"Homes for the Handicapped, Roselle, Illinois."
    Architectural Review. 162 (October 1977), 253.

"Kunz House, St. Charles, Illinois." Architectural Review.
    167 (June 1980), 369.

"Strong Forms Drawn from Solar Strategies." AIA Journal. 70
    (January 1981), 50.

Viladas, P. "Bradford Exchange." Interiors. 138 (June
    1979), 104-105.

EXHIBITIONS:

Chicago Architects Design: A Century of Architectural
    Drawings. Chicago: The Art Institute of Chicago and
    Rizzoli Pubs., 1982, p.2.

Chicago Historical Society. Chicago Women in Architecture,
    1974-1984. Insert: Inland Architect. 28 (November-
    December 1984), p. 27.

WHEELER, CANDACE (1827-1923)   DESIGNER

Some of Candace Wheeler's letters are at Yale University in the Stimson Papers. The Metropolitan Museum of Art, New York and the Cleveland Museum have examples of textiles.

PRIMARY WORKS:

"Art Education for Women." Outlook. 55 (January 2, 1897), 85 + .

"The Art of Embroidery." Home Needlework Magazine. 1 (April 1899), 99-102.

Content in a Garden. New York: Houghton Mifflin, 1902.

Corticelli Home Neddlework. Florence, Mass: Nonotuck Silk Co., 1899.

"Country House Interiors." Christian Union. 45 (April 30, 1892), 840 +.

"Decoration of Walls." Outlook. 52 (November 2, 1895), 705 + .

"Decorative Art." Architectural Record. 4 (April-June 1895), 409-413.

"The Decorative Use of Flowers." Atlantic Monthly. 95 (May 1905), 630-634.

The Development of Embroidery in America. New York: Harper and Bros., 1921.

Doubledarling and the Dream Spinner. New York: Fox, Duffield & Co, 1905.

"A Dream City." Harper's New Monthly Magazine. 86 (May 1893), 830-846.

"The Fine Arts Group Exhibitors." Critic. 26 (January 26, 1895), 70.

"Furnishing of Country Homes." Christian Union. 45 (April 23, 1892), 792 + .

"Home Industries and Domestic Manufactures." Outlook. 63
    (October 14, 1899), 402-406.

Household Art. New York: Harper and Bros., 1893.

"How I Devised an Attractive Kitchen." Ladies Home Journal.
    20 (July 1930), 20.

How To Make Rugs. New York: Doubleday and Co., 1902.

"Interior Decoration as a Profession for Women." Outlook.
    52 (April 6, 1895), 559-560; (April 20, 1895), 649.

"Interiors of Summer Cottages." Christian Union. 45 (April
    16, 1892), 741 + .

"The New Woman and Her Home Needs." Christian Union. 43
    (June 25, 1891), 845.

"Practical Use of Art Education." Christian Union. 44
    (September 26, 1891), 582 + .

"The Principles of Decoration." Outlook. 53 (February 15,
    1896), 284 + .

Principles of Home Decoration. New York: Doubleday, Page
    and Co., 1903.

"The Study of Design." Art Amateur. 26 (December 1891), 18.

"Weaving Rugs From Rags." Ladies Home Journal. 22 (November
    1905), 56.

Yesterdays in A Busy Life. New York, London: Harper, 1918.

SECONDARY WORKS:

Anscombe, Isabelle. A Woman's Touch: Women in Design from
    1860 to the Present Day. New York: Viking, 1984, pp.
    35-41, 45, 46.

"The Associated Artists." Art Amateur. 12 (January 1885),
    38.

"The Associated Artists Needlework." Art Amateur. 6
    (December 1881), 13.

Bolton, Sarah K. Successful Women. Boston: Lothrop, 1888.
    Chapter nine is devoted to Wheeler and her work.

"Candace Wheeler." Biographical Cyclopedia of American
    Women. New York: Halvord Pub. Co., 1925, v. 2, pp.
    186-190.

"Candace Wheeler." In: International Dictionary of Women's
    Biography. New York: Macmillan, 1982, p. 495.

"Candace Wheeler." Notable American Women. Cambridge:
    Belknap Press, 1971, pp. 574-576.

Faude, Wilson H. "Associated Artists and the American
    Renaissance in the Decorative Arts." Winterthur
    Portfolio. 10 (1975), 101-130.

_____. "Candace Wheeler, Textile Designer."
    Antiques. 112 (August 1977), 258-262.

Keith, Dona Wheeler. "The American Tapestry as Invented by
    Candace Wheeler." Wellesley College Bulletin. 2
    (January 1936), 9.

Logan, Mrs. John A. The Part Taken by Women in American
    History. Wilmington, Delaware: Perry-Nalle, 1912, p.
    753.

Lynes, Russell. The Tastemakers. New York: Harper, 1954,
    pp. 181ff.

"Mrs. Candace T. Wheeler." Art News. 21 (August 11, 1923),
    6.

"Mrs. Candace Wheeler Dies at 96." New York Times (August
    6, 1923), 11.

Peavy, Linda and Ursula Smith. Women Who Changed Things.
    New York: Charles Scribner's Sons, 1983, pp. 159-176.
    (Juvenile literature)

Prather-Moses, Alice I., compiler. The International
    Dictionary of Women Workers in the Decorative Arts.
    Metuchen, N,J,: Scarecrow Press, 1981, pp. 172-173.

"Some Work of the Associated Artists." Harpers Monthly

Magazine. 69 (August 1884), 343.

Stern, Madeline B. We the Women. New York: Schulte, 1963,
    pp. 273-304.

Williams, V. "Nineteenth Century Profile: Candace Wheeler,
    Textile Designer for Associated Artists." 19th
    Century. 6 (Summer 1980), 60-61.

WHITMAN, BERTHA YEREX (1892-1984) ⁜   ARCHITECT

Burnham Library at the Art Institute of Chicago has the
work of Bertha Yerex Whitman on roll no. 38 of its
architectural microfilm project.

The American Institute of Architects Archives has an
unpublished manuscript by Whitman entitled, My Life with
Perkins, Fellows and Hamilton Architects.

PRIMARY WORKS:

My Grandfather and Me. s.n.: s.p., 1979.

A Tyro Takes A Trip. Written about her trip around the
    world, 1965-66, privately printed, [1966].

SECONDARY WORKS:

Berkeley, Ellen Perry. "Architecture: Towards a Feminist
    Critique." In: New Space for Women, edited by Gerda
    Wekerle and others. Boulder, CO: Westview Press, 1980,
    pp. 208-209.

"Bertha Yerex Whitman." In: Contemporary Authors. Detroit:
    Gale, 1985, v. 114, p. 462.

"Bertha Yerex Whitman." Michigan Alumnus. 83 (February
    1977), 26-27.

Cole, Doris. From Tipi to Skyscraper: A History of Women in
    Architecture. Boston: i Press, 1973, pp. 74-76.

Stevens, Mary Otis. "Struggle for Place: Women in
     Architecture, 1920-1960." Women in American
     Architecture. New York: Whitney Library of Design,
     1977, p. 89.

EXHIBITION:

Chicago Women Architects: Contemporary Directions. Chicago:
     Artemesia Gallery, 1978, p. 2

WILLIS, BEVERLY (1927-   ) *   ARCHITECT

PRIMARY WORKS:

Articles by Beverly Willis In Lambda Alpha Land Economics
     Journal, 3 (1981) 174-175.

editor. AIA. The Architect and the Shelter Industry.
     Washington, D.C.: AIA, 1975.

"Conservation: Beverly A. Willis, FAIA." Architecture
     California. 7 (January-February 1985), 16-17.

"Development of a Methodology for Environmental Data
     Evaluation." Western Building Design. 12 (December
     1975), 9, 10.

"How a California Firm Grew Up with the Computer." AIA
     Journal. 65 (January 1976), 48-64.

"People on the Way Up." Saturday Evening Post. 235 (May 5,
     1962), 26.

"The Revitalization of Union Street." Urban Land. 33 (May
     1974), 10-13.

"San Francisco: City Shapers." Architectural Forum. 138
     (April 1973), 24-49.

and Ravinder Jain and Bruce M. Hutchings, eds.
     Environmental Impact Analysis: Emerging Issue in
     Planning. Chicago: University of Illinois Press, 1978.

SECONDARY WORKS:

Armstrong, Leslie, and Roger Morgan. Space for Dance: An
    Architectural Design Guide. Washington, D.C.:
    Publishing Center for Cultural Resources, 1984.

"Design News." Architectural Record. 172 (July 1984), 49.

"Design Skill Rehabilitates Old San Francisco Buiding."
    American Journal of Buiding Design. 1 (July 1965),
    10-15.

Green, Lois W. "The Willis Way." San Francisco Sunday
    Examiner & Chronicle (December 11, 1983), 38-40.

Heymont, George. "Model Home: San Francisco Ballet's
    Spacious New Headquarters." Ballet News. 5 (April
    1984), 28-30.

Marlin, William. "The Struggle for Affable, Affordable
    Buildings." Christian Science Monitor (October 20,
    1977), 27.

"Northern California AIA Design Awards Honor 17 Projects in
    1967 Progam." Architecture/West. 74 (July 1968), 11.

Powell, Jim. " Beverly Willis Listens." Savvy. 3 (November
    1982), 46-51.

Rich-McCoy, Lois. Millionaires: Self Made Women of America.
    New York: Harper and Row, 1978, pp. 169-188.

Rochlin, Harriet. "All in a Day's Work." Ms. 5 (December
    1976), 15.

Ryder, Sharon L. "Getting at the Issues." Progressive
    Architecture. 55 (1974), 82-87.

"Twenty-one City Scenes." House Beautiful. 107 (August
    1965), 72-73.

WOOD, EDITH ELMER (1871-1945)   HOUSING REFORMER

The Schlesinger Library at Harvard University has in its
manuscript collection a biographical file on Edith Elmer
Wood.

PRIMARY WORKS:

"Housing in My Time." Shelter. 3 (December 1938), 10-15.

Housing of the Unskilled Wage Earner. New York: Macmillan,
    1919.

Housing Progress in Western Europe. New York: Dutton, 1923.

"Library on Housing." Architectural Record. 103 (February
    1948), 20.

"Recent Housing Work in Western Europe." Architectural
    Record. 53 February 1923), 173-183.

Recent Trends in American Housing. New York: Macmillan,
    1931.

Slums and Blighted Areas in the United States. Washington,
    D.C.: Government Printing Office, 1935.

"Slums and the City Plan." American City. 20 (1929), 93-97.

"The Statistics of Room Congestion." Journal of the
    American Statistical Association. 15 (1928), 37-41.

and John J. Murphy, and Frederick L. Ackerman. The Housing
    Famine, How to End It. New York: E.P. Dutton, 1920.

SECONDARY WORKS:

Birch, Eugenie L. Edith Elmer Wood and the Genesis of
    Liberal Housing Thought: 1910-1942. Ph.D.
    Dissertation, Columbia University, 1976.

"Edith Elmer Wood." American Reformers, edited by Alden
    Whitman. New York: H.W. Wilson, 1985.

"Edith Elmer Wood." American Women, 1935-1940. Detroit:
    Gale Publishers, 1981, p. 1001.

"Edith Elmer Wood." Macmillan Encyclopedia of Architects.
    New York: Free Press, 1982, v. 4, p. 412.

"Edith Elmer Wood." In: Notable American Women. Cambridge,
    MA: Harvard University Press, 1971, pp. 644-645.

"Edith Elmer Wood: Obituary." Journal of Housing. 2 (May
    1945), 88.

"Edith Elmer Wood: Obituary." Pencil Points. 26 (July
    1945), 28.

"Edith Elmer Wood: Obituary." Public Housing. 17 (May
    1945), 1-4.

"Emergency Housing Proposals." Architectural Forum. 74
    (April 1941), 18 + .

Fant, Barbara G. Slum Reclamation and Housing Reform in the
    Nation's Capital, 1890-1940. Ph.D. Dissertation,
    George Washington Univ., 1982.

Logan, Mary S. The Part Taken by Women in American History.
    Wilmington, Delaware: Perry-Nalle, 1912, p. 854.

"Obituary." Architectural Forum. 82 (June 1945), 72.

"Recent Trends in Housing." Architectural Forum. 55
    (December 1931), 10.

"What Has Kept Costs Down During England's House Building
    Boom?" Architectural Record. 84 (July 1938), 79-82.

WRIGHT, JOSEPHINE CHAPMAN ※   ARCHITECT

SECONDARY WORKS:

Knowlton, Elliott. Worcester's Best: A Guide to the City's
    Architectural Heritage. Worcester: Worcester Heritage
    Preservation Society, 1984, p. 78.

"Novel Apartment House Planned by Woman Architect!"
     Architect and Engineer. 49 (April 1917), 92.

"Woman Architect Plans Apartment." Southern Architect and
     Building News. 37 (October 1916), 36-37.

"A Woman Who Builds Homes." Ladies Home Journal. 31
     (October 1914), 3.

"The Woman's Club-house, Worcester, Massachusetts."
     American Architect and Building News. 78 (December 27,
     1902), 103 + plate.

Wright, Gwendolyn. "On the Fringe of the Profession: Women
     in Architecture" In: The Architect. New York: Oxford
     University Press, 1977, pp. 290-291.

YEATMAN, GEORGINA POPE (1902-1982) *   ARCHITECT

The MIT Museum has sketches of a prize winning project by
Yeatman.

SECONDARY WORKS:

Coit, Elisabeth. "Georgina Pope Yeatman." Technology
     Review. 39 (1937), 255.

"Director of City Architecture, Philadelphia."
     Architectural Record. 79 (February 1936), 32.

"Philadelphia's City Architect." Architectural Forum. 64
     (January 1936), 38.

YOCH, FLORENCE * (fl. ca. 1920's - 30's) LANDSCAPE
                                        ARCHITECT

PRIMARY WORKS:

"The Court Garden of the Woman's Athletic Club, Los
     Angeles." Landscape Architecture. 17 (October 1926),
     37-39.

Dobyns, Winifred. California Gardens. New York: Macmillan
      Co., 1983.
      Much of Florence Yoch's landscape work is published in
      this volume.

SECONDARY WORKS:

Brown, Catherine R. Women and the Land. Baltimore: Morgan
      State University, 1979, p. [28].

Deitz, Paula. "Designing Women." Metropolis (December
      1982), 14-19.

"Fitting the Land for Human Use." California Arts and
      Architecture. 38 (July 1930), 19-20.

Palmer, Donna. An Overview of the Trends, Eras and Values
      of Landscape Architecture in America. MLA North
      Carolina State University, 1976, p. 32.

EXHBITION:

Catalogue of the Architectural Drawing Collection. Santa
      Barbara, CA: University Art Museum, 1983. p. 873.

Index

227

chintz 82

Church of all Souls 85

churches 161, 180, 183, 211

Citicorp Center 176, 190, 191, 211

cities 12, 37, 115
    building of 117
    Canadian 114
    future of 38
    garden 38
    great American 114
    growth of 116
    new 140
    our 106

citizens 37

city 23, 25, 26, 116
    beautiful 187
    planners 38
    planning 105, 106, 107, 117, 139
    segments 27
    shapers 221
    zoning 106

Civic improvement 117

Clark House 206

Clark, Wayne E. 173

Class, Robert A. 3

Clay, Grady 12

Clements, Robert M. 143

Cleveland, H.W.S. 106

Cleveland Museum 217

Cliff, Ursula 12, 49, 93, 105, 110

Close, Elizabeth Sheu 54-55

closets 158, 206

clothes 188

Clymer, Eleanor 82

Coatsworth, Patricia 2

Coffin, Marian Cruger 55-56

Cohen, J.H. 12,

Coit, Elizabeth 57-58, 225

Cole, Doris 3, 12, 31, 57, 58-59, 64, 78, 93, 103, 113, 128, 134, 143, 151, 153, 155, 173, 220

Cole, Susan 41

Collins, Peter 142

Colony Hill 173

Colonial 118

Colquhoun, A, 27

Colter, Mary 59-63

Columbia 13, 91, 136, 186, 192, 200,

Columbus, Ohio 179

Colybes, Annick 12

communications 48, 52

Community